Black resistance to British policing

MANCHESTER
1824

Manchester University Press

Racism, Resistance and Social Change

Black resistance to British policing

Adam Elliott-Cooper

Manchester University Press

Published by Manchester University Press
Altrincham Street, Manchester M1 7JA
www.manchesteruniversitypress.co.uk

British Library Cataloguing-in-Publication Data
A catalogue record for this book is available from the British Library

ISBN 978 1 5261 5707 2 hardback
ISBN 978 1 5261 4393 8 paperback

First published 2021

Typeset by
Servis Filmsetting Ltd, Stockport, Cheshire
Printed in Great Britain by
TJ Books Ltd, Padstow

Series editors' foreword

John Solomos, Satnam Virdee, Aaron Winter

The study of race, racism and ethnicity has expanded greatly since the end of the twentieth century. This expansion has coincided with a growing awareness of the continuing role that these issues play in contemporary societies all over the globe. *Racism, Resistance and Social Change* is a new series of books that seeks to make a substantial contribution to this flourishing field of scholarship and research. We are committed to providing a forum for the publication of the highest quality scholarship on race, racism, antiracism and ethnic relations. As editors of this series we would like to publish both theoretically driven books and texts with an empirical frame that seek to further develop our understanding of the origins, development and contemporary forms of racisms, racial inequalities and racial and ethnic relations. We welcome work from a range of theoretical and political perspectives, and as the series develops we ideally want to encourage a conversation that goes beyond specific national or geopolitical environments. While we are aware that there are important differences between national and regional research traditions, we hope that scholars from a variety of disciplines and multidisciplinary frames will take the opportunity to include their research work in the series.

As the title of the series highlights, we also welcome texts that can address issues about resistance and anti-racism as well as the role of political and policy interventions in this rapidly evolving discipline. The changing forms of racist mobilisation and expression that have come to the fore in recent years have highlighted the need for more reflection and research on the role of political and civil society mobilisations in this field.

We are committed to building on theoretical advances by providing an arena for new and challenging theoretical and empirical studies on the changing morphology of race and racism in contemporary societies.

Contents

Figures

Acknowledgements

It has taken nearly a decade for me to research and write this book. It has been rewritten countless times, through journal articles and a thesis, blogs and workshops, conversations and activism. First, I am indebted to all the youth workers and young people I was blessed to work with in community organisations in Nottingham and London, whose energy and insight sparked my interest in this topic. In turning my work into a doctoral thesis, Patricia Daley's supervision was central. Without her encouragement and guidance, I would not be where I am, and while the learning experience of doctoral research is rarely smooth, it is a necessary, and ultimately enriching, struggle. I am profoundly indebted to many activists, both those who participated directly in my research and those who informed it indirectly. Stafford Scott and Suresh Grover, in particular, have (perhaps unknowingly) tutored me from the beginning – their insights mark every chapter of this book. The time and thought given to both my ideas and my personal development by Vron Ware, Yasmeen Narayan and Gargi Bhattacharyya have been invaluable.

A special thanks to everyone who read a chapter or chapters, or even the whole book, offering criticism, direction and at times some much-needed affirmation. I am eternally grateful to: Luke De Noronha, Mohammed Elnaiem, David Featherstone, Virinder Kalra, Alex Wanjiku Kelbert, Kojo Kyerewaa, Nivi Manchanda,

Acknowledgements

Sofia Mason, Gavin Rand, Robbie Shilliam, Sivamohan Valluvan, Joshua Virasami and Musab Younis. And I have to shout out my informal intellectual communities: 'RICE', 'Kusoma', 'Badminton Bolsheviks', 'Elma Francois 2.0' and 'Afropessimism Ate My Baby', who have all brought insight, analysis and laughter through their curiosity, comradeship and cutting analysis of racial politics. I never cease to feel fortunate to be in the company of such brilliant minds.

Many thanks to the family and close friends who indulged me by reading through my rough ideas, summaries and the introduction to this book: Terence Elliott-Cooper, Rianna Augustin, Shikila Edward, Susanna Allam and Conrad Appiah. My parents, Colette Elliott and Nigel Cooper, while each quite different, have both played such an integral role in my intellectual and political development; I shall never be able to express how important you both are. Aimée Allam, your patience and support during the many trials I've faced over the course of my writing have kept me, and this book, in one piece.

Abbreviations

Unless stated or obvious, entities are UK-based. They may be historical or present-day, or both.

ANPR   Automated Number Plate Recognition
BAME   Black, Asian or Minority Ethnic
BLM   Black Lives Matter (US, UK, worldwide)
BPM   Black Parents Movement
CBO   Criminal Behaviour Order
CPS   Crown Prosecution Service
iNAPP   interim National Afrikan People's Parliament (UK)
JE   Joint Enterprise (legal procedure)
JENGbA   Joint Enterprise Not Guilty by Association
KCPO   Knife Crime Prevention Order
LCAPSV   London Campaign Against Police and State Violence
MNLA   Malayan National Liberation Army
NMP   Newham Monitoring Project
NPMP   Northern Police Monitoring Project
NWCSA   Negro Welfare, Cultural and Social Association (Trinidad)
OWAAD   Organisation of Women of African and Asian Descent (their newsletter was FOWAAD)
PNM   People's National Movement (Trinidad, then UK)

Abbreviations

RUC	Royal Ulster Constabulary
SYV	Serious Youth Violence
TDC	Tottenham Defence Campaign
UFFC	United Family and Friends Campaign
XR	Extinction Rebellion

Introduction

In 2008, I volunteered part-time at Hyson Green Youth Centre in Radford, Nottingham. I worked with young people excluded from secondary school in this multicultural working-class neighbourhood in the East Midlands. Most of the staff and young people were Black, and posters of Black inventors and pre-colonial African monuments lined the walls. The other youth workers were Nottingham locals, knowledgeable about the history of resistance in the area, often recalling the rebellions against racism and policing in the 1980s.

Although our main focus was on developing core curriculum subjects, some of the best learning exchanges took place during periods of recreation. Between games of table tennis or pool, my colleagues and I were interested in engaging the young people in social issues. We might try to bring up the class struggles around exploitation at work, or problems with housing. But these problems were often too distant for these young people to engage in meaningfully. While their parents or other adults in their lives might have struggled with these issues, they were not problems these young people had to engage with directly. The shame of surviving in a low-income household also made talking openly about these issues difficult, particularly given that poverty has long been positioned as a personal failing. Raising the issue of historic racist crimes or contemporary racial injustices was met with dismissive eye rolls – 'Come off all that Black stuff … it's boring'. Conversations about racism often portray Black people as passive victims, weakened by a system of stereotypes and prejudices by which no one wants to be defined.

But as soon as we mentioned policing, something clicked. While some young people would recount their frustration with harassment or detention by police, others would talk about the violent experiences of their friends or family members. Rather than being disempowered by these stories, the young people framed these grievances with the police as a collective experience. Many of the adults they respected and the artists or athletes they looked up to articulated encounters with the law to which they could relate. Policing was an obstacle that was in their immediate reality, with stops, questioning and searches a common occurrence, making arrest and imprisonment a constant threat.

During one session, the staff and young people agreed that the role of the police is to protect people and property, but we then went on to ask: which people, and whose property, are they protecting? Few in the room considered that a police presence made them feel any safer, and through these discussions, class and racial injustices could be discussed in ways that felt relevant. This point of entry allowed us to embark on critical discussions about the operation of power within our society, and how it might be addressed (see Chapter 4). These conversations inspired me, first to become more involved in organised resistance to policing, and eventually to think and write about it. I started planning formal research on the topic following the civil unrest of 2011. When I told people I was looking at how Black communities were organising to defend themselves from the police, I was often met with a puzzled expression, followed by: 'Oh, in the US?' Over the years, fewer people have presumed that research on resistance to policing must have a US focus, and by the end of 2020, more researchers were interested in challenging police power in Britain.

In 2020, the young people in Nottingham who had sparked my interest in resisting policing would have reached their mid-twenties. Britain was swept up in the largest anti-racist protests against policing in its history. A video of George Floyd, a Black man killed by police in Minneapolis on 20 May, shook America and then the world. The harrowing footage of Floyd lying on the road with a knee on his neck, surrounded by police officers, resulted in millions viewing this man pleading for his life as he was tortured to death on camera. For many taking to the streets in protest, this racist strangulation of a Black man had sinister echoes of America's past – George Floyd's death wasn't just a brutal killing, it was the most public lynching in human history. America erupted into nationwide rebellion not seen since the 1960s.

Protests continued for months, bolstered by anger at the nationalist bigotry of the Trump presidency, and the devastating effects of his administration's handling of the COVID-19 pandemic in which millions were denied essential healthcare or welfare provision. I often wonder whether the young people I worked with in Hyson Green Youth Centre attended the protests in Nottingham, or recollected our conversations about state power and resistance. The largest demonstrations, in London, saw mobilisations of over 30,000 on some days, with smaller towns and villages throughout England and Wales holding rallies, donating funds and placing Black Lives Matter (BLM) posters in their windows.[1] I attended the London protests as a legal observer, monitoring police activity, gathering evidence of violence against protesters, and providing legal and other support to the people who had taken to the streets.

While this wave of protest began in the US, in many ways the UK faced related, yet materially different, problems. The Boris Johnson-led Conservative government used nationalist rhetoric to win a general election using just a three-word manifesto: Get Brexit Done. Many were aware of Johnson's long-running, bigoted journalism in the *Daily Telegraph* and *The Spectator*. The world was in the grip of a pandemic. The treatment of NHS workers, who lacked the necessary equipment, had solicited widespread outrage. Revelations that Black people were both more likely to die of COVID-19 and were more likely to be fined by police for allegedly breaking lockdown rules compounded decades of institutionalised racism, bolstering popular discontent. The 'special relationship' between the US and the UK endured, with Boris Johnson embracing the Trump administration. Many protesters taking to the streets in 2020 saw the Brexit slogan 'Take Back Control' as part of the same project of right-wing nationalism as Trump's 'Make America Great Again'. Thus, while the protests began in solidarity with those marching for George Floyd, the connections and parallels with the racisms faced on the other side of the Atlantic were central to British mobilisations.

Belly Mujinga, a British-Congolese public transport worker in London with underlying health conditions, had recently died from COVID-19 after a member of the public spat in her face. In 2019, Shukri Abdi, a young British-Somali who had endured sustained racist bullying at her school, had drowned in the River Irwell in Bury, Greater Manchester. Shukri was surrounded by five white children, some of whom had been accused of bullying her in the lead-up to her death. The authorities failed to investigate her death and her former school's management offered extensive support to the girls her family believed played a role in the tragedy. A fire in the multi-ethnic council housing block Grenfell Tower in west London in 2017, where at least seventy-two people lost their lives in a preventable tragedy, also featured in slogans on placards and in the chants of protesters. Alongside the names of those who had died at the hands of police, prisons and border enforcers, these British anti-racist protests connected them to racism in housing, healthcare, schools and the workplace.

As the media circled the protests, looking for a hook or an angle, the most obvious was the now over-rehearsed challenge – that Britain is different from America. But this only proved one thing – that Britain is a nation uncomfortable with discussions of 'race' and British racism. Britain's liberal press and popular common sense imply that racism is the crude business of the US, something that used to happen in South Africa, and only occasionally happens in Britain, on football terraces or in working-class pubs.

Few conversations during the protests captured this better than an interview on BBC Newsnight, in which George the Poet, a Black writer and political commentator, was told by the presenter: 'But you're not putting Britain and America on the same footing ... our police aren't armed. They don't have guns. The legacy of slavery is not the same.' George visibly recoils at this newspeak, perhaps thinking of Mark Duggan, Azelle Rodney, Jean Charles de Menezes or Jermaine Baker: which people in uniform shot these people, if 'our police' are not armed? Are the officers who hold automatic firearms at airports and major train stations invisible to the presenter? George responded by pointedly addressing the other wholly misleading statement in the interviewer's assertion: in fact, Britain's colonial past haunts it just as much as America's history of settler colonialism and slavery.

Imperial amnesia enables Britain to remember America as a racist aberration, rather than a former British settler colony. The fact that, unlike America, Britain didn't have plantation slavery on its mainland was not for moral or ethical considerations. Slave labour was most profitable in the Caribbean; this is why Britain trafficked Africans to Barbados and Grenada, rather than Bristol or Glasgow. Indeed, England and Scotland both had colonies in the Americas before the Acts of Union that created the United Kingdom of Great Britain in 1707. Put simply, the UK has never existed without colonies and racial governance – this is how racialised categories, structural power and organised violence are imposed.[2] Colonisation in Australasia, the Caribbean, the Middle East, North America, South and South East Asia and nearly a third of the African continent made racism one of Britain's most enduring ideological exports.[3] This book will trace the patterns of racism which were central to Britain's capacity to exploit and control the lands and peoples of its colonies, shaping the racisms of the twenty-first century.

Keeping the dirty business of slavery, genocide and racist rule physically distant from the British mainland is one of the ways Britain was able to absolve itself of its shameful endeavours and retain its national pride. The thousands of miles that separated the British mainland from the overt racial governance of its colonies meant that it could also construct a conceptual barrier between racism and its own self-image.[4] This was all the more necessary as Britain gained vast wealth from its Empire – yet racism, to paraphrase Stuart Hall, is as British as the sugar in a cup of tea. Therefore, this book urges us to reckon with colonialism and its racist legacies in order for us to better understand recent histories of policing and resistance on the British mainland. Just as America is indelibly marked by racism through its histories of settler coloni- alism and slavery, Britain is similarly shaped by its own legacies of enslavement, colonial exploitation and violence.

In an attempt to awaken Britain from its colonial amnesia, the wave of protest in the summer of 2020 saw its colonial monuments targeted. A statue of slave trader Edward Colston was torn down in Bristol; overseer of colonial genocide Winston Churchill was dubbed 'a racist' with spray paint; and Oxford's Oriel College agreed to take Cecil Rhodes down from his pedestal following prolonged protest from students. So, despite this movement's focus on Britain's racist present, it was compelled to constantly refer, in both action and words, to Britain's colonial past.

In a similar vein, most chapters in this book will return to a series of cases which draw on the experiences of racism and resistance to it in Britain's colonies. I should make clear from the outset, that my intention is not to flatten racial governance into something that was uniform across Britain's many colonies, or worse, to imply that the racism of the past is the same as racism today. I seek instead for these histories to contextualise and better inform our understand- ing of contemporary racism. These histories will help illuminate

6

the varied ways in which violence and control were deployed and justified, drawing on some of the racial thinking and stereotypes from philosophers, policy-makers, activists and popular writers. It is through this racial thinking that concepts of order and morality, crime and justice, honour and shame, became normalised, even revered, throughout Britain and its colonies.

Structure and methods: what to expect when reading this book

This book is broadly chronological, beginning in the immediate post-war period, and providing a selective overview of Britain's Black political movement in the twentieth century. Specific moments in this period are examined in detail to better unpack how Black resistance to policing is linked to the revolutionary politics of anti-colonialism, Black internationalism, Black feminism and anti-capitalism. These radical movements posed the question of why Black people were in Britain in the first place. The Black Power movement provided, through its newspapers and speeches, the response: 'We are in Britain not by choice or by chance, but because of the historical fact that Britain first came to our countries'. This movement also identified racism as structural: this means that the normal functioning of institutions and cultures reproduces racism. As they put it: 'Black people now face mounting racism and exploitation in immigration, employment, housing, education as well as increasing persecution and brutality by the police'.[5]

Chapter 1 looks at cases of police brutality, including the under-researched experiences of women, connecting campaigns of resistance which analysed both racism and patriarchy. By patriarchy, I mean the structural power of men and masculinity over women, queer and trans people, spaces and ideas.[6] This structural power is reproduced in the home and family, in work under capitalism, and in state institutions (Chapters 2 and 3 look at how patriarchy is also reproduced by imperialism). Too often overlooked are many of the Black women's activist groups in England, active during the 1970s and 1980s, which identified policing as one of their primary concerns. FOWAAD (the newsletter of the Organisation of Women of African and Asian Descent, OWAAD) documented cases of police racism, and the Brixton Black Women's Group organised marches against police brutality.[7] The International Black Women for Wages for Housework supported the Tottenham Three, wrongfully accused of killing Police Constable Keith Blakelock during the Broadwater Farm disturbances in 1985.[8] Other examples include the United Black Women's Action Group and the Paddington Black Women's Group in 1979, both using police mistreatment of Black youth as an impetus for mobilisation.[9]

Britain's Black political movements helped shape understandings of racist tropes of Black criminality, and by extension the presentation of migration from the colonies as an alien invasion, disrupting an imagined harmonious, culturally uniform, respectable Britain. All of this led to fears of moral decline brought about by Black migrants, seen as drifters, pimps, drug dealers, criminal Rastafarians, Black militants and muggers.[10] It is in this context that violent racist policing is intensified through powers such as the 'Sus' laws, resulting in the urban uprisings across England in 1980, 1981 and 1985. In the final section of Chapter 1, I look briefly at the ways the capitalist liberal democratic state reacted to this movement, not simply to repress it, but to co-opt anti-racism from the 1980s and the rise of neoliberalism.

While the popular image of the criminalised 'Black folk-devil', such as the mugger or, more recently, the gangster, is usually a man, Black British feminists have also discussed how these traits are projected onto women.[11] Discourses framing Black women in late twentieth-century Britain reflected earlier colonial ones, which communicated excessive fertility, sexual deviance and 'dysfunctional' familial relations.[12] Encapsulated by the critique 'Ain't I a woman?', different categories of women are essentialised as respectable or deviant through classed and racialised discourses.[13] Building on the work of Black feminists in North America, Chapter 2 shows how Black feminisms in Britain have drawn on colonial legacies in Europe, identifying multiple sites of oppression and resistance, including the family, the workplace and the police.[14] The chapter also finds aspects of queer theory useful, concepts which seek to disrupt sexual norms and liberate people from the constraints of those norms. Thus, while Black families are systematically framed as dysfunctional, the Black family as a site of resistance is also, I argue, an opportunity to think beyond the nuclear family, to a wider, more liberatory conception of kinship and care.

Given that many of the anti-racist critiques of policing have focused on the experience of Black men, it is important to highlight the Black women who are also subjected to overt violence from state actors.[15] One of the most high-profile cases was that of Joy Gardner, who died when her home was raided on suspicion of immigration offences in 1993. Officers described her as being in a 'fury' and exhibiting 'superhuman strength', so that it took one officer to hold her arm, and others using belts to bind her waist, wrists, ankles and thighs, before covering her face with elastic adhesive bandage.[16] The officers implicated in this death testified that Gardner's supernormal strength justified use of such extreme force that resulted in her asphyxiation; this led to their acquittal at the subsequent trial. Later campaigns include the death of Sarah Reed in Holloway Prison in 2012[17] or the Free Siyanda Campaign challenging the 2019 imprisonment of a young woman for defending herself from a racist attack in Wales.[18] Importantly, almost every campaign against a Black death in police custody is led by a woman. Chapter 2 picks up the Stephen Lawrence Campaign led by his mother Doreen, beginning in 1993 when Stephen was killed, to over a decade later when a police whistleblower revealed that he had been tasked to spy on the campaign. The chapter analyses a number of campaigns led by women resisting violent police racism, both before and beyond the civil unrest of 2011.

Chapter 3 examines the criminalisation of Black men, providing a prelude to the criminalisation and killing of Mark Duggan, which led to the revolts in August 2011. Britain, like many other countries, faces an expanding wealth gap and reduced welfare provisions for those who need them most; this has galvanised the fear of criminality and bolstered the authority of the state to inflict violence. Chapter 4 analyses the 2011 unrest itself, focusing on the police response and the community defence campaigns which challenged the escalation in state violence in the summer of 2011. Chapter 5 provides an overview of the cutting edge of police power, analysing how new forms of surveillance, control and violence are reproducing older racisms. I argue that police and prisons bring more violence into already violent situations, exacerbating rather than solving problems. The prison population in Britain has almost doubled in the last forty years, with police given more power and weaponry, supported by mushrooming public relations machinery. In the twenty-first century, the use of imprisonment as a disciplinary force against women is rapidly expanding. More people are being sent to court for drug charges, with the majority of incarcerated women being imprisoned for offences related to their own drug use, or the drug use of someone else.

A high proportion of incarcerated people have experienced trauma before being imprisoned, or suffer from mental ill-health. Inadequate provision means that these cases are often undiagnosed, but the Office for National Statistics reports that 40 per cent of incarcerated women have required support for their mental health prior to imprisonment, and almost a quarter of those on remand had previously been admitted to a mental health hospital. Special educational needs, self-harm and suicide are also common among all people in prison, and more common among incarcerated women.[19] Around a quarter of Britain's prison population are racially minoritised groups, and as prisons specifically for 'foreign nationals' are set up, the system is locking up Black people in Britain at the same rate as Black Americans in the US. We should be unsurprised that the radical demands of the BLM protests of 2020 have been derided and misreported: their demands to defund the police have a clear, abolitionist vision.

Chapter 6 looks to the future, analysing both the emergence of BLM and the spontaneous and everyday forms of resistance too often overlooked by political analysts. Here, I make a case for working towards a world in which police and prisons are obsolete, a radical vision gaining popular currency in the third decade of the twenty-first century.

Chapters 1 to 5 of this book begin with a section on history, including anti-colonialism, colonial discourses, racist cultures and colonial policing. These historical sections do not simply provide context for the analyses of twenty-first-century resistance to anti-racism that follow, but are fundamental to understanding Black resistance to British policing. 'Race', Patrick Woolf argues, 'is a trace of history: colonised populations continue to be racial-ised in specific ways that mark out and reproduce the unequal relationships'[20] – ways that shape structures of exploitation, control and violence. By identifying the traces of racist colonial discourses and practices, we can better understand police racism and resistance to it. In other words, policing reflects a pervasive colonial norm that reproduces racial thinking and governance. Examining how colonialists and their advocates viewed and treated subjugated populations enables us to better understand the ways racism is constantly changing, yet is always connected to the racisms in different historical or geographical settings. As Cedric Robinson argues, 'Race presents all the appearance of stability. History, however, compromises this fixity'.[21] Racism's slippery nature, its ability to adapt to different contexts, makes anti-racism both a complex phenomenon and a struggle which must be informed by transnational and transhistorical racisms and anti-racisms.

Chapter 1 turns to life in colonial Trinidad in the 1930s, showing how radical anti-capitalist and anti-colonial uprisings influenced Britain's Black political movement. Chapters 2 and 3 look at how the racialised tropes that shape popular perceptions of criminality in contemporary Britain can be traced back to eighteenth- and nineteenth-century notions of respectability, and how they were established through emergent discourses in fields such as literature, science, philosophy and theology.[22] While analyses of imperialism often focus on aspects of the colonial state such as the armed forces or private property laws, an analysis of gender compels us to look more closely at how colonised people were governed. Controlling gender and sexuality involved disciplining subjugated populations in both public life and in their private intimacies.

European imperial discourses of respectability and the nation reorganised social life in the imperial centres and the colonies.[23] This historical moment saw gendered, sexual and abled norms become hegemonic, in contrast to both the British mainland's poor and its colonised Others.[24] In other words, gendered and sexual attributes of Europe's bourgeoisie became the yardstick with which morality was measured. Britain's imperial expansion, in the Americas, Australasia, Africa and Asia provided a racialised Other, with which its own genteel and honourable men and women (the only two acceptable genders in any 'civilised' society) were contrasted. The white, heteronormative nuclear family stood at the zenith in this hierarchy of respectability, and a cult of domesticity demarcated the roles for man, woman and child.[25]

The public spheres, in both the domestic class system and the international racialised order, were defined by the nation: 'Nationalism and respectability assigned everyone his place in life, man and woman, normal and abnormal, native and foreigner; any confusion between these categories threatened chaos and loss of control'.[26] This potential for chaos exhibited itself in the lower classes and in racialised Others. For instance, in justifying their subjugated social position, Jewish men in Europe were framed both as behaving like women and as unable to practise sexual restraint.[27]

Racialised and classed tropes that signified disorder were also extended to Europe's colonies, where the colonised were framed as sexually promiscuous, violent and in need of moral uplift. It is important to note that respectability is not binary, but slippery, context-specific and broadly defined. The British poor were thus considered more respectable than the colonised, exhibited through the development of Britain's Poor Laws which provided aid to the 'deserving' destitute. Significantly, the 'whitening' of Britain's working classes carved out a novel elevated identity by which the frontiers of settler colonies could be populated by newly respectable bodies.[28]

Framing poor and colonised families as chaotic and disorderly, with uniquely promiscuous and unrestrained sexual relations, was contrasted with the self-image of civility and bourgeois order that the European colonial powers wished to promote. Imposing European norms onto Black family life during the colonial period was a means of achieving order and civility in public life in the colonies. In a form of body politic, colonised families were compelled to follow a strict hierarchy, with the man at the top, the woman taking on care and domestic responsibilities, and children respecting this hierarchical division of labour. The hierarchy of the nation would then also be protected, with colonial state authorities acting as the head of the national family. However, since racism essentialised the degenerate traits projected onto Black families, this colonial civilising project was never complete – the Black family was forever precluded from achieving the civility of its colonial master. It is within the bind of conflicted racial logic such as this, that imperialism continually reproduced its legitimacy.

While Chapter 4 offers a more recent history, detailing the rise of 'gangs' discourse in twenty-first-century Britain, Chapter 5 returns us to the colonial era. Here, we look at policing in the dying days of Empire, as applied to insurgent groups in colonies such as Kenya and Malaya. For the Kikuyu in British Kenya, the prison system evolved into labour camps in the 1950s. Over 150,000 suspected Mau Mau were imprisoned and tortured; others were subjected to 'attacks that included wiping out an entire village of men, women, and elderly (the children were spared) using bayonets, rifles, machine guns, and fire'.[29] Such policies and practices were implemented in response to anti-colonial resistance, which was characterised as a sexualised and animalistic attack on whites, particularly endangering white women.

This counterinsurgency policing, repressing anti-colonial revolt, was carried out by the British colonial administration. But it was overseen, in part, by the man voted the greatest ever Briton – Winston Churchill. His role in advocating racial violence in the colonies, as well as wanting to campaign under the slogan 'Keep England White' in the post-war period, makes him an ironically poignant symbol of British nationalism. Seen in this light, it is perhaps unsurprising that his statue was the target of anti-racist protesters in the summer of 2020. Etching the words 'Was a Racist' underneath his name on the statue in Parliament Square was unpalatable for Churchill's advocates, both in the liberal media and on the far right – yet I think their response can be paraphrased as: 'Yeah, so what?'

In Chapter 6, there is no historical section – instead this final chapter focuses firmly on the future. Here, I develop the work of public intellectuals and activists such as Angela Davis, Michelle Alexander and Ruth Wilson Gilmore in the US, pitching them alongside British activist demands for defunding the police. Perceptions of criminality are used to legitimise the authority of a failing government, with racial folk devils such as the gangster, the terrorist or the immigrant paving the way for a 'war on gangs', a 'war on terror', and the notorious 'hostile environment' for undocumented migrants. Schools,[30] colleges, domestic violence services,[31] hospitals,[32] housing,[33] community centres and workplaces are among the institutions of public life where the police have monitoring powers to identify and punish suspected 'gang members', 'extremists' or 'illegal immigrants'. Reports and inquiries have been followed by policy changes that have done little to reduce either institutional racism in policing, or the harm and violence that exist within British society. This final chapter argues that the police and prison system are beyond reform, and new solutions beyond these institutions of violence and punishment are urgently needed.

Between 2012 and 2019, over seven hundred youth clubs in the UK closed.[34] While university tuition fees have gone from zero to £9,000 in a generation, the meagre £30 a week to support low-income students' attendance at further education colleges has disappeared. Cuts to social care mean that those who experience violence or abuse in the home are less likely to be supported, and the massive reduction in new council housing, particularly in cities such as London, makes a secure place to live in their local community a pipe dream for much of the younger generation. The deregulation of work, through the weakening of union power and the growth in zero-hour contracts, makes it harder for those on lower incomes to make ends meet.

Police are being put into schools, while young people trying to access mental health support are being turned away. The groups of people on the sharp end of these reforms seem endless and growing, much like the criminal justice system which they are ever more likely to encounter. It has been left to the police and prison system to incarcerate away society's problems, which could be better addressed by reducing inequalities. Defunding the police is therefore a demand which challenges us to imagine a world in which we do not rely on violence to deal with the problems we face. It does not demand that we sack every police officer and close every prison tomorrow, but that we find progressive solutions to take power and resources away from the police, and divert them into communities and social services. The demands made by protesters across the world in the summer of 2020 were therefore not simply about making Black lives matter. They were about envisioning the steps needed to move towards a world free from violence and oppression for all people.

Beyond racism and racial prejudice

Racism is best defined as a historically constituted system of power used to discipline, exploit and facilitate violence. In other words, racism must be understood in its historical context, and as a way of controlling racialised populations. Importantly, racism is a colonial, rather than simply a social, construct and the legacies of colonialism shape racism today.[35] It is used by capitalism to exploit workers by categorising them differently – this is known as racial capitalism. Imperialism, the process through which capitalism expands across the globe, uses racism to categorise and control populations differently. The imperial expansion of capitalism does not make workers more similar – the 'proletariat', as orthodox Marxism claims; it makes them different, in order to wield power over them differently.[36] Finally, racism is a system of violence, 'the state-sanctioned or extra-legal production and exploitation of group-differentiated vulnerability to premature death'.[37] This means that the violence of racism is not just the brutality of police and prisons, but all the forms of harm and exploitation.

This is not principally a book about racism, however – it is a book about resistance to it. It does not seek to convince the reader that policing and other forms of British governance are institutionally racist. Every year, thoroughly researched reports, articles and books are published on the myriad ways in which racism still structures society. Various statistical analyses of institutional racism evidence unequal opportunities, unequal treatment and unequal outcomes.[38] New cultures of racism, through media representation,[39] popular rhetoric,[40] policy[41] or political campaigns[42] are continually documented and analysed, demonstrating the ways in which racism reproduces and justifies itself. This book is heavily indebted to these ongoing projects, and they are used throughout to illustrate the specific racisms that are being confronted by the campaigns I describe. It is through analysing these racisms that the focus on resistance can be better framed, enabling a fuller picture of the ways in which policing and racism are being challenged in twenty-first-century Britain.

Neither is this book an exhaustive account of every anti-racist campaign against policing in twenty-first-century Britain. I have not selected the campaigns and struggles that are necessarily the most important or the most 'radical'. They are the campaigns I became most familiar with while working with young people in London, before this book was conceived. Volunteering with groups such as the Newham Monitoring Project and the Tottenham Defence Campaign (TDC) in the early 2010s, I learned about the histories of resistance in these communities, attending meetings and demonstrations, and writing about the anti-racist campaigning against policing taking place in different parts of London. It is from here that I began to make more national and historical connections, learning from activists in cities across England. This book is based on twenty-five formal interviews with activists, as well as my experiences and conversations at hundreds of anti-racist public meetings, protests and events challenging policing between 2010 and 2020.

This book focuses on policing, not because it is necessarily the most important racial issue in Britain; rather, it is because police harassment and brutality are always a point of antagonism which galvanises a collective consciousness against state power and racism. From the shock and grief following a death at the hands of police, to the day-to-day indignities of criminalisation and harassment, resistance to policing is a focus for anti-racists seeking radical social change. Importantly, police racism illustrates how racism should be defined as mode of governance – a system of control – employed by the state.[43] Racism emerged during the colonial era to justify and govern enslaved and other colonised people. The statues of Colston and Churchill are symbols of racism, not because these were racist men, but because racism was fundamental to their economic and political power. It is this understanding of racism which must guide our thinking today – the pursuit of capitalist profits and the maintenance of state power still instrumentalise racism. This enables us to push back against popular, but misleading, interpretations of racism that are gaining currency in the twenty-first century.

Racism, I argue, cannot be reduced to the prejudices or 'unconscious bias' that lead to 'micro-aggressions'. While the subtle forms of bigotry, prejudice or other mistreatment are certainly real problems, they are the effect of the structural racial ordering of the world and its populations.[44] Chapter 3 analyses an instance of individual prejudice and bigoted language to illustrate the structural racism from which these thoughts and actions emerge. Indeed, challenging bias and prejudice, learning and unlearning the ways in which we and other people see and experience the world, are vital if we are to live healthier, happier and more prosperous lives. However, as I argue in Chapter 6, challenging these things *alone* will not stop racism from placing people into racial categories which influence how they are (under)valued as workers, framed as morally degenerate and consequently controlled by the violence of police, prisons, borders and military forces. It is by connecting the interpersonal to the structural that we can better understand the social, political, cultural and economic structures which use racial ordering and governance to control, exploit and enact violence.

Related to this, the language of 'hate crime' does not help us to understand racial violence adequately. Individuals and groups do not attack racialised minorities (or any other oppressed group) simply because they 'hate' them. Structural racism is not the sum total of racist individuals in a silent conspiracy, but the product of histories of entrenched cultures of racism, alongside the market imperatives of racial capitalism, which seek to discipline and maximise the exploitation of people and the environment. In other words, violence is used against oppressed people because it forms part of a wider system of control, from the violence experienced by exploited workers, to the brutality of fascists on the streets or police in the back of a van.[45] These forms of violence are connected and interdependent, and the reduction of them to an act of hatred, or any other emotion, strips racial violence of its political underpinnings, of its fundamental utility as a system of control for capitalist profit and state power. Specifically, de-politicising racial violence in this way allows the state to offer its own top-down solutions to racism, using initiatives from the very institutions that are themselves the primary reproducers of racism, such as the police or the Home Office. Such endeavours do not simply lack the necessary imagination or specific tools to tackle racism, they often bring new sources of violence, inequality and exploitation to oppressed peoples.

This book is also sceptical about how useful the concept of 'privilege' is in effectively understanding or critiquing racism. The problem we face is not simply that some people are 'privileged' by racism; the problem is that capitalism and the state use racism to reproduce their power – they categorise people in order to control them more effectively. Pointing out the 'privilege' of an individual or group of individuals, demanding that they reflect on or 'check' their privilege, reduces racism to an interpersonal act, rather than the system of control that it is. Additionally, and perhaps most importantly, detailing Black resistance to British policing stands firmly against the idea that race or Blackness is simply an identity. Black resistance is not any Black person who is resisting something, and Black politics is not simply any Black person engaged in any political act.

Experiencing racism can give those subjected to it first-hand experience of both its interpersonal nuances and its more violent structure of control and exploitation. But Black people don't fully understand how racism functions simply because they experience it, any more than they understand anti-racism simply by dint of being Black. If that were the case, forming a mass movement of Black resistance to racism would be simple and straightforward. Chapter 4 will expand on this point, through an analysis of Black conservative activists who deny the existence of structural racism in Britain. This book demonstrates that Black resistance isn't fixed: it shifts and changes across different times and places, developing crucial solidarities with radical liberation movements across the world. Consequently, abolition, anti-colonialism and anti-racism are long, messy, protracted struggles, riddled with contradictions, disputes and setbacks. As the first chapter in the book argues, Black politics emerges across the Atlantic world as part of a political process – it is an assertion of radical resistance to imperial racism, a system of control which capitalism uses to expand its reach from Europe to its colonies.

Racism and capitalism became inseparable through European colonialism, and the Black politics that emerges in resistance to these systems of control, exploitation and accumulation cannot be separated from them. Consequently, Black resistance cannot be about privileging Black people or Black liberation over other freedom struggles. It is a movement which identifies the interconnection of the globe's oppressed peoples and radical movements. At the risk of labouring the point, it is not about illuminating the 'privileges' of non-Black people in a pessimistic kind of one-upmanship – it is a Black politics for which solidarity is a moral and political, as well as a strategic, imperative.

In other words, Black liberation is not possible without the liberation of all people – otherwise it would result in a narrow nationalism destined to 'become not even the replica of Europe, but its caricature'[46] through the creation of new hierarchies that echo the oppressions it purports to counter.[47] Police racism is not about a lack of Black people in positions of leadership, or 'bad apples' who 'hate' Black people, or 'privileged' or 'ignorant' police officers who are consequently biased in their use of aggression. The policing of Black people, in its many forms, has always been a fundamental component of the power and wealth of the British state. Racism is not a system that can be checked, trained or diversified away; it is a mode of governance which is fundamentally linked to capitalism through imperialism. As such it requires a collective, international and revolutionary response if it is to be defeated.

1

'We did not come alive in Britain': histories of Black resistance to British policing

The more prosecutions, the more jail sentences, the more ill-treatment of the workers by the police, the more hatred the workers will have for a British Colonial Imperialism. In the West Indies, the moment you say strike you get jail sentences because you are Negro and East Indian workers: but in England and all over the world, the strike is a common thing. (Elma Francois, Speech at her trial for sedition in Trinidad and Tobago, 1937)

Dem said deh Babylon dem went too far
So wha? wi ad woz fi bun two kyar
(Linton Kwesi Johnson, *The Great Insurrection*, 1981)

In 1976, John La Rose addressed an audience in Brixton (south London), the unofficial capital of Black Britain, and delivered a speech about coming 'alive' to racism. Marking the first anniversary of *Race Today*, Britain's most influential radical Black magazine, La Rose laid out the political urgency of such a journal, through a retelling of the history of Black resistance to British power.[1] The often-repeated narrative, La Rose explained, is that all Caribbean people arriving on the British mainland were full of an almost naive excitement. Britain, their mother country, would welcome them with open arms, particularly following the sacrifices made by Caribbean soldiers in two world wars, and the urgent need of their labour to rebuild the heart of Empire. To the shock and surprise of some, as the number of coloured immigrants swelled, they faced discrimination in housing, work and social life. It is from encountering racism in Britain that Black communities organised to change policy and legislation, demanding civil rights and liberties, and challenging racist stereotypes and violence.

An examination of how anti-colonialism against the British Empire is linked to anti-racism on the British mainland is fundamental to understanding Black struggles against policing in the twentieth century. This chapter looks at how Black political action and thought resisted capitalism and imperialism, organising movements with international links of solidarity and deep roots in local communities. Crucially, this history offers a damning critique of the state-led forms of anti-racism that gained traction in the final decades of the twentieth century. This liberal, state-friendly anti-racism is limited to demands for representation in government and business, or for diversity training which challenges interpersonal prejudice. This is particularly important for the topic of this book – Black resistance to policing, which requires direct confrontation with state power, rather than amalgamation into its institutions. The history of grassroots mass movements, organised through colonial experience and anti-capitalism, provides an urgent alternative to this trend, which extends into the twenty-first century. This is because it points us in a different direction for thinking about racism and resistance – not as a set of prejudices that arise from 'coloured' migration to Britain, requiring reform, training or better representation. Rather, histories of resistance to British colonialism understand Black politics as a struggle against imperialism, the globalised manifestation of racist capitalist exploitation. Black resistance to policing, like all struggles for Black liberation, is therefore necessarily anti-capitalist and internationalist. The movements and campaigns analysed in this chapter will help illustrate the history of these political formations, and situate Black resistance to policing in the twenty-first century.

La Rose's history of anti-colonialism detailed how anti-racism is always a challenge to state power. He exposed the myth that what came to be known as the Windrush generation (named after the arrival in 1948 of the ship of that name) marked the genesis of British racism and anti-racism. Rather, it began a new chapter in a longer history. Anti-racism has always been a transnational struggle linked to anti-colonialism, forming part of a wider history of campaigns by Jewish communities, the Irish and other racialised outsiders.[2] Black struggle against British racism also, of course, took place in the colonies, with Black scholar-activists such as Arthur Lewis illustrating how Caribbean workers were already aware of the racism which underpinned British governance. Lewis recounts how land, factories and high-level political and economic decision-making in the colonies were dominated by whites. According to the 1915 census in British Guiana, nearly half the eligible 'European' men were able to vote, whereas only 6.8 per cent of eligible 'Africans and Coloureds' and 0.6 per cent of 'Indians' were permitted to cast a ballot.[3] These inequalities were compounded by laws in the British colony from previous decades, which prevented Africans and Indians from purchasing or irrigating land.

In an effort to sow divisions between Africans and Indians, particularly following the riots of 1856, in which both racial groups destroyed tens of thousands of pounds worth of European-owned property, Indians were eventually given rights to purchase and irrigate land, but not beyond the rice sector.[4] In other Caribbean colonies, African and South Asian labourers either worked in white-owned mines and industrial facilities (e.g. alumina or baux-ite in Jamaica and oil in Trinidad) or rented small agricultural plots from the European landowning classes. Farmers in British Honduras (now Belize) worked the land for half a wage, with the other half made up with a provision of rations from the landlord.

These examples of working conditions in the Caribbean dem-onstrate how racism was fundamental to capitalism in Britain's colonies. Many of the people migrating to Britain in the post-war period had already experienced racist governance, through the colonial administration, policing and the ownership of land and industry. Others had experienced racism through joining the regiments of the British army in the world wars, including the 'race riots' of 1919 which led to many Black troops being deported from Britain back to the Caribbean.[5] It is this racism, bound to the power of the state and capitalism, that encouraged engagement in political antagonism, through labour organising and anti-colonial rebellion. Given the tiny white elite populations, racism was not experienced through the everyday as it is in Britain. There was less familiarity with what, by the twenty-first century, came to be termed 'micro-aggressions', 'white privilege' or 'hate crime', but a more material and structural conception of racism.

In other words, an understanding of racism that was linked to capitalist and imperial power relations already existed in the Caribbean through the experiences of, and resistance to, colonialism. Therefore, while some forms of assault, abuse and insult are symptomatic of racism, the function and source of racism are material – to classify people differently, ordering them into hierarchies which control, exploit and enact violence upon those lower down the racial order. Racial orders are necessary for the control of capital, natural resources and land, with racist state violence emerging as a disciplinary force to maximise the exploitation of workers and repress resistance.

Elma Francois was one of the lesser-known Black workers coming alive to British racism from beyond its shores. Born to a poor family on the tiny Caribbean island of St Vincent in the late nineteenth century, Francois picked cotton with her mother and then worked in a sugar factory. She was soon dismissed following her attempts to organise the other workers to push for improvements in their pay and conditions. Migrating to Trinidad in 1919 at the age of 22, she took work as a domestic servant in a wealthy household in the island's capital, Port of Spain. Further exposure to the gendered divisions of labour in domestic servitude, and to the racist nature of colonialism among oil-rich

Trinidad's European investors, spurred Francois into more militant organising.

Francois soon became well known in Port of Spain as a committed communist, feminist, trade unionist and Black international
organiser. Co-founding the Negro Welfare, Cultural and Social
Association (NWCSA) and the National Unemployed Movement,
she organised hunger marches among the unemployed and strikes
among the working poor during the interwar recession. The
NWCSA, in particular, had international links with equivalent
groups in Britain, such as the Negro Welfare Association. Founded
by Black seafaring communists from the Caribbean, this group campaigned against imperialism and racism in interwar Britain, building transnational connections through activists such as George
Padmore.[6] These international links helped activists like Francois
better understand the global nature of Black politics. She delivered educational speeches in public squares and collected funds to
resource Black liberation movements across the globe, particularly
in defence of Ethiopia following the Italian invasion in 1935.

In the late 1930s, Francois was at the centre of a transnational
labour movement which spread across the Caribbean, demanding rights and freedoms from the British colonial authorities. The
forces standing in the way of this people's movement were not
just the bosses, but also the police. Members of unions such as the
NWCSA were angered by poor living conditions, low wages and
the common arrest and extrajudicial killing of striking workers.
On the night of 13 October 1937, before what became a general
strike and a popular uprising in Trinidad, Francois delivered a
rousing speech to workers in Port of Spain. At The Greens on
Piccadilly Street, she spoke of the movement for land rights against
British settlers in Kenya, protests in Nigeria against colonial taxes,
the terror of workers in fascist Germany and the victories won
by working-class strikers in England. 'I spoke', Elma Francois
recalled, 'about the Negro and East-Indian workers who sleep
under the Town Hall and in the Square through poverty', linking

the suffering of colonised people in the Caribbean to colonised and working peoples across the globe.[7]

Francois used these public meetings to demonstrate the inter-connectedness of racism, capitalism and imperialism. While affirming how the racialised divisions of labour within Trinidad reflected the global divisions of labour in a world still flounder-ing under the heel of European colonialism, she did not dismiss European proletarian struggles as inconsequential. Encouraging Caribbean workers to observe the victories and suffering of Europe's poor facilitated a better understanding of the weaknesses of Europe's political and economic elite, wielding power over the masses in both the underdeveloped colonies and the expanding economies in the heart of Empire. Through this international-ism of both action and thought, activists such as Francois could formulate political positions and social strategies that contested the power of an Empire struggling to maintain global dominance. Racism was not a question of identity, lack of diversity, or some groups being privileged; it was a system of governance instrumen-tal to the division and exploitation of workers, a system unafraid to wield state violence in the discipline of racialised populations that dared engage in organised resistance.

The largest strike in Trinidad started with oil workers in June 1938, soon spreading to dockworkers, shop clerks and agricultural workers, as well as domestic workers – mainly women, with whom Francois was a key organiser. The strikes and protests eventually turned into a popular uprising. Indeed when police attempted to arrest one of the union leaders, Tubal Uriah 'Buzz' Butler, the crowd came to his defence. This led to the death of Corporal Charles King, one of the servicemen involved in the arrests. Following the uprising and this death, a state of emergency was declared. Two warships, HMS Ajax and HMS Exeter, manned by 2,200 mainly white expatriate troops, were summoned to the island's shores, tasked with crushing the rebellion. Both police and military had extraordinary powers to search, arrest and shoot at will. Fourteen civilians were killed, and over fifty seriously wounded, according to official reports (local witnesses claimed that the death toll was higher).

Over five hundred arrests were made, including Elma Francois, who became the first woman in the island's history to be charged with sedition. The police claimed that her speech of the previous year had the intent of 'causing disaffection among his Majesty's subjects'.[8] The focus of the prosecution's case was the disturbances which had led to the destruction of property, police injuries and the death of a serviceman. But for those charged, the events of 1937–38 were part of a wider movement against state violence, racism and capitalist exploitation. Unlike her co-defendants, Francois went against the wishes of her attorney, and insisted on representing herself in court. Facing an all-male, property-owning jury, she used the opportunity to recount how innocent civilians had been killed by the bullets of soldiers and police repressing the rebellion. With sharp political prescience, she asserted:

> war clouds are now hanging over Europe and political howlers will soon be coming to ask you, the same people who when you ask for bread are shot like dogs and given jail sentences, to fight for them. But we will tell them that we will not fight in any war. The only war we will fight is the fight to better conditions, peace and liberty.[9]

This fight, Francois stated, was enshrined in the commitments of the NWCSA to the 'welfare of negro people … solidarity with the oppressed negro people across the West Indies and the entire world … [and] to win the masses of oppressed people the world over'.[10] Francois understood that while the struggles against capitalism and imperialism in other parts of the world were different from those in the Caribbean, freedom for Black people was bound up with the liberation of all oppressed people. She used her platform to highlight these connections, and to call for the links of solidarity necessary to overthrow the militarism and capitalism which used racism to control oppressed peoples across the colonised world. Francois was the only defendant of all the NWCSA members charged with sedition to be found not guilty.

The surveillance of labour organisers by the colonial police was common in the British Caribbean, often leading to trumped-up charges or extrajudicial killings, particularly during the uprisings of the 1930s. By 1938, British troops were stationed in Trinidad, with a new Sedition Bill proposed to limit press freedom, trade union organising and other civil liberties, in what George Padmore called colonial fascism.[11] But despite the violent policing and widespread imprisonment of activists, far-reaching victories were achieved. Fixed minimum wages, increases in public welfare expenditure, pensions and compensation for industrial injuries were among the improvements to the lives of ordinary people won through the strikes and protests. Importantly, these uprisings also transformed the working classes across the Caribbean into a more politically strategic, internationally connected and radically organised social movement.[12] Elma Francois and the NWCSA is one of many anti-colonial stories seldom remembered and too often disconnected from resistance to British racism on the UK mainland. The final part of this section briefly analyses the importance of anti-imperialism and anti-capitalism to the formation of Britain's Black political movement.

The popular education disseminated through informal lectures from activists like Francois, or through trade unions and other organisations, led to an understanding of British colonial imperialism and to a thirst for both local and international solidarities. These ideas, forged through the colonial experience, would lay the foundations for a radical Black politics that saw anti-colonialism and anti-racism as one and the same. The uprisings which took place across the Caribbean in the late 1930s were thus a prelude to the anti-colonial movements which won formal independence in the post-war period, and to the Caribbean Black Power uprisings of the 1970s and 1980s. These movements built ideological and material links of solidarity with Black freedom struggles in the US as well as liberation struggles across Africa, Asia and Latin America.[13] What is less often recalled, however, were the ways in which these Caribbean labour and resistance movements of the late 1930s formed part of the historical memories and political cultures of those who migrated to Britain in the post-war period.

John La Rose, in maintaining that Black people did not come alive in Britain, saw the story of Elma Francois as a key example of the history of Black resistance to British racism. He corresponded with Francois' biographer Rhoda Reddock and arranged for the book to be published by New Beacon Books, the radical Black press he co-founded. Starting the story of anti-racism in Britain's colonies, rather than on the British mainland, doesn't simply uncover the histories of less-remembered activists and social movements; it also uncovers a Black politics which is committed to an international struggle against capitalism and imperialism. The racism of British colonial policing was intimately linked with white colonial control of land and resources. While not every Caribbean migrant to Britain arrived as a committed anti-racist, those who were involved in trade unions were often those who helped to shape Britain's radical Black movements in the 1950s and 1960s.[14] Imperialism and capitalism were understood as so interwoven with racism that they could never be resisted in isolation from one another. What surprised many Caribbean trade unionists migrating to Britain, La Rose argued, was not racism from bosses, government or the police, but the racism they experienced from the working class. Organised racism from their neighbours and co-workers, including British trade unions, was a new problem with which they had to contend.

Maintaining links to the colonies meant that many of the first radical political organisations set up by Caribbean people in post-war Britain were British branches of Caribbean trade unions. Organisations such as the Caribbean Labour Congress were dominated by anti-colonial communists intimately connected with independence struggles back home. As *Race Today* and other radical Black publications of the time attested, these solidarities encompassed the Black Power movements in the US, those sparked by the Rodney Riots in Kingston, Jamaica in 1968, and the wars for liberation in Southern Africa in the 1970s – as well as the trade union and socialist movements which defined the Cold War politics of Latin America, Africa and Asia. Crucially, this global outlook did not cloud the need for local action. Britain's Black Power movement, together with radical publishers and anti-racist community organisations, took on the racism emanating from institutions that shaped the lives and livelihoods of colonial migrants and their descendants. Like racist governance in the colonies, law-and-order policing was where many Black people felt or witnessed the most overt forms of racial violence. Harassment, incarceration, brutality and death at the hands of the state made resistance to the police a fundamental part of Black grassroots organising in the twentieth century.

Anti-colonialism and anti-racism in Britain

Resisting racial violence has been central to Black political movements in Britain, particularly during the early years of post-war migration. It involved defending physical places – which were then termed coloured quarters[15] – from far-right racism on the streets, an issue ignored or even sanctioned by the police.[16] By the 1950s, Blacks were not simply responding to individual racist attacks from whites, but were engaging in pitched battles against violent white mobs in Nottingham (East Midlands) and Notting Hill (west London). Notting Hill is now best known for its Caribbean Carnival; the costumes and sound systems were first brought to the area in part as a response to racism. When the Black community became firmly established in the Notting Hill and Ladbroke Grove area, the fascist Union Movement whipped up panic about an 'invasion' by coloured people. Attacks from groups of whites, who were often armed, were an increasing concern. By

September 1958, Black residents collectively fought back, defending themselves with petrol bombs. This street-based confrontation
marked a political rupture which intensified the militancy of Black
resistance to racism.[17] Many Blacks considered the police to be on
the side of the racist mobs; racists who were arrested for brutal
attacks were often released on bail, or not charged at all.[18]

The overt and violent racism in this part of west London stimu-
lated not only spontaneous rebellion but also grassroots organising.
The threat of attack, and the tacit complicity of the state, meant
that Black people were obliged not only to resist racial aggression
on the streets, but also to organise more sustained political defence
campaigns. The most high-profile incident was the death of Kelso
Cochrane, a young Antiguan carpenter who was stabbed to death
in a racist murder in 1959.[19] A multitude of organisations was set
up in the wake of these events, and they became a focal point for
Black activism. London-based, yet internationally oriented, coali-
tions developed around the 'riots' and Cochrane's murder, involving activists and groups which included Amy Ashwood Garvey's
Association for the Advancement of Coloured People, the *West
Indian Gazette* co-founded by Claudia Jones, and a London branch
of Trinidad's People's National Movement (PNM).[20]

While those organising around the murder of Cochrane were
sensitive to the grief and mourning experienced by his family
and friends, they also highlighted the fact that this racist murder
required a political response. Lobbying politicians, writing articles and organising public gatherings was not simply a struggle
against racism in Britain, and these international activists continued to connect this campaign with anti-colonial movements
across the Caribbean and Africa, with which they maintained
strong political connections. London provided a unique cruci-
ble in which colonialism and racism, and the struggle against
them, combined. By the 1950s, Amy Ashwood Garvey had decades
of experience organising in and against the British state. She had
campaigned against British support for the 1935 Italian invasion of

Ethiopia and she had co-organised the Fifth Pan-African Congress, held in Manchester in 1945,[21] which, like the congresses that preceded it, brought together Black anticolonialists (including George Padmore, W. E. B. Du Bois and Kwame Nkrumah) from across the world to one of the centres of Empire.[22] Thus, Garvey's Black nationalist and anti-racist politics were not simply informed by anti-colonialism, they were forged in it.

Claudia Jones moved from Trinidad to the US as a child, but was deported from the US as an adult for 'un-American activities' and violating the McCarran Act (she was a non-US citizen and a member of the Communist Party). She was refused re-entry to Trinidad by the British colonial administration in 1955, as they were concerned that her commitment to communism and Black liberation could lead to unrest. Eventually admitted to Britain, where the authorities could keep a closer eye, Jones, alongside Garvey, edited the *West Indian Gazette*. From 1958, this periodical reported on the anti-colonial and workers' movements from across the Caribbean, keeping Black and anti-racist activists in Britain connected to these international struggles.[23]

Jones also organised London's first Caribbean Carnival in St Pancras Town Hall in 1959, providing the inspiration for the Notting Hill Carnival from 1966. The Caribbean migrants to Britain who founded British branches of Caribbean political organisations, such as those in Trinidad, used these links of solidarity to strengthen claims for independence. Despite the PNM not formally positioning itself as a socialist or trade union-oriented political party, until Trinidadian independence it supported grassroots struggles.[24] The transnational activists and organisations involved in campaigning for justice following the murder of Kelso Cochrane formed part of a broad coalition of anti-racist and anti-colonial organisers. These groups consistently used their activism to demonstrate the links between the violent racism on the streets of Britain, and the violent colonialism facing contestation across Africa and the Caribbean. Capitalist exploitation in the colonies and Europe, enforced by racial governance from the police and other state institutions, was confronted by the radical politics of activists such as Claudia Jones, who had a profound influence on a generation of Black Marxists involved in movements in the decades that followed.

Britain's Black Power movement emerged from this combination of international interconnections and racist violence in Britain. As a declining colonial power in the first half of the twentieth century, Britain attracted increasing numbers of anti-colonial activists who migrated to its cities, to study, work and organise against Empire. The ensuing militancy led to the reformist Universal Coloured People's Association being succeeded by the revolutionary Black Unity and Freedom Party in 1970, with branches in London and Manchester. Inspired by the Black Power movement in the US, as well as anti-colonial groups internationally, the British Black Panthers began in London in 1968, followed by other groups such as the Black Liberation Front. Branches of these organisations, as well as myriad other groups, were also established in many other cities.[25]

Like their US contemporaries, they organised independent services for working-class Black communities, including supplementary schools, youth clubs and healthcare provision. They delivered rousing speeches in public spaces, organised marches and demonstrations, and published magazines and pamphlets. Many of their members were born in Britain's colonies, and those who were British-born had strong links through family connections. It is worth noting that almost all these Black Power movements conceived of Black as a political colour. Like Walter Rodney[26] and Steve Biko,[27] they identified all the oppressed peoples of the colonised world as Black. These social and cultural links strengthened the political solidarities with a world that was decolonising around them, and these solidarities informed the principles of the organisations. With the Cold War raging and armed struggle the liberatory norm, a militant hope of a world free from imperialism and capitalism underpinned the goals of radical activists across Black

Britain. However, in order to get a better idea of how Black communities resisted British policing in the 1970s and 1980s, we turn next to campaigns and organisations which may, on the surface, not appear to be part of a Black Power movement.

Black parents on the move

In the 1970s and 1980s, the family became an important site for Black struggle against policing. These new Black movements offer a wider understanding of Black resistance, illustrating how both police racism and resistance to it are gendered. Later in this section we will look at Black women's groups who were involved in organised resistance to policing, but first we will consider the Black women who entered activism through the defence of their children. One such organisation was the Black Parents Movement (BPM), a network of Black parents' organisations which spanned the country. One of the first was founded in north London in 1976 by Black activists from different political backgrounds. Some had been part of militant Black Power groups such as the Black Panther Movement and the Black Unity and Freedom Party; others had worked in solidarity with Caribbean trade unions through the West Indian Standing Conference in the 1960s. Many were Black parents who were concerned with the racism their children faced, particularly in school and on the streets from the police. While focusing on the racism on their doorstep, which plagued the day-to-day realities of Black communities, these Black parents simultaneously challenged the racist myth of the degenerate Black family and that of the violent criminality projected onto Black youth. The BPM's political position was also anti-colonial. In their newsletter, *Battle Front*, they explained:

> First, there was the battle to carve out a decent life under the tough conditions of British Colonial Rule. Then there was the long, hard struggle to get established in Britain in the face of racism and hostility.[28]

The BPM lived this anti-colonial history through their activism, supporting the anti-apartheid movement in South Africa and Black Power struggles in the Caribbean such as the Grenada Revolution in the early 1980s. This international solidarity was maintained as the BPM network spread across Britain. One local case became known as the Harlesden Six, a campaign to defend a group of young Black women and girls harassed, assaulted and arrested by police in this area of north London in June 1976.

As they were leaving the Burning Spear nightclub, these women saw a young Black man being arrested by a group of police officers. His sister was protesting his innocence as they forced him into their vehicle. Leaving the scene, the young women turned back when they heard a scream – they returned to find the sister lying on the pavement and being assaulted by the officers. Challenging the assault, the group of young women and girls were, in turn, badly beaten by the officers. Later in court, one the officers claimed the women had been 'hysterical', which had forced the police to slap them, on the assumption that this would free them from their purported hysteria. The misogynistic logic of irrationally emotional women requiring the physical discipline of the rational man was accompanied by racial abuse. A local man, Erwin Andrew, witnessed the assault and immediately went to the police to file a complaint. In addition to brutality, the witness reported the officers hurling racist and sexist abuse at the young women – 'You women are animals, look at the way they behave' – before arresting and taking them all to the police station.

The women and girls reported that the assaults, both verbal and physical, continued in the police station. One of the young women passed out; the police doctor dismissed all of them as showing no signs of injury. They were charged with a range of offences, including threatening behaviour and assaulting a police officer. The BPM formed part of a campaign to defend the Harlesden Six. Organising public meetings and pickets, and ensuring that left-wing legal representatives took on the case, the BPM reproduced a model which put the demands of the defendants at the centre of an anti-racist community campaign.

In court, the racist and sexist abuse from the violent officers was painfully recounted. Some of the women had criminal records, and the prosecution used this to argue that these Black women were delinquents, describing them as 'convicted criminals' in order to undermine their credibility. When it was reported that a slap was necessary to calm 'hysteria', the witness Mr Andrew responded, 'There was nothing therapeutic about the fact that when he slapped her he called her a Black bitch'. While this did little to challenge the sexist assumption that physical violence can and should be used to relieve 'hysterical' women, it did suggest to the magistrate that the explanation provided by the officers was insincere.

The evidence of the police unraveled further as the officers were cross-examined. First, while PC Elliston claimed that his statement and testimony were taken from the records made in his notebook, the verbal threats he claimed were made by the young women were nowhere to be found in his notes. When asked what his relationship was like with the Black community, he claimed that this was good. PC Elliston was then asked if he had heard of a Mr Mullins. Reports from the trial recount an uneasy silence – this was a local Black community worker who had recently been badly beaten, along with two other Black youths, in Harlesden Police Station. Elliston had been accused of being one of the assaulting officers, making him very unpopular among the local Black community. PC Elliston refused to answer the question about Mr Mullins, but the damage was done. These inconsistencies were compounded by a letter from the GP of one of the young women, which reported internal bruising following the arrest.

Despite the overwhelming evidence from witnesses and medical reports, as well as the inconsistency of the officers' accounts, the court remained unconvinced. After eight days of evidence spread over five weeks, the magistrates took less than fifteen minutes to bring in guilty verdicts to five of the six young women and girls. The accusations of hysteria and criminality projected onto these Black women and girls by the police overrode the evidence and testimony on which their defence relied. Punishments ranged from probation to suspended prison sentences.

Avoiding incarceration for such serious offences was considered a partial victory for the Harlesden Six by the BPM. However, coverage in community newspapers and leaflets following the trial declared 'Guilty Verdicts Are Unacceptable' and 'The Fight Goes On!' The courtroom was just one arena in which organisations such as the BPM challenged British racism. The activists involved hoped to demonstrate how the power and testimonies of the police were not all-powerful, given that they had been humiliated in court, and the young women had walked out with their freedom. It is through activism like this that campaigners learned to organise with the community, put together legal and media campaigns, and understand the nuances of state racism.

The Harlesden Six is one of the many less-remembered cases of police brutality resisted by Black women. The BPM, as well as the other campaigns led by Black parents, such as 'Scrap Sus', were markedly different from the Black Power organisatons that had come before them, such as the Black Panther Movement. These self-identified parents' groups were not only responding to the racism faced by children and young people. Their existence was also indirectly a response to the racist pathologising of Black families, which were framed as chaotic or even non-existent. Yet, rather than simply trying to mimic the ideal of the nuclear family which represented British values, these groups of Black parents built radical alliances with Black youth movements across the country, extending notions of family and parental responsibility, and using them as a vehicle for radical change. It is therefore unsurprising that, for many other Black campaigns against policing, family and parenting continued to inform the political positions and experiences of those involved.

For subsequent campaigns, such as Scrap Sus, started by groups of Black women coming together in south London, the experience of care for Black children and young people in the face of police racism formed a vital part of a lived political education.[29] The 'Sus' laws, laws of 'suspicion', which empowered police officers to stop and search individuals, were a reinterpretation of the 1824 Vagrancy Act. Relaunched in the 1970s, police used the tactic to deal with a new category of crime: mugging.[30] This term, borrowed from the US, wasn't a crime in itself, but rather a word used to describe a collection of street-based offences, including theft, threatening behaviour or assault. Collecting all these crimes under one umbrella term aided the press, politicians and police in creating the impression that these crimes were on the rise in a new way.

The spectre of the 'mugger' set the foundations for a moral panic centred on the idea that society was going into decline, attributing blame to cultures and communities that were alien to British life. Reports of the mugger were therefore projected onto young Black men, considered to embody the antithesis of English values by a police and media campaign during the 1970s, exemplifying how 'Crime is summoned ... as the "evil" which is the reverse of the "normality" of "Englishness"'.[31] This campaign identified 'areas of above-average crime rates, even though at the time Black immigrants were under-represented in the crime rates of these "criminal areas"'.[32] The racist logic which underpinned this moral panic criminalised Black communities, and led to an escalation of harassment, arrest and brutality in the mid-1970s.

Before long, activists, parents and public sector workers were challenging this moral panic and the violent policing that accompanied it. Campaigners in Bristol travelled to London to protest youths being harassed by Sus laws. In Liverpool, young people organised a sit-in at a local church to protest police violence and racism, while in Manchester's Moss Side, complaints of police

violence and racism were dismissed by senior officers.[33] Some
of the resistance was spontaneous, with activist Jan McKenley
remembering how people would challenge the police whenever
they saw them using Sus powers against a young person in their
community. Many of the campaigns were localised, initiated by
mothers such as Martha Otito Osamor, who was then part of the
United Black Women's Action Group:

> as young mothers we were trying to avoid those things happen-
> ing to our children ... We started from a council estate and then
> other people hear about us so we were meeting in our front rooms
> but we got bigger and we had to go into a community centre in
> Stanley Road [Tottenham, north London] where we meet every
> third Sunday of the month. So other women were coming to this
> meeting and they were bringing issues that were real, you know,
> they will come and say 'my son's been arrested by the police' or 'he's
> in prison' or, you know, and so on.[34]

Beverley Bryan recalls that most of the people organising against
Sus were women, and Stella Dadzie[35] has recounted the move
within OWAAD towards organising against the police following
the rise of Sus. Gee Bernard[36] helped to establish 'West Indian
Parents Against Sus', 'Sus Against Us' and 'Scrap Sus'.[37] State
violence was coupled with hostilities from far-right groups. In
1977, the National Front were confronted by counter protests in
Lewisham, a target of the far-right and fascists owing to its anti-
racist campaigns. This became known as the Battle of Lewisham,[38]
but despite the victory here, violence from the far right continued.
In 1981, thirteen Black teenagers died in a house fire which many
believe was a case of arson, in keeping with other racist attacks
in the area. Police refused to investigate the deaths as suspicious,
and what came to be known as the New Cross Massacre led to the
Black People's Day of Action, the largest anti-racist demonstration
Britain had ever seen.[39] The 1980s were decisive years for Black
struggle for many reasons, and mass protest against racist violence
formed part of a wider movement of Black rebellion.

Where will this all end?
Rebellion, repression and co-optation in the 1980s

Throughout the first half of the twentieth century, militarised policing, mass imprisonment of suspect communities and other forms of violence were generally reserved for Britain's colonies. The account of the repression of strikes in Trinidad earlier in the chapter provided one example. Kenya and Malaya (detailed in Chapter 4) provide key cases in which the army and police were almost indistinguishable, shooting and detaining strikers, protesters and other suspected dissidents with impunity. However, during the Troubles in Northern Ireland between the 1960s and the 1990s, the violence and militarism of colonial policing made their way to the UK. Northern Ireland, part of England's oldest former colony, is a long-disputed territory whose history is beyond the scope of this book. Shoot-to-kill policies and imprisonment without trial were sanctioned by the British government, and imposed upon suspected nationalist dissidents in Northern Ireland. Riot police with armour and weaponry not used on the British mainland became routine in towns with large Catholic populations, such as Derry[40] (I return to this in Chapter 5).

Between the 1960s and 1990s there was, of course, another colonial legacy changing the face of Britain as migrants from its colonies and former colonies settled in significant numbers. Both the conflict in Northern Ireland and the existence of 'coloured' immigration brought changes to how law and order were understood. Stereotypes about Black violence, promiscuity and criminality created the illusion that Black and migrant communities were bringing new crimes (e.g. mugging) to the nation, crimes the criminal justice system was unequipped to deal with. And so, in the wake of the expansion of colonial forms of policing in Northern Ireland, a more militarised form of policing was introduced across the UK, with the aim of providing new tools for racist state violence on the British mainland. This section now examines how new forms of state power and racism in the final decades of the twentieth century were used to repress urban revolt and Black political movements. These include both paramilitary tactics and forms of co-optation, which displaced radical politics with a more liberal reformism.

On 2 April 1980, police raided the Black and White Café in St Pauls, Bristol. A crowd quickly formed to defend the café, and within two hours the police were outnumbered. The police quickly retreated from the hostile crowd, which continued to grow as buildings and vehicles were attacked and looted.[41] Two hours later, a hundred more officers arrived with riot shields. They too were forced to retreat by the anti-police gathering, which a local cleric described as the first genuinely multiracial event in St Pauls' history.[42] Rumours spread that coachloads of Black youth from Birmingham were planning to join the revolt. By 3.30 a.m. over a hundred Black people had been stopped by police on the M5 motorway between Birmingham and Bristol based on this suspicion. National connections were being made, however, with slogans including 'Bristol yesterday, Brixton today'.[43] Similar events occurred that year in Nottingham, and then in 1981, Black youths in Brixton (south London) engaged in a similar revolt following an attempted arrest. Uprisings eventually spread across multiracial working-class areas of cities and towns across England. These rebellions were described by *Race Today* as an insurrection.[44]

Toxteth (the Liverpool 8 district), a low-income area with the city's largest Black population, had experienced considerable police brutality and use of Sus laws. Planting drugs and running 'coon races' to arrest local Black youths were common accusations from the local community against the police.[45] Alongside a large Irish population, Black and other working-class youth in the city engaged in some of the most violent rebellions of that year. CS gas, which had hitherto been used by British police only in Northern Ireland, was used on the UK mainland for the first time, in an attempt to disperse those engaged in the conflict.[46] And alongside the mass arrest of over five hundred people, another tactic from Northern Ireland was employed in Britain for the first time: vans were driven into crowds of people. While this successfully forced people to flee, the police killed a disabled man, David Moore. The officers in charge of the vehicle were cleared of any wrongdoing a year later.[47] The Home Secretary William Whitelaw drew comparisons with Northern Ireland when visiting Liverpool in the aftermath of the rebellions. In an interesting example of nominative determinism, Whitelaw proposed the deployment of combat troops to maintain order in communities such as Toxteth, working with Defence Secretary John Nott to arm police with more offensive weapons.[48] The communities affected by these uprisings soon formed organisations to defend the young people from the response of the state and to try and hold police to account. The Liverpool 8 Defence Campaign, Brixton Defence Committee, St Pauls Defence Committee (Bristol) and Moss Side Defence Committee (Manchester) were among the groups which engaged in campaigns and legal proceedings to defend those criminalised in 1981.

In Manchester, nearly five hundred people were arrested and charged with offences relating to the rebellions in the summer of 1981. Mass arrests and police vehicles intentionally driven into crowds were, as in Toxteth, key police tactics.[49] Fifty-four vans of 'snatch squads', inspired by similar tactics in Northern Ireland, seized people off the streets in a frenzy of arrest and brutality.[50] The Moss Side Defence Committee, like their equivalents in other cities, were focused, localised struggles that strove to expose police racism and limit the number of young people sent to prison following the disturbances. Yet, as Gus John, one of the organisers of the committee, explains, these campaigns also helped young people to gain a greater sense of their own power.[51] They demonstrated that spontaneous rebellions were not separate from organised campaigns, and that the two fed off and reinforced each other, each resisting British policing in different ways.

Unable to repress the discontent, the government set into motion a new approach: community policing, liaison committees, an independent complaints system, and (in the words of *Race Today*) 'other such trivialities'.[52] Activists criticised these reforms as attempts to incorporate the defence committees into police and government-moderated consultancy groups. Yet a more covert approach was also being developed.[53] Paramilitary policing methods used by British police in Northern Ireland and Hong Kong were introduced to police forces wholesale on the British mainland. These colonial police forces were trained to use CS gas, make mass arrests, shoot firearms and impose curfews. By 1983, police forces across England had received procedural training in this form of policing, formalising the techniques that had been used on an ad-hoc basis during the disturbances of 1981. The assistance that the police received from part of Britain's few remaining colonies was a secret at the time.[54] We cannot understate here the importance of colonial policing to the development of police power and racism on the British mainland. These strategies and techniques have colonial roots, and should be central to the story we tell about police racism.

A year later, in 1982, Sir Kenneth Newman was brought in to head London's Metropolitan Police. Newman was previously a colonial detective in the Palestine Special Branch before 1948,[55] and later moved to Northern Ireland, becoming Chief Constable of the Royal Ulster Constabulary (RUC).[56] He was awarded a knighthood for his work in transferring power from the British army to the RUC in the 1970s. It would be less than three years until widespread unrest and paramilitary policing returned to urban areas of England. In 1985, Brixton and Tottenham (in London), and Handsworth (Birmingham), would be among the communities which saw uprisings return.

> I was first alerted when I heard a noise ... which I now know was the breaking-in of the door. I opened my eyes, and I saw my mum walking towards the door ... then I heard another noise, and when

> I jumped up, I just saw, my mum was on the floor. She looked like she'd been pushed ... I stood up on the bed, and there was a policeman standing there with a gun in his hand, standing over my mum.[57]

The above quotation is from Lee Groce – he was eleven years old when police raided his family home in Brixton in September 1985. Officers were allegedly searching for Lee's elder brother, who was not in the house when police broke through the front door. The police shot their mother Cherry Groce in the back as she ran up the stairs in her nightdress, paralysing her from the waist down. In response to this shooting, Brixton revolted against the police for the second time in four years, forcing officers to retreat from the area.

While the violence and resistance following the shooting of Cherry Groce appeared to be confined to Brixton, these events reverberated in other Black communities in London, particularly Broadwater Farm, a large housing estate in Tottenham. The police described Broadwater Farm as an estate 'where normal policing methods are resisted by a vociferous minority and where unprovoked attacks on police are all too common'.[58] Stafford Scott, spokesperson of the Broadwater Farm Defence Campaign in Tottenham, provides a different perception of community-police relations in the context of Cherry Groce's death:

> When we in Tottenham hear about a Black sister, a Black mother, being shot in her back as she's turned and running away, running up the stairs, we felt it in Tottenham. We may not have kicked off there like they kicked off here [in Brixton], but believe me we felt it, we talked about it. Everybody in our community heard about it, and we were enraged.[59]

A week after Cherry Groce was shot, on 5 October 1985, police in Tottenham arrested Floyd Jarrett for what they claimed was a vehicle tax infringement. On the pretext of searching for stolen goods, the officers used his keys to enter the property where Jarrett's mother and younger sister were living. During the unlawful search, Floyd's mother, Cynthia Jarrett, died. This police raid on the home of a Black suspect led to the second tragedy suffered by a Black mother at the hands of the state in as many weeks.

A march to the local police station was ignored, and riot police arrived to confront a mobilisation on Broadwater Farm led by young people. By the end of the night, a police officer had been killed in the midst of the ensuing conflict. Sir Kenneth Newman gave the green light for officers to be armed with guns loaded with plastic bullets, but he ordered them not to fire.[60] Newman's oversight of the Broadwater Farm uprisings in 1985 was the first time this kind of paramilitary policing had been deployed on the British mainland. The introduction of CS spray and other tactics would soon complete the move into a more paramilitary and colonial approach to policing in England.[61]

The estate was under police occupation for several months, with between 200 and 400 officers patrolling Broadwater Farm at any given time.[62] One mother living on the estate told *Race Today*:

> Doors were broken down, people beaten up, searches made and photographs taken. Phones have been cut off, or tampered with. We have learnt that the police question our visitors, and notes are made of people entering and leaving the estate ... The police question the residents. We were asked about our country of birth.[63]

This level of blanket violence and harassment against a specific community is reminiscent of colonial policies which saw mass arrest and detention routinely used during periods of anti-colonial unrest. Boys as young as fourteen were arrested in school grounds and taken to police stations for questioning. The police even targeted schools for children with special educational needs. *Race Today* were told:

> Children have been arrested and kept in detention ... Parents have been refused access to children, who are being moved to different institutions around the country.[64]

Young people on Broadwater Farm endured horrific violence and false imprisonment, some of which took years of campaigning to overturn.[65] Yet at the same time, there was an escalation of forms of soft power, which attempted to co-opt different sections of 'suspect communities' to erode the radicalism of Black struggle.

Unlike other parts of England, Birmingham did not see widespread uprisings until the mid-1980s. On 9 September 1985, when revolts had already taken place in many parts of the country, Handsworth also went up in flames. The uprising began after police got into a dispute with a local resident over an alleged parking ticket. Over three hundred residents engaged in pitched battles against police which raged throughout the night and continued for the next three days.[66] Handsworth was also the site of the last major rebellion of the 1980s, and the state then took a different approach to challenging urban revolt. The rest of this section looks at how the state tried to co-opt different sections of Britain's Black communities. I analyse how government used racialised and classed cleavages to disrupt solidarities, turning radical demands into narrow appeals for representation and funding for specifically *ethnic* or *cultural*, rather than political, initiatives.

The Handsworth Defence Campaign, a multi-ethnic community campaign, was organised to defend those arrested, most of whom were Black, although a number were Asian or white. The political establishment echoed the police and media narrative, and soon the Home Secretary, Douglas Hurd, visited the area. He asked a member of the local African-Caribbean community why the unrest had taken place, to which the man responded by citing rising levels of unemployment. Moments later, groups of young people began to pelt Hurd with rocks, and he was rushed into an armoured police vehicle for protection. Hurd dismissed this analysis, later commenting that 'All this ground has been ploughed over quite a lot and I am not sure there is a lot of good soil to be turned up'.[67] Here, we see the connections between race and class made explicit by community activists. As Stuart Hall said, 'race is the modality in which class is lived'[68] – in other words, racism is experienced through the poverty, exploitation and violence of capitalism.

According to the radical local *Asian Youth News*, the police tried to turn the South Asian and African-Caribbean community against each other when a post office fire killed two people. The *Asian Youth News* also claimed that this tactic was not new:

> Only a few months ago, three Birmingham Asian businessmen were caught bringing heroin in. The police only harass the African youth for small amounts of soft drugs while they leave their rich friends alone.[69]

Here, we see activists from the Asian Youth Movement dissect how ethnic and class cleavages are exploited in an attempt to better control racially subjugated populations. Handsworth saw radical resistance on both sides of this attempted division. A statement released by an African-Caribbean community meeting expressed their condolences, and 'Asian and African members of the community laid wreaths at the post office as a mark of respect'.[70] Institutions also racialised those responsible for the violence as specifically African Caribbean in attempt to further contain the parameters of debate regarding the cause of the disturbances. The contradictions of this racist and divisive narrative were also challenged by the *Asian Youth News*:

> a Tory magistrate has attended a meeting where Asian businessmen have started to set up vigilante squads of Asian youth to go against the African community. The police would like to have us fight each other so that we do not organise against the brutality and poverty we face.[71]

When Asian business owners invoked racial prejudice and class privileges against working-class Black youth, they were challenged by radical voices organising against racism. These critiques of Handsworth's petite bourgeoisie should be understood as a continuation of how the colonial bourgeoisie was mobilised to re-entrench white domination throughout the British Empire. The moderate wealth which privileges small-scale business owners over lower-income people gives them a stake in a racist system, an investment they defend by aligning themselves with the state.[72] These class cleavages were compounded in Handsworth by the ethnic divisions between people of African or South Asian heritage. Attempts to co-opt grassroots anti-racist activism were not confined to Birmingham: central government began constructing a national campaign to encourage ethnic and class cleavages among communities of resistance.

Following the urban rebellions of the early-to-mid-1980s, the government began discussing possible avenues for the avoidance of future uprisings. While many of the proposals involved harsher policing and sentencing, the government also discussed softer approaches. Confidential discussions between Prime Minister Margaret Thatcher and Home Secretary Douglas Hurd, declassified in 2015, indicate the government was concerned that the pool of disaffected, mostly Black, young people in the cities should not be allowed to increase, and that visible action should be taken to better the 'life chances of this very difficult group'.[73]

The final three words of the above quotation are underlined in the original correspondence, signalling that the state considered the problem of urban revolt to be attributable to the young people involved, rather than to the policing or other forms of racism they resisted. One proposal in the confidential government correspondence was an 'Inner City Initiative' that would 'encourage small Black businesses' in areas such as Tottenham and Brixton. Ministers and civil servants considered the 'Black Business in Birmingham Initiative'[74] a model for Black areas in London. The approach of the government served two functions. First, as we have seen above, the government found that local business owners could be easily co-opted and mobilised against Black people who engage in civil unrest. A proliferation of Black businesses could potentially make managing urban revolts easier, as the state would be more likely to have aspirational allies within Black communities, who could be used as a proxy against the low-income 'disaffected, mostly Black, young people'.[75]

Secondly, the Inner City Initiative served the ideological interests of the state. Rather than the government using tax revenue to generate public sector employment or other social, health or educational services, they saw the private sector as primarily responsible for job creation. The proposals formed part of the wider economic movement of neoliberalisation promoted by Margaret Thatcher's government in the 1980s. This shifted the role of the state from welfare provider to facilitator of market growth, encouraging individuals to compete for waged labour or a share in the market through entrepreneurship.[76] Within this logic, low incomes and unemployment are the fault of inefficient, lazy or financially irresponsible individuals falling behind in a competitive market, rather than racialised capitalist exploitation reproducing and entrenching existing inequalities. This approach would enable the state to more easily malign any future rebellions as the nefarious behaviour of deviant communities, unrelated to social injustice.

It is important to note that, despite these government proposals, little became concrete policy. This can be partly attributed to critiques from the conservative right. In 1985, government advisor Oliver Letwin argued that state funding for Black businesses would be wasted on 'Rastafarian arts and crafts workshops' and the 'disco and drug trade'. According to Letwin, 'Lower-class unemployed white people had lived for years in appalling slums without a breakdown of public order on anything like the present scale', implying that violent unrest resulted from the uniquely 'bad moral attitudes' of Black youths. Letwin has since apologised for his comments, conceding that they were 'badly worded'.[77] Like many 'apologies' for racism, the intention or sentiment is not deemed problematic, rather the manner and phrasing is acknowledged to have aged poorly. This is a notion that reflects the contemporary emergence of professionalised anti-racism, whose primary concern is representation, diversity training and politically correct language, resulting in only superficial reforms.

Today, a state-managed anti-racism, in which Black politics has been stripped of its radicalism, is the most enduring legacy of the state's attempt at using soft power to quell Black rebellion. Bureaucrats, politicians and commentators framed Black politics as being any Black person doing anything, from council workers to MPs, investment bankers to captains of industry, or indeed any Black person achieving public renown or influence (even marrying into the royal family). We see its digital iteration in #blackexcellence. Furthermore, by manipulating youth sector funding, it became more difficult for young people to engage in radical politics, as resources grow ever more focused on anti-gangs workshops, anti-terror initiatives or employability skills.[78] Many of the monitoring groups and law centres challenging the police were offered government resources with conditions that limited their ability to scrutinise the state. Equality and diversity consultancy, implicit bias training and racial awareness workshops reduced racism to individual prejudice, privilege and hatred.

This depoliticisation of Black politics treated the state and its institutions as a tool for anti-racism, rather than recognising it to be a significant reproducer of racism. The language of interpersonal prejudice and privilege misrepresents racism as purely an individual matter to be unlearned, educated or diversified away, rather than racism being a fundamental system of control intrinsic to capitalist exploitation and state power. Targeted funding denudes radical Black politics of its commitment to solidarity, instead focusing on individuals who should change their personal knowledge and thoughts and their interaction with friends, colleagues or members of the public. Today, this has left different communities to compete over resources limited by the state and market capitalism. At its most crass, communities are encouraged to argue over who is most marginalised or most privileged, in order to justify who should be platformed, financed or centred. To be clear, this is not an argument for ignoring difference, but rather for the need to work through difference in order to build connections of mutuality and solidarity. Otherwise, state-sanctioned anti-racisms produce a superficial Black politics which pays lip service to anti-capitalism and anti-colonialism, but does little to build practically on the radical anti-colonial and Black Power movements which shook Britain and its colonies in the twentieth century.

Conclusion

Having a more diverse organisation, workplace or curriculum is, of course, a good thing. Being more aware of the ways power is reproduced through our interpersonal interactions is vital if we are to live, work and organise together. Anti-racists all want to live and work in environments which are diverse, and with people who are aware of the ways different people navigate a deeply unjust and discriminatory world. But reducing anti-racism to these processes alone misinterprets racism as a problem of prejudice, and not as a process which better enables capitalism and state power to perpetuate exploitation and violence. This enables policies and practices which elevate 'politically correct' language and state-led equality and diversity programmes to anti-racist tools in and of themselves. While we cannot overlook the necessity for resources coupled with progressive reforms, these will have little effect unless they are connected to the real motors of social change – grassroots mass movements. The Black movements against British policing detailed in this chapter were not led by purists, blindly committed to Marxism or any other ideology. But they remained focused on racism as intrinsically connected to capitalism through colonialism, and the battle against the first cannot be separated from the latter two.

Black politics arises in Britain not as a signal of a new multiculturalism in which Black people are simply present in British economic, political and social life. Rather than caring because one is a West Indian from Jamaica or an African from Nigeria, people begin to identify with a Black political struggle through social movements that connect colonialism and imperialism to racism in Britain. When John La Rose asserts that 'We did not come alive in Britain', he is not simply acknowledging histories of migration from the colonies to the centre of Empire. He is demonstrating how anti-racism must be rooted in anti-colonialism, and the capitalist exploitation which connects them. This radical appraisal of 1970s Britain provides powerful lessons for the twenty-first century.

When the 'Windrush generation' is presented as the dawn of Britain's relationship with Black people, it suggests that racism emerged in Britain when Black migrants stepped off that ship in 1948. The myth that racial difference arrived on British shores and that this gave rise to racial prejudice and discrimination not only erases centuries of anti-colonial resistance to British power, it also enables the state to reduce racism to a problem which can be eradicated by diversified institutions, race equality education and legislation to make overt discrimination unlawful. Britain's Black Power movements understood that racism is fundamental to the extraction of resources and the exploitation of people which drive international capitalism. While not reducing racism to merely a tool of economic profiteering, these movements still understood capitalist exploitation as a fundamental part of racism. By separating racism from class struggle and imperialism, the state could use the aftermath of the radical uprisings of the 1980s to pick off individuals and organisations willing to be incorporated into a liberal anti-racism that worked with, rather than against, the state. The chapters that follow will detail some of the campaigns that have resisted the allure of government-led responses to British racism and policing.

2

Into the twenty-first century: resistance, respectability and Black deaths in police custody

To despise and to degrade the female sex, is the characteristic of the savage state in every part of the globe. (William Robertson, *The History of America*, four volumes, 1777)

We are strong, or people perceive us as strong, but we are no different from any other human being. (Marcia Rigg, interview with author, 2018)

In 1993, Stephen Lawrence, a Black teenager from south London, was killed in a racist attack. His mother, Doreen, became one of the most prominent and influential anti-racist campaigners of the decade, challenging both racial violence on the streets and uniformed institutional racism. The Lawrence family, and the campaign that surrounded their struggle, exposed the under-policing of racial violence, and the institutional racism of British policing which led to Black communities being treated as a violent, criminal threat. Following Stephen's murder, his friend Duwayne Brooks and the Lawrence family were all treated as suspects rather than victims. Duwayne, who was with Stephen during the attack but had managed to get away and call an ambulance, was never asked by the police if he had been injured. They instead interrogated him, asking whether he had been carrying a weapon, insisting that he knew who had attacked Stephen. Police also repeatedly asked him what he and Stephen had done to provoke the ambush that had led to his friend being stabbed to death.[1]

One of the questions officers asked Duwayne was whether he and Stephen had been harassing white girls outside the local McDonalds earlier that evening. This line of questioning appears to suggest, at best, suspicion of an unrelated offence. But, given the racist context of the police's handling of the case, it is more likely that officers' minds were fixed on this alleged violation of white women by Black men, to the extent that it took precedence over the care of a victim of a racist attack, or the investigation of a racist murder. Particularly unsettling is the line of questioning that implies that Stephen's murder was part of a series of confrontations, suggesting that their harassment of white women could explain, or even justify, the attack. Accusing Duwayne and Stephen of being sexual predators, who had been forced to face the consequences of white mob justice, draws on racist stereotypes and histories of lynch logic in British ports during the 1919 'race riots'[2] and attacks on Blacks in Nottingham (East Midlands) and Notting Hill (west London) in 1958.[3] It also echoes British colonial penal systems and the chilling violence associated with Jim Crow America. While there was no evidence that Duwayne knew their attackers, or harassed the women in question that evening, he was effectively detained as a suspect – police refused to allow him to travel in the ambulance with his dying friend.

Less than an hour after the attack, a carload of young white men drove past the scene twice, jeering. They were identified as Jason Goatley and David Copley – both of whom were involved in an attack two years earlier that had led to the murder of Rolan Adams. Also in the car was Kieran Highland, an influential member of an organisation called Nazi Turn Out. No attempt to pursue the vehicle or these individuals in connection with the attack on Stephen and Duwayne was ever made. Within days of Stephen's murder, a number of anonymous witnesses cited two individuals as possible suspects, who were said to have been involved in previous racially motivated attacks. Another witness visited the Lawrences' home to tell them the names of people she saw washing blood off their clothes the day after the murder. However, these witnesses and a number of others were ignored by the Metropolitan Police, even though Doreen Lawrence pushed for them to do everything in their power to pursue the suspects. Years later, in the inquiry into Stephen's death, Doreen recalled:

> There was one incident that stuck out in my mind when I was asking about the boys [suspects] in prison. I was asking: 'Why couldn't they put a bug in with them in the room to listen to what was being said', because if they wouldn't talk to the police they would talk to individuals. [Detective Chief Superintendent] Ilsley said: 'We don't do things like this. No way.' I could remember he was very angry.[4]

This request, quoted in the report by Sir William Macpherson into the death of Stephen Lawrence, underlined the frustration felt by Stephen's mother at police inaction in the pursuit of her son's killers. While this was received as an outlandish suggestion at the time, the Stephen Lawrence Campaign's pressure on the police ultimately forced them to record incriminating conversations and footage of the men who would eventually be convicted of Stephen's murder. But Doreen's request now takes on a painful irony, as the murder suspects were not the only people being covertly investigated by the police. In 2013, ex-police spy turned whistleblower Peter Francis revealed that a number of anti-racist campaigns had been infiltrated by undercover officers. The Stephen Lawrence Campaign was key among them, and Doreen Lawrence herself was covertly spied on and investigated. One of the ways in which the police attempted to spy on, and potentially smear, the Lawrence family, was through the use of 'family liaison' officers:

> Family liaison is an important aspect of any case. Mr Crampton [who initially headed the police investigation into Stephen's death] ... picked DS Bevan for family liaison because he believed that DS Bevan had some training in 'human awareness'. He picked DC Holden because she was a woman, and it was felt desirable that there should be a woman involved in the liaison with Mr and Mrs Lawrence.[5]

Family liaison officers were ostensibly created in order to provide a more caring role for police officers interacting with a distressed family while carrying out an investigation. Doreen Lawrence said she always thought it strange that grieving relatives and friends visiting her home had their names recorded by police. The reasons for this were not explained at the time, but the evidence which follows indicates that they were under surveillance. The intelligence gathered by family liaison officers was allegedly passed through Special Branch to undercover officers whose job it was to spy on the Lawrence family, their friends and campaign members.

Francis, the ex-undercover police spy, states that he was tasked with finding out if any of the people visiting the Lawrence's home had attended demonstrations or were drug dealers, with the intention of painting members of the Stephen Lawrence Campaign as political extremists or criminals. Echoing the presumption of criminality exhibited by the officers who interrogated Duwayne Brooks, Special Branch appear to have been confident they could find dirt on the Lawrences. Racist stereotypes of Black people could be exploited by bringing prosecutions under the flimsiest of evidence. As Doreen Lawrence foresaw, over a decade before the whistle was blown on police spying: 'Coming across a Black family who have no criminal background is new to them, an alien concept. It was like you have to be a criminal if you are Black'.[6] The movement led by the Lawrence family won battles with the press, public and courts despite their resources being dwarfed by those of the police – the latter including the covertly gathered evidence on the family intended to subvert and smear them and their supporters. The police failed in their attempts; not only did the Lawrence family have copious evidence, international support from Nelson Mandela, and even the *Daily Mail* on their side, but also their public image as a *respectable* family was unassailable.

The legacy of the Stephen Lawrence Campaign – with regard to both the violent racist crime itself, and the corruption and institutional racism of London's Metropolitan Police exposed by the inquiry into his death – has made Stephen's name synonymous with the Black struggle against both forms of racist violence. Stephen's image is not simply that of a victim of one of the most brutal episodes of racism in Britain, but a symbol of Black justice and resistance.[7] The Stephen Lawrence Campaign was, perhaps on the surface, the story of a respectable, grieving family seeking truth and justice. But it was also a movement of resistance which took on the most powerful state institutions, forcing London's Metropolitan Police to concede publicly their own institutional racism in the face of irrefutable evidence and widespread community support.[8]

The Stephen Lawrence Centre in Deptford, south London, went on to host a range of anti-racist community projects, such as Shake! – an arts project which runs workshops on topics including police racism and other legacies of colonialism. Part of the Stephen Lawrence Trust's mission is to help young Black students fund architecture degrees, as Stephen had intended to study architecture: highlighting these academic aspirations radically changed how his image was conceptualised. Importantly, the campaign didn't simply display Stephen Lawrence as a respectable young man from a respectable family; it also showed a human side to a young Black man whose life was devalued by racism.

Another lasting gift of the Stephen Lawrence Campaign is how it has shaped resistance to racial violence. Almost every campaign calling for justice following a Black death at the hands of police in Britain is led by a woman. Doreen Lawrence was by no means the first mother, sister or partner to lead a campaign following the racist murder of a loved one. But what is made clear in the interviews with women engaged in similar struggles that followed, is that she had a huge impact on how a successful campaign could be run, from grassroots community building and protest, to victories in the courts and mainstream media.

This chapter demonstrates how racism frames Black families as chaotic, and Black women as promiscuous and deviant. Thus, an important component of anti-racist campaigns such as those led by the Lawrences, is an image of the Black family as *respectable*. This involves pursuing a necessarily complex and delicate tension – while the politics of family respectability is fraught by its heavily gendered assumptions, it is also the conduit through which brave, bold and, not unimportantly, successful assertions of anti-racist activism have often been channelled. To understand better the relationship between gender, anti-racism and the family, this chapter charts some of the connections between imperial cultures of respectability and nationalism in eighteenth- and nineteenth-century Europe, and twenty-first-century racisms. This critical history of racist discourses builds on Black feminism,[9] which affirms that for Black activists, the family, rather than simply being a decisive site of oppression as some interpretations of feminism argue, can also be a site of resistance against racism.

The chapter does not attempt to provide a definitive answer as to why women lead almost every campaign concerning Black death in custody, but it aims to contextualise this pattern of resistance by tracing the routes of British racism through imperial discourses of respectability. I argue that, by tracing the colonial routes of respectability, gender norms and racism, we can better understand police racism and resistance to it. In other words, policing reflects a pervasive colonial norm that reproduces cultures of both racism and patriarchy; tracing racialised and gendered norms through discourses of respectability is fundamental to understanding contemporary cultures of racism and anti-racism. Importantly, as Hortense Spillers affirms, 'there is no absolute point of chronological initiation, [but] we might repeat certain familiar impression points that lend shape to the business of dehumanised naming'.[10] In other words, the 'naming' and other racial discourses which dehumanise colonised women do not signify the genesis or root of racism, but how contemporary racisms are moulded by their histories.

As Black feminists have long attested, contemporary struggle against police racism illustrates how the Black family can be a space of resistance. This is exemplified through a range of different actions and explanations, which, as this chapter outlines, includes demanding justice for lost loved ones in the face of state racism, media representations that frame Black familial relations as deviant and dysfunctional, and a police force that violently suppresses peaceful protest. These are articulated by activists through the legacies of slavery and ongoing racisms, the love and care for a family member subjected to police violence, and the multiple sites of labour and oppression navigated by the women engaged in Black struggles against policing. Thus, I will argue that these campaigns can disrupt racist cultures of respectability by demonstrating the radical potential of Black familial relations. These campaigns reject both a national order which demands civil obedience from citizens fighting for justice, and a domestic order which feminises care work.

Importantly, this account of Black struggles led by women which use the family as a site of resistance does not seek to define the 'right' or 'radical' family. Rather, it details how gendered and familial categories are subverted, following anti-racist queer theories, in illuminating the radical potential of these sites of struggle.[11] Queer theory challenges structural discrimination of LGBTQI+ life, seeking to liberate all people from gendered and sexual norms. But this chapter shows how the struggle for the right to familial relations can also form part of a struggle against the oppressive nature of the nuclear family. Specifically, women engaged in Black resistance to policing have to fight for respect as a grieving parent or caregiver. Simultaneously, many of these same women are challenging the norms of motherhood that limit women to the category of caregiver, which does not challenge the hierarchies of the home or of wider society. Importantly, as we shall see, there is therefore no uniformity among women activists with regard to the significance of women in Black deaths in custody campaigns. While many of the activists who feature in this chapter reject the problematic tropes of respectability, others utilise the politics of respectability as a political tool. Through this, I argue that these forms of resistance to contemporary racisms also challenge essentialism, exhibiting uneven perspectives, experiences and political goals.

The next section of this chapter explores imperial history, and how gendered and sexual norms were imposed on colonised populations. I show how women were framed as sexually deviant, violent and morally degenerate, providing a context for the racism experienced by women engaged in Black resistance to policing in the twenty-first century. The section after that looks at the racism and sexism directed at Black women in modern Britain, with a specific focus on Black conservativism and its preoccupation with 'single parent' households. Finally, we turn to campaigns against Black deaths in police custody in twenty-first-century Britain, almost all of which are led by women. Using interviews and first-hand accounts from protests and public meetings, I analyse the significance of these struggles. Illustrating their battles against patriarchy, police violence and racism, these campaigns make radical demands for a Black family life which is neither destroyed by racial violence, nor constrained by the imposition of dominant familial norms.

Imperial discourses of respectability and nationalism in eighteenth- and nineteenth-century Europe

Demonstrating how colonialism shapes the private, domestic sphere, as well as the public terrain of the nation, unveils a relationship between an imposed order within the family and the imposed order of the nation.[12] In eighteenth- and nineteenth-century Europe, the order of the family acted as a symbol for the order and coherence of the nation. Specifically, it was vitally important that man, woman and child within the home knew their place. The man as husband and father – the marital patriarch – reflected the authority of the nation. The woman, as wife and mother, represented national gentility and innocence. Each well-ordered family would thus respect the order of the nation, upholding the stability of national positions held by the nobility, parliament and property owners. Central to the domestic order was the perceived civility of women. However, the British working class were considered morally undeveloped.

Edward Long's account of slavery in the British West Indies in 1772 noted that the 'lower class of women in England, are remarkably fond of the Blacks, for reasons too brutal to mention'.[13] Poor white women could not represent virtue like their wealthier counterparts, yet were still worthy of protection from the indignity of miscegenation. So it was the middle classes that reflected the nation's self-image.[14] Imperialism bolstered the necessity of a national stereotype against which colonised Others could be contrasted. It is through its non-respectable, colonised opposite that European culture could affirm its own identity and perception of itself. This essentialised view meant that gender relations among the colonised were considered to be uniquely repressive, and there was particular emphasis on the tyrannical violence of colonised men.

Women in the so-called Orient – the Indian subcontinent, Indochina, the Middle East and North Africa – were invisiblised, with Muslim women, in particular, framed as being imprisoned in the home by pathologically controlling men.[15] Black women in Africa were portrayed as wild, strong and consequently dangerous, hardened by the male violence and polygamy which defined sexual relations on that continent.[16] It was polygamy which many evangelicals and scientists considered most abhorrent, with such familial relations (real or imagined) being construed as the cause of low birth rates, small populations and therefore stunted civilisational development.[17]

Despite the contrasting ways in which different colonised women were seen in the colonial imagination, the sexual relations of colonised societies were generally racialised as promiscuous.

These racial pathologies were attributed to fluid or non-European gender, sexual and familial norms. Some of these assumptions, such as the lack of a fixed nuclear family structure, were partially informed by concrete observations. However, many others were invented – in the Caribbean context, for instance, Black women's framing as sexual deviants justified their suitability for both the reproduction of enslaved labour and the sexual desires of their owners.[18] Dominant pro-slavery discourses framed Black women as scheming Jezebels, arguing that they began sexual activity at an early age, preferred multiple male partners, and were eager sex workers.[19] Charles Leslie, writing an account of Jamaica in the mid-eighteenth century, explained to his British readership:

> The Negroe Women go many of them quite naked, they don't know what Shame is; and are surprised at an Europeans Balefulness, who perhaps turns his Head aside at the Sight. Their Masters give them a Kind of Petticoat, but they don't care to wear it.[20]

This fantasy of the immodest enslaved woman and the bashful, respectable European man was a necessary racist image, given the sexual violence systematically deployed by white men against enslaved Black women. Indeed, this misrepresentation of enslaved women served to legitimise, or at least exonerate slave-owners from accusations of sexual misconduct.[21] The sexual component of slavery was only ever alluded to for British audiences, with Edward Long informing readers of his *History of Jamaica* (1774) that 'Negro women were sexually more desirable for physiological reasons left unexplained'.[22] Enslaved Black women were also considered to possess an animalistic strength, pain threshold and propensity for violence. Consequently, forced labour was not simply considered easily manageable for Black women, but a disciplinary and civilising influence.[23] These discourses went even further, arguing that the necessity of continuing the trade in enslaved Africans must continue, partly owing to the promiscuity of Black women. It is worth quoting Leslie at length here, citing a slave owner in Jamaica who

[d]oes not think that the number of negroes sufficient to cultivate sugar estates can be kept up by propagation, for these reasons – more males imported than females, from the Africans being all Polygamists, and of course unwilling to part with their females – the early and promiscuous intercourse of the sexes – the venereals – young females procuring abortions ... the negro woman suckling too long ... the little care too many of the negro women are apt to take of their children.[24]

Here we see the deviance, ineptitude and chaos of Black sexual relations projected onto enslaved women in the Caribbean.[25] So polemical is this mythology that Black women simultaneously take too little care of their children, and in the same sentence over-care by suckling too long. This colonial anxiety – that is simultaneously obsessed with the excess and the deficit – is key to many representations of the colonised.[26] While the rape of enslaved women and girls was instituted into the system of slavery, it was the enslaved who were allegedly precocious and promiscuous in their sexual relations.[27] The reader is given further assurance of Black sexual deviance by being reminded that their alleged 'promiscuity' is rooted in African polygamy, rather than the sexual power of the slave master and the system through which he derives this power.

The intention of this report was not simply to demonstrate how the deviance of Black women justified their enslavement, but that such deviance explains why the numbers of enslaved people in Jamaica were diminishing, and that it was therefore necessary to continue the transatlantic slave trade. Such misrepresentations conceal the gynaecological disorders which proliferated due to the poor healthcare, violence, malnutrition and backbreaking labour endured by pregnant women.[28] It is important to note that Black women across the Americas helped build and maintain families despite the racist violence and discourses of the slave system. Some mirrored normative European family structures, but many pushed the boundaries of the nuclear family, building kinship networks and intimacies which resisted the brutality of the plantation.[29] The family, kinship and other networks of care will be returned to in later sections, as they continue to shape resistance to racism in the twentieth and twenty-first centuries.

The Caribbean was among many areas of the British Empire in which colonised women were considered to be sexually promiscuous. In his 1934 novel *Burmese Days*, George Orwell narrates a story that centres on how colonised women were bought as concubines by British settlers who had not been able to find a European woman to marry. Being framed as subservient saw many women from Europe's colonies across Asia being racialised in this way. Non-respectable colonised women could also, in contrast, be depicted as sexually vulgar. This was the case in Ireland, where women were characterised as loud drunks.[30] In southern Africa, women were categorised as having oversized sexual characteristics, causing both alarm and intrigue, such that Saartjie Baartman (dubbed the 'Hottentot Venus') was persuaded to travel to Europe, where her naked body was exhibited and studied by curious scientists and captivated festival goers.

The manner in which colonised women were imaged and denigrated through imperial discourses and practices always, albeit in differing ways, served the colonial imperative to impose order onto the allegedly chaotic family lives of the colonised. The racist mythologies underpinning the colonial imposition on the private lives of the colonised reflected an authority over their public lives within the national order of the colony. As the ordered, nuclear, middle-class family represented the civility of the British nation, the purported deviance of the colonised family confirmed its savagery. In other words, racist ideas about colonised people performing the 'wrong' gender roles shaped by discourses of respectability helped to justify colonialism itself.

More liberal apologists of Empire saw colonised women, and the racialised promiscuity that was projected onto them, as an invitation for a less violent civilising project. Formerly enslaved Black people, First Nations peoples in North America, Indians, Africans, and Aborigines in Australia were among those targeted by evangelical missionaries in the late nineteenth and early twentieth centuries. Women from these colonised societies were considered uniquely oppressed by the indignities of slavery's legacies (in the Caribbean context), or by the inherent violence, hyper-sexuality or oriental despotism of their men (in the Asian context).

The tradition of *sati* in India, in which widows would die by suicide, became a popular rallying call among colonial progressives. Petitions and reports were submitted to the British Parliament, lobbying for greater powers to eradicate the practice in the nation's most profitable colony. The character Phileas Fogg in Jules Verne's classic novel *Around the World in Eighty Days* makes a stop in rural India to rescue an Indian widow. The widow, intoxicated with hemp and opium, is 'young, and as fair as a European', guarded by 'stupid fanatics … a violent contrast to her, armed as they were with naked sabres hung at their waists'. Fogg's shock at the widow's fate is directed towards the colonial administration, and he questions why 'these barbarous customs still exist in India, and that the English have been unable to put a stop to them?' His guide responds that the administration does not have the capacity to rule the entire region, and 'we have no power over these savage territories'. Our hero uses his twelve short hours in India to save the widow before continuing his journey.[31] Such feminist missions to South Asia in which the honour and courage of the respectable white man made liberating its women imperative, became a popular civilising fantasy encapsulated by Gayatri Spivak's cutting appraisal: 'white men saving brown women from brown men'.[32]

Away from the world of adventure novels, missionary endeavours that required compassion and intimacy with colonised women would have been inappropriate work for a man – such a task could be completed only with a British woman's civility. Respectable white women set out to impose European gender norms on what were perceived as chaotic and promiscuous family relations and sexual practices.[33] Encouraging women to dress in modest European-style garments and promoting home-making, bible-reading and good table manners formed part of this liberal, feminist, civilising project.[34] Later feminists encouraged women to contribute to imperial war efforts, such as suffragist Millicent Fawcett who advocated Britain's use of concentration camps to 'protect' women and children during the Boer War.[35] This mission enabled early European feminists to join the imperial project, active outside the home while maintaining their civility by remaining connected to the domestic sphere.[36]

Both the liberal-progressive and the more violent and reactionary civilising projects were connected by an assumption that Blackness connoted backwardness; the closer their proximity to whiteness, the more civilised colonised women would become. Such women across Britain's colonies were trained to carry out the domestic labour in the respectable homes of the coloniser. Raising children, cooking meals and organising household affairs was laborious and poorly paid, but was presented as prestigious training in European civility. This proximity to civilisation became complicated as Britain's imperial power went into decline. Following World War II, citizens from Britain's colonies – particularly in the Caribbean – were recruited for jobs that needed doing in the centre of Empire, not only to work, but to stay. While there was widespread concern among policy-makers about encouraging white British women into full-time employment, and its possible repercussions on the sanctity of the nuclear family, such considerations did not extend to Black women.[37]

In the late 1950s and early 1960s, newspapers were informing readers that 'for the Black man, sexual relationships outside of marriage were normal',[38] confirming the disregard for Black family life. Indeed, as one 1961 study in the East Midlands concluded, 98 per cent of the children of Jamaican women working in Nottingham had to be left behind in the Caribbean.[39] Many children of Caribbean migrants to Britain were either reunited with their mother once she had become financially secure enough to send for them, or never developed a relationship with a mother who could neither afford to bring her children to Britain nor return home. This served only to perpetuate the stereotype that the perceived problems faced by colonised people lay in their non-respectable home lives – stereotypes that had inspired the earlier feminist civilising missions to Britain's colonies. This stereotype aided the justification for breaking up Black families to deal with labour shortages in post-war Britain, exemplifying a wider indifference to family breakdown that migration and restrictive migration policies often represent. It also paved the way for other kinds of racism that emerged in the final decades of the twentieth century.

While they were considered a useful source of cheap labour in Britain, Black women were considered a 'high promiscuity risk' by the medical establishment, and had their fertility classified as a symptom of moral degeneracy. This resulted in unwanted sterilisations and abortions imposed upon many Black women, as well as forms of contraception which prioritised birth control over patient health. This medical racism was a legacy of the eugenics of pre-war Britain, in which controlling the birth rates of people deemed undesirable was considered a matter of public health. This was compounded by the sexist assumption that state authorities should have power over women's bodies. This racist state power over women's sexuality went to extremes as virginity testing was imposed upon women migrating to Britain from South Asia to marry British-based South Asian men.[40] This state-sanctioned sexual violence was fiercely resisted by Black and Asian social movements, but spoke volumes about the chauvinistic power of the immigration authorities in protecting the mother country from promiscuous racial Others.

When demands for abortion and contraception were made by feminist movements in Britain in the 1970s, Black feminists recalled this racist history of coercion. Rather than denying access to birth control as had previously been the case, medical professionals now actively sought to control the bodies and fertility of women by encouraging birth control for Black and working-class women they considered the producers of degenerate families.[41] Racist discourses that pathologise Black woman as bad single parents were not only continued in the twenty-first century by white conservatism; as we are about to see, they have also become the preoccupation of a Black conservative agenda.

Single parent households and Black conservatism

In the 1980s, at the height of Thatcherism's conservative revolution, low-income, unemployed and racialised women became the target of renewed scrutiny over their alleged promiscuity, parental ability and respectability. These inquiries revolved around their position within the nuclear family – specifically, whether they formed part of a heteronormative two-parent household, and whether they governed the home effectively through the disciplining of their children. Margaret Thatcher's infamous decree that 'there is no such thing as society' is often foregrounded as the definitive hallmark of Thatcherism and its articulation of neoliberal individualism's popular appeal. Often forgotten, however, is that the above quotation is incomplete; what Thatcher originally stated was that 'there is no such thing as society … there are individual men and women, and there are families'.[42] Put differently, the myth of the well-ordered, respectable, British nuclear family was central here to the wider moral economy that was being promoted during this era – a cult of entrepreneurial individualism on the one hand, and a wider conservative attachment to the family on the other.[43] Like the colonial discourses outlined in the previous section, the Black family was framed as the antithesis of Britain's national self-image.[44]

As in the imperial discourses of the eighteenth and nineteenth centuries, the order of the nuclear family is articulated as a symbol for the order of the nation. In the 2000s, the pathology of Black families was given a new lease of political life. Both the Conservative

Party[45] and Black conservative activists were concerned that the purported chaos of Black families headed by single mothers was responsible for the moral decline of the nation. Often in partnership with Conservative politicians and commentators, some Black conservatives said things that their white counterparts were hitherto uncomfortable to utter in public – that the Black family needed order imposed upon it, if law and order in the nation were to be restored. These conservative voices argue that it is anti-racism which creates the false impression that social problems are connected to racism, when in fact race does not matter[46] as much as hard work and the right attitude. 'Black pupils and bad behaviour – only a Black academic can state the obvious', exclaimed one *Telegraph* journalist,[47] applauding the work of Tony Sewell, the CEO of the educational charity Generating Genius. Through his public talks and journalism (for a time he wrote a column in Britain's biggest Black newspaper, *The Voice*), Sewell passionately argued against the relevance of institutional racism and generally ignored the classed cleavages across different schools.

In July 2020, Sewell was made chair of the Conservative government's newly formed Commission on Race and Ethnic Disparities. Through a career that spans academia, journalism, government policy and education, Sewell has focused on the Black family as the source of moral degeneracy among Britain's Black population, seen to be dragging down the nation's productive capacity and moral self-worth. Based on his educational work and practice, for which he was awarded a CBE, Sewell argues that racial inequalities are due to a cultural pattern that makes Black boys 'feminised'.[48] Often describing the Black boys he worked with as living in 'single parent households', Sewell echoed sentiments in the US,[49] long critiqued by Black feminists for misrepresenting Black women as problematic matriarchs.[50] Sewell himself explained this 'feminisation' by drawing on psychology. His claims are premised on a prescribed division of parental labour: mothers provide security, while fathers are reassuring partners in play.

Generating Genius takes Black boys away from their mothers and provides intensive educational science training, often leading to above-average examination results. Yet Sewell laments the fact that, even after achieving top marks in their exams, the problems faced by these boys have not been completely overcome:

> many of the boys, once freed from the arms of their single mothers, suddenly had to cope with a world run by adult Black males – figures in their lives who were mostly absent, unreliable, despised by their mothers, and usually unsuccessful. These boys kicked up against us. It was like we were their dads who had walked out of their lives, and suddenly we demanded their respect.[51]

At best, Sewell claims that, owing to their home environment, these young boys have not learned to respect men. But what also appears to be implied, is that the rebellion of young boys is an outcome of a lack of respect that can *only* be demanded by men. Sewell's psychological separation of the sexes means that only a man and a woman, together, within the nuclear family, can raise a respectable child. This respectability is manifested by responding appropriately to the disciplinary power of men in authority, both inside and outside the home. It is only through this family structure that Black boys can perform their prescribed gender roles, and break free from the purported femininity in their character that is holding them back. In becoming the masculine ideal in the home, Black men and boys can play a moral and productive role within the nation.

Shaun Bailey (discussed further in the next chapter), former adviser on youth and crime to Conservative Prime Minister David Cameron, and Conservative candidate for the 2021 London mayoral election, casts similar aspersions on the Black family, or apparent lack thereof. Bailey claims that 'Marriage does not exist amongst the Black community. It is why we have so many problems with the men'.[52] This echoes the chaos of Black families lamented by his conservative colleagues. He attributes partial blame to the welfare state and goes on to clarify that 'we [Black people] are trapped by government policy. Because it discour-ages us from raising our children in nuclear families. The nuclear family should be the norm'.[53] Drawing on well-trodden tropes of single mothers claiming welfare benefits, Bailey reaffirms the Black family as deviant. He illustrates this both within the private sphere of the home and, publicly, through Black interactions with the welfare state and criminal justice system.

Ray Lewis, former advisor to former Conservative London Mayor Boris Johnson, also asserts that the problems faced by Black boys in Britain stem from poor parental discipline, given that 'there are no males in our [Black British] households'[54] to reproduce the patriarchal norm of the nuclear family unit. This is reflected in Conservative policies such as an advertisement for the Mayor's Mentoring Scheme which read: 'Wanted: Positive role models for Black boys in London'.[55] Here, we see the state make an intervention which attempts to fashion the components that make a 'respectable' Black family – replacing absent fathers with local volunteers. The point here is not that mentorship among Black people is racist in itself. The problem lies in the fact that these programmes explain away racial inequalities through a char-acter deficit within each member of the Black family.

So we have the absent Black father, the incapable (albeit some-times for reasons beyond their control) Black mother, and the feminised, deviant Black boy (Black girls are rarely mentioned in the writings of these Black conservatives). This apparent deficit is remedied through the use of role models and mentors, simultane-ously ignoring or underplaying structural racism and reproducing stereotypes about chaotic Black families as the root of racial ine-qualities. The popularity of mentor and role-model programmes among conservative and liberal institutions alike, enables such pro-grammes to divert attention away from the institutional racisms of the organisations that fund, and often run, such projects, as well as the structural racial inequalities from which such institutions draw their power and legitimacy. While those on the reactionary end, such as Sewell, may shout 'Racism is not the problem', the more liberal advocates of such an approach simply avoid using words like racism at all.

I would like to highlight here that mentoring, and projects that provide mentorship for young people, are not racist in themselves. There are countless youth projects that combine mentorship with other forms of support for young people, through initiatives that are both community-led and underpinned by a more critical understanding of racism. However, the 'pull yourself up by your bootstraps' logic, be it explicitly articulated by conservatives or implied by more liberal advocates, is a particular strain of racial thinking which, I hope this section has made clear, requires critical examination. Importantly, the racial stereotypes drawn upon by conservative commentators did not emerge in the post-war period as Black people migrated to Britain in significant numbers. They are rooted in colonial discourses that framed Black women as promiscuous, and the Black family as consequently disorderly, requiring scrutiny, imposition and re-ordering by the state. It is in this context that women do not simply challenge the racial violence of policing. They contend with wider cultures of racism and respectability that frame Black women as neglectful, inept parents, myths upon which racial inequalities are blamed.

Women and resistance to police racism

While civil unrest, mass protests and inquiries dominate many of the discussions on resistance to racist policing in Britain, an analysis of the smaller-scale organising, often led by women, can also provide useful evidence for analysing gendered forms of racism and anti-racist struggle. Marcia Rigg, campaigner against deaths in custody and sister of Sean Rigg, who died in Brixton Police Station in 2008, discussed women's activism extensively in the course of an interview with the author. Sean Rigg was diagnosed with paranoid schizophrenia as a young man, but with the combined support of family, friends and social services, he was able to travel, make music and live a relatively healthy life. He lived in a hostel in south London where he could receive support from professionals and relatives. One morning it became apparent that he had not taken his medication and was experiencing paranoia. Unsure of how to respond, hostel staff called the police. Three hours later officers arrived on the scene – they eventually tracked Sean down in a local park where he was reported to have been acting erratically, and took him into custody. Within minutes of the arrest, he was pronounced dead.

The police claimed Sean had assaulted an officer and was then taken to hospital, where his heart simply stopped beating. Concerned about the circumstances surrounding the death, Sean's siblings requested the CCTV footage from the custody suite where Sean was held, as well as a viewing of his body. During the viewing, they discovered a mark on Sean's temple, which had not been reported by the police, either to the family or in their press statements. None of the officers could explain how the mark appeared on Sean's head, and the CCTV footage the police provided failed to show a clear picture of Sean and the officers who had brought him into custody. After their lawyer requested a plan of all CCTV cameras in Brixton Police Station, the police conceded that there were two additional cameras from which footage had not been shared. This additional evidence led to an inquest in 2012 concluding that police restrained Sean face-down in a manner deemed 'unnecessary' and 'unsuitable'. It is this use of force which had contributed to the cardiac arrest from which Sean had died. Yet, as has been the case with every death at the hands of police since 1969, a 2019 hearing cleared all the officers involved of misconduct.

Marcia Rigg spoke to me in detail about the community build-ing, protest and legal campaign she had led following her brother's death. She began the interview by talking about a coalition of campaigners against deaths in police custody called the United

Family and Friends Campaign (UFFC), which was founded by a group of Black families in 1997:

> Brenda [Weinberg] was the main campaigner for Brian [Douglas], who was his sister, and the mother of Joy Gardner, Myrna Simpson, was carrying the campaign for her daughter. And the Sylvesters was actually the husband and wife, that is Roger Sylvester's parents ... it was the women, it usually is. And that I think is because mostly they kill our brothers and our sons and our fathers and so it's the women that are the ones that have to take up the baton and the fight for justice for them.[56]

When Marcia Rigg expanded on her reflections about why it was usually women who organised the campaigns, she ranged from talking about post-colonial perspectives to discussing care work and familial relationships:

> Our life is a struggle, it's just because that is just the way it is, which dates back from slavery ... and I think it is because of the struggle and the times that we go through, that is what makes you strong, when you have to fight against injustice, what else should you do? There is no other option but to fight and so we have to find that strength. Any woman, Black, white or Asian, it doesn't matter, when it is your children you go to the ends of the earth, you do anything, you would die for them.[57]

Referencing slavery and its legacies exemplifies a radical analysis of state racism in contemporary Britain. This analysis does not simply contextualise racial violence in order to better understand the death of a family member or the issue of Black deaths in custody. Marcia uses the histories of colonial racism and anti-colonial struggle to reaffirm the argument that racism is systemic and therefore requires fundamental societal change. Resistance is the necessary response to racism. More than this, Marcia acknowledges that fighting against injustice is also an act of love – a love which, despite campaigning for her brother, she associates with motherhood. Marcia expanded on this, by describing Black women as both mothers to, and leaders in, Black movements of resistance:

I think people see that we are women of strength, particularly because we are Black and the struggles that we have been through. They admire us because we don't give up, we cannot afford to give up, because of our future generations. If in slavery women didn't fight for our freedom, we would still be enslaved. So they have passed the baton on to women like me.[58]

A maternal connection to Black struggle was voiced by other activists, such as a founding member of the London Campaign Against Police and State Violence (LCAPSV), who explained the circumstances from which the group emerged:

It was my son, my eldest son actually. He was using a public phone box in the area that he lives in Camberwell, and the police felt like they had the right to go and search him ... So they keep doing this to him and they beat him up over at Borough High Street before. He has had a lot of problems with the police. And when I heard what they did to him ... and [he] says, 'Mum, is this going to be my life from now on?', I really got mad. I got mad.[59]

The same activist went on to reflect Marcia Rigg's perspective on the strength that is developed by women engaged in Black struggle, and the necessity for resistance:

But you see, the women, when their children or their husbands are in this situation, then really and truly who else is left? They have got to stand up because if they don't then no one else will. And there is one thing with women, that it doesn't matter how old your children become they are still your children. And you just cannot sit back and see the wrong that is being done to them and ignore it, you just cannot do that. And it is not that we are more passionate, but we are more durable. And we endure a lot.[60]

Black women who hadn't lost a loved one, but campaigned in solidarity with those who had, also drew on motherhood:

This kid was one of our kids, and it doesn't matter where we are, it just seems like the Black male is [treated like] a threat across the world, and I'm just fed up with it ... I felt very strongly about ... just something about his face because it reminded me of family members. He didn't look too dissimilar from my children.[61]

Other women confirmed the leadership of Black women, again focusing on mothers:

> If you look at the family campaigns, I think the vast majority of them are led by Black women and a lot of the time it is Black mothers.[62]

> [Police violence] predominantly happens to our men, although it does happen to our women and we know it is also [racially] disproportionate, and it is women who are often left holding the pieces together, and they are the ones left having to maintain the families and communities and homes and having to bring up the children, with minimal resources, oftentimes with broken family networks themselves.[63]

These assertions resonate with key Black feminist concepts which identify the Black family as not simply an institution of gendered order, but also a potential site of radical resistance.[64] By challenging the legitimacy of the existing national order, this approach disrupts norms of respectability which frame the family as an institution that should reproduce order in the public sphere. The same activist drew on Black feminism to explain this pattern of resistance:

> By virtue of being Black women, we have had to reckon with various forms of oppression at one time. And not only in terms of oppression against us and our own people, but in terms of our family members who often are also men, and so we had to learn how to straddle various levels. So we couldn't just be a woman. We couldn't just be Black. We couldn't just be poor. We couldn't just be any one thing, we had to develop a methodology, an organising methodology and we have had to develop an analysis which takes into consideration multiple sites of oppression.[65]

However, another female activist argued:

> There is a role for Black feminist analysis. The issue being though, is if people within communities, Black and white, would actually listen to that analysis. Because feminism is deeply marked as something that is negative. Black feminists here are a very small group.[66]

These quotations exemplify the diversity of opinion among campaigners about how women leading Black deaths in custody campaigns understand themselves, and how they are understood by others. The women interviewed reaffirm arguments made by Black feminists that critiques of patriarchy are often absent from Black resistance to policing. This can be attributed to the dominance of patriarchal thinking among Black men, as well as in wider society.[67] One woman from an activist group in Ladbroke Grove (west London) provided a different explanation for why she thought women played such an important role in Black community struggles against police violence:

> I think that, you know, maybe that has got something to do with it, the sense that we haven't been profiled as our men are being profiled. We have been able to walk relatively safely without being watched, without being profiled, without being harassed, without being stalked [by the police].[68]

While Marcia Rigg added:

> Women perhaps come with a softer approach … we may be listened to more … And the Black man is [considered] a threat to the judicial system.[69]

These perspectives underline a view that Black men are subject to state violence and harassment, from a form of policing which reproduces notions of Black men as criminal, aggressive or political militants.[70] This is contrasted with a degree of agency and freedom to protest among Black women, who, while subjected to racialised stereotypes framing them as deviant, are at less risk of being detained or killed by the police.

It should not, however, be assumed that the police, press or wider society are generally restrained when dealing with women relatives of those killed at the hands of the state. In 2011, I was present when the annual March Against Deaths in Custody, organised by UFFC, demonstrated outside Downing Street. Every year, the families of those killed hand-deliver a letter to the Prime

Minister at the gates of Downing Street, with a list of demands. On this occasion, protesters were refused access to the gates – this may have been linked to the killing of Mark Duggan earlier that year and the resulting civil unrest and police repression. In response to this refusal by police, some demonstrators sat down in front of the Downing Street gates in protest. Without warning, hundreds of police officers emerged from surrounding buildings, and began to close in on the protest, forming a 'kettle'. Marcia Rigg recalled: 'I just remember a sea of police officers surrounding Downing Street ... that could have kicked off a riot in itself'. The mother of Ricky Bishop, a young man who died in Brixton police station (south London) in 2008, was dragged across the pavement by police in front of me. Marcia Rigg confirmed that at least one protester was arrested, and two Black mothers made formal complaints to the police after being assaulted by officers.

In our interview, Marcia Rigg said that she could not think of any other context in which a women-led march would be subjected to that kind of police violence. In isolation, the incident could be seen as an ill-thought-out decision by officers. But in the historical context of colonial discourses and practices, as well as the criminalisation and over-policing of Black people in Britain, it was predictable that a protest led by Black women would be pathologised as violent or treated heavy-handedly by the police. This association between Black campaigns and violence was compounded after these protests, as police and the media questioned the connotations of slogans such as 'No Justice, No Peace', with one commentator claiming that it 'sounded more like a threat than a prediction'.[71] Here, we see campaigns against police violence being framed as violent in themselves, with the words being used at protests interpreted in a way that portrays Black women as threatening.

Marcia Rigg proclaimed at a demonstration: 'How can there be peace, when there is no justice?' Indeed, it is the existing order, in which Black people face harassment, brutality and incarceration, which the state interprets as 'peace'. Any disruption, or proposed disruption, to this purported peace is interpreted as a violent threat. The damage to property during the 2011 riots, sparked by the killing of Mark Duggan (discussed in more detail in the next chapter), is another example of this threat to the existing order. While Marcia Rigg does not advocate violent resistance, she rejects the term 'riot', asserting that 'People call it riots but I call it an uprising, and my community calls it an uprising'.[72]

In the months and years following Mark Duggan's death and the resulting protests, he was described by police as one of the forty-eight most violent criminals in Europe,[73] and by much of the mainstream press as a gangster[74] – a label which remains both unsubstantiated[75] and racially charged.[76] The child of a Black father and a white mother, Duggan received all the stereotypes that a Black man with two Black parents could have expected. Mark Duggan's father died in the months following Mark's death, and Mark's white aunt, Carol Duggan, became the primary spokesperson for his justice campaign. A newspaper article described her as 'a cross between Ali G and Liam Gallagher of Oasis. Manc meets Jafaican'.[77] Ali G is a character created by Jewish comedian Sacha Baron Cohen parodying a working-class British-Caribbean; Liam Gallagher is a singer from Manchester ('Manc'), a city characterised as violent and working class. This description thus constitutes a racialised, classist denigration of Mark Duggan's aunt; as part of a Black family as well as of a Black community campaign, she is described as 'Jafaican' (a fake Jamaican). This attack on Carol Duggan thus deploys crude class stereotypes and slurs, and deepens this non-respectable imagery by emphasising her proximity to an imagined Blackness.

These examples demonstrate how women engaged in campaigns against Black deaths in police custody are not afforded the respect of a caring family member grieving for their lost loved one. Rather, these campaigns are read as threats to civility and public order, by both state actors that violently repress protest and by newspapers that deploy racialised tropes to frame activists as deviant. Importantly, however, women campaigning against Black deaths in custody challenge respectability and its norms on their own terms. While the norm of the caring mother reflects the hegemonic order of the *private* sphere, these campaigners use the family to resist the order of the *public* sphere and the institutions that reproduce it. Engaging in acts of civil resistance through the occupation of roads, questioning the state's expectation of peaceful protest and declaring the police and judicial system racist, they resist the norms of civic order and challenge its legitimacy. This radical approach is reaffirmed through activists' analyses which draw explicitly on Empire and its legacies, drawing parallels with resistance to the injustices of enslavement in the colonial period.

Norms that essentialise poor and Black women were also implicitly challenged through the ideas, as well as the actions, of the women involved in these campaigns. In the above interviews, activists articulated a range of perspectives, political goals and explanations of why and how women lead these campaigns. This diversity negates attempts to essentialise women campaigners against police racism as uniform in their action and thought. Some women engaged in resistance to policing employed a Black feminist analysis of work and care. They identified multiple sites of oppression (gender, race and class) and resistance across waged labour, domestic work and activism, a common observation made in Black British feminism. Other women echoed the Black feminist notion that all forms of mothering and care in Black communities should be considered important components of anti-racist and anti-sexist struggles.[78] This highlights the ways in which Black feminist thought often associated with the academy continues to be bound up with the material struggles of grassroots campaigners.

However, while the women interviewed considered care work to be an asset to their activism, feminists have also highlighted the additional burdens that the emotional labour of this kind of work can impose on women.[79] Rather than this political work being necessarily liberatory, we also see the notion of the Black 'superwoman' uncritically invoked to justify unpaid female labour. Doreen, the mother of Stephen Lawrence, had to campaign for nearly a decade to see the police publicly exposed as institutionally racist. The sisters of Sean Rigg pored over the documents relating to Sean's death in 2009, finding inconsistencies that were missed by lawyers and institutions such as the Independent Police Complaints Commission, and they continue their campaign to this day. Much of this work is tedious, beset with bureaucratic barriers and attracting limited public support, especially in the early stages of campaigning. We therefore see a tension around the extent to which we should understand the gendered nature of this resistance as a signifier of female leadership or of an unequal distribution of labour. This is compounded by the work often done by women which is often not seen as political – coming to the aid of Black men and boys whose own chauvinistic behaviour within a system of racist criminalisation can provoke a violent response from the state. This kind of care and protection from criminalisation is the norm for many women who may not always see this work as a form of anti-racism.

It is important that we unpack how these justice campaigns operate, and what, in particular, dominant men can learn from the gendered nature of resistance. The work of women in Black community struggles against police violence further underlines the urgency for an anti-racism which takes seriously the role of patriarchy in shaping racism. While some activists maintain that women's resistance against racial violence is also a struggle against patriarchy, this does not necessarily mean that campaigns against Black deaths in custody are politically uniform in their analysis of, and commitment to, women's liberation. Some activists said that patriarchy meant that there was still little space provided for feminist politics in Black struggles against policing. Other women resolutely focused on the violence experienced by Black men as the primary impetus for Black women's leadership in these campaigns. Thus, despite the significant number of women leading campaigns against violent police racism, there is not a politically homogenous position among them on the role of women's liberation.

Many Black feminists have acknowledged the imperial cultures from which contemporary tropes of Black women as sexually deviant,[80] superwomen[81] and animalistic[82] emerge. From the conservative right, women not only have their work undervalued, but are dismissed as failures, incapable of carrying out the patriarchal defence of the Black family, which only a man can embody. The degradation of Carol Duggan as an unfit carer, or households headed by single Black mothers as a source of Black boys' criminalisation, echoes the eighteenth- and nineteenth-century discourses framing the poor or colonised family as dysfunctional. But this challenge to the racist tropes projected onto racialised families is not an argument for achieving the ideal of the nuclear family. Indeed, when Hortense Spillers analyses the distortion of Black women in the family, she is 'less interested in joining the ranks of gendered femaleness than gaining the insurgent ground'[83] in the struggle against patriarchy. Specifically, oppressed women do not have the choice as to how their familial relations are organised, and can use the family to subvert gendered norms, racism and state power.

This chapter has focused on how families are damaged by police violence, but they have also been torn apart through the histories of colonialism and slavery[84] as well as contemporary forms of imperialism and border regimes.[85] The family therefore remains a potential site of struggle, even if a radical vision of the future would seek its emancipation from patriarchy. It may therefore be useful to think of the family in the way that we think of racialised categories or the working class – our vision is to be liberated from these inequalities, but until then, they remain categories which aid our understanding of oppression and sites of struggle.[86] In other words, incorporating the radical potential of the family into our understanding of Black struggle speaks not only to how racism is reproduced, but also how resistance is forged. While some of the women interviewed emphasised the ways in which Black men are racialised as violent and dangerous, Marcia Rigg said that she could not envisage any other protest led by women involving the intimidation, violence and arrests that these Black death in custody campaigns featured. Contrasting white bourgeois respectable women with the deviant and animalistic Black is thus an imperial discourse which continues to inform the logic of police violence and how it is deployed.

Conclusion

Under various colonial regimes, authorities used both the hard power of the whip and the gun, and the softer power of the Bible and the school, to impose law and order on colonised women. While men dominated the thick wedge of colonial violence, it was often women who took up the task of the missionary, attempting to civilise colonised women through cultural imperialism. Over a century after the formal end of Empire, comparable tactics were used by London's Metropolitan Police. Family liaison officers – a man with 'human awareness' and a female officer chosen simply for her gender – were deployed to record the names and details of the Lawrences' friends and family as they struggled against the fatal violence of racism. Any evidence which could link the Lawrence family to crime would shame them out of their respectable image, confirming the assumptions of a society centuries deep in racist thinking. While the police were unable to uncover any such deviance from societal norms, the exposure of their surveillance, infiltration and intentions confirms the perception of the Black family as chaotic and deviant.

Historians have recounted how imperial cultures in the eighteenth and nineteenth centuries helped shape sexual and gendered norms through racist cultures of respectability and nation. But this focus on colonial history goes further than simply providing context for contemporary racisms. Such historical discourses expose the hegemonic cultures through which racism is articulated by the press and politicians, implemented by the police, and legitimised through popular images and stereotypes. Importantly, these discourses also frame the women who lead campaigns against fatal police racisms as deviant rather than caring family members, as threats to civic order rather than active citizens, and as provocateurs of violence despite their commitment to peaceful protest.

Imperial discourses of respectability and nationalism sought to maintain distinctions between women and men, rich and poor, white and colonised, with defined intellectual capacity, moral worth and social positions. Yet these gendered, sexual and racialised categories are disrupted by both the radical activism of women in Black death in custody campaigns, and the unevenness with which notions such as family, feminism and political strategy are articulated by these campaigners. In other words, the variety of perspectives, articulations and actions of women engaged in Black struggles against policing, particularly in Black death in custody campaigns, poses a challenge to the essentialisms inherent in racist discourses.

Indeed, it simultaneously pushes back against discourses which essentialise Black women through the aforementioned racial tropes, and against reductionist conceptions of resistance that homogenise the Black experience or Black political action and thought. The responses from the activists interviewed reaffirm that there is no single explanation why women lead almost every campaign against a Black death in custody, and explain why there should in fact not be a single, straightforward explanation.

The imperial cultures of respectability and nation in which racism and gendered norms became entrenched are fundamental to our understanding of Black activism and racism in twenty-first-century Britain. The violence of colonial settlement, enslavement, order and violence deployed racisms which framed colonised societies as deviant and as unable or unwilling to adhere to the norms of respectable gender relations. Framing the Black family as dysfunctional or abnormal has contributed to racist discourses which criminalise Black people, while at the same time stimulating radical Black familial relations that challenge the civic order. By disrupting norms of respectability and the national order, women's leadership in campaigns against Black deaths in custody goes beyond attaining justice for a loved one or a community member. These activists challenge us to radically rethink gender, race and class relations in light of their global, historical constitution, while remaining grounded in material struggles against state power.

The next chapter further analyses how gendered norms are used to criminalise Black people, this time focusing on masculine norms. Returning to imperial discourses will illuminate how binary, prescribed gender roles were reproduced to frame colonised men as deviant and violent. As in this chapter, we shall see how these colonial cultures shape contemporary racisms, enabling us to better understand racist criminalisation, and the Black resistance to policing which challenges it.

3

Black masculinity and criminalisation: the 2011 'riots' in context

> What we are dealing with is not a general social disorder; but specific groups of people who for one reason or another, are deciding not to abide by the same code of conduct as the rest of us … this gang culture that is killing innocent young Black kids. But we won't stop this by pretending it isn't young Black kids doing it. (Tony Blair, Callaghan Memorial Lecture, Cardiff Chamber of Commerce, 2007)

> All the noble savage's wars with his fellow-savages (and he takes no pleasure in anything else) are wars of extermination. (Charles Dickens, *The Noble Savage*, 1853)

In the 1990s, concern around 'football hooligans' led to the Conservative government giving the police new powers very similar to the Sus laws detailed in Chapter 1. Section 60 of the Criminal Justice and Public Order Act 1994 gave police the authority to stop and search anyone, without reasonable suspicion, across a given area (generally around a football stadium) for twenty-four hours.[1] By 2008, New Labour had extended these powers to any area where police 'intelligence' anticipated violence or where a violent incident had recently occurred, while also making it easier to extend or renew a Section 60 order.[2] When the Conservatives returned to power, they allowed the police to expand the powers further, in initiatives such as Operation Blunt 2, which targeted 'gangs'. This Metropolitan Police programme sought to 'blunt' sharp implements used by 'gangs' in London. Between May 2008 and April 2011, London was divided into three areas, known as tiers. Tier 1, covering London's most multicultural and deprived boroughs, comprised areas that police intelligence allegedly indicated had the largest amount of gang activity (not the highest crime levels), and stop and search powers were increased massively in these boroughs. Tier 2 had a medium amount of gang activity, it was claimed, and had a moderate increase in stop and search. Tier 3, mainly wealthier suburban areas of London, had little or no gang activity, and saw a very small increase in the power.

The use of Section 60 powers effectively saw Sus laws reintroduced across London for three years, as police were legally sanctioned to use stop and search with little restraint. Research[3] and experience suggest that police rarely use reasonable suspicion when using conventional stop and search powers. However, applying Section 60 over the whole of London for three years prevented legal challenges from police action lawyers and community organisations.

By May 2009, an 11 per cent decrease in crimes involving knives and guns was announced, with the commander of the operation informing the public:

> We targeted the dangerous places where knife crime is most prevalent and young people are most concerned. Stop and search has helped create the environment where the carrying of knives is now less common than when we started. Seizures are substantially down despite maintaining the high level of activity. Officers carried out 287,898 stops and searches since May last year.[4]

What the police argued was that, despite the fact that they were not seizing as many weapons as expected through their searches, stop and search was working as a deterrent. However, the tier system employed by the Metropolitan Police allows us to look more closely at the effectiveness of Operation Blunt 2 by comparing different areas. While it is true that gun and knife crime across London decreased by 11 per cent, violent crime fell across every tier, including in those areas with a moderate increase, or no increase, in Section 60 stops and searches. An analysis of the operation in its entirety found that:

> A conditional difference-in-difference regression analysis found no statistically significant crime-reduction effect across eleven offence types from the increase in weapons searches, when comparing boroughs with the biggest increases in stop and search activity with those that had much smaller increases.[5]

In fact, recorded crimes involving a sharp implement fluctuated at roughly the same rate across Tiers 1, 2 and 3. Levels of stop and search therefore had no effect on violence reduction. Spring and summer generally see increases in violence, while the colder, wetter months, when fewer people are out on the streets, see a decrease in recorded offences. Put simply, the operation proved that stop and search has no effect on reducing violent crime.

Despite this, and numerous other studies demonstrating the ineffectiveness of stop and search in reducing levels of violence, an attachment to this approach to violence reduction prevails. The police continually pressure the government to remove all requirements for 'reasonable suspicion' under stop and search.[6] The mantra of 'evidence-based' policy remains as hollow as it has ever been, while further alienating working-class youth generally and Black working classes in particular. Instead, it is a different set of ideological props that upholds the continued commitment to such practices. Inevitably, it is the concept of moral panic, so frequently tied to the spectre of the violent, criminal Black figure lurking in the cities, that enables politicians, the police, the press and eventually 'common-sense' racism, to legitimise the policies necessary to 'police the crisis'.[7] This chapter analyses political rhetoric, the conservative press and the policing of Black men to unpack the ways in which Black masculinity is framed as deviant, dangerous and alien to Britain. It is contrasted with legitimate white masculinities that manifest themselves through success in the market economy, state power, or the nuclear family. Building on the previous chapter, I argue that these gendered norms are disrupted by some of the grassroots Black campaigns against policing, which necessarily challenge gendered norms as well as racism.

There is, however, a risk that these characterisations of a rabid Black masculinity are read in a parochial context, as implicating only the racisms faced by Black people in Britain and as being uniquely consolidated by the escalation of stop-and-search powers. On the contrary, it is vital that racist criminalisation, stereotypes and tropes are seen in the context of imperial history.[8] This chapter highlights three key ways in which police racism becomes entrenched through Britain's imperial discourses, rehearsed over several centuries. First, gender and masculinity are framed and regulated to reproduce imperial power and the racialisation of subject populations. Specifically, ideas about both gender and race are imposed on colonised people to better exploit, control and execute violence upon them. Secondly, racialisation is constantly changing: presenting itself as fixed, it is in fact in constant flux across time and space. For example, Black men may be framed as weak and infantile in one context, but hyper-masculine, cunning and with super-human strength in another. Thirdly, building on the previous chapter, both radical anti-racism *and* Black feminism are vital conceptual tools for analysing the perception that Black men require a distinctively punitive control. As before, we now turn to a closer reading of the historical record.

As in Chapter 2, this chapter begins with a brief trip into Britain's imperial past, investigating cultures of racism across Britain's slave colonies in the Caribbean and other colonial possessions in Africa and Asia. There will be a particular focus on how the masculinity of the colonised was constructed. As we saw in Chapter 2, colonised men were framed as falling outside the norms of honourable men, with laziness, hyper-sexuality and violence among the tropes used to justify Britain's imperial ambitions. In the second section, we will return to some of the Black conservatives analysed in Chapter 2. Here, we will look at how these campaigners for Black respectability contrast the 'success' of their own families and careers with the 'failures' of criminalised men. The final section of this chapter focuses on one particular incident – in which a criminalised Black man is confronted by the police – in order to illustrate how masculine violence can be considered legitimate if it is state-led, or criminalised if it is associated with the colonised, Black or working classes.

Imperial discourses of Black masculinity

Moral panics in twentieth-century Britain often associate immigration and Blackness with violence and crime. Yet these stereotypes did not emerge abruptly in the post-war period, when people from Britain's African, Asian and Caribbean colonies and former colonies began to migrate to the centre of the declining imperial power in significant numbers. Indeed, even a partial recycling of such a reading of history serves to legitimise the mainstream assumption of Britain's uneasy relationship with 'race' – that the problems of racism arise primarily as a result of immigration and its undoing of an otherwise coherent, homogenous, united Britain. In other words, the myth that race started becoming a British preoccupation when Other people and Other cultures arrived on British shores, disturbing the uniformity and unity of British political, cultural and social life. This proposition argues that it is the problem of difference ('incoming' minorities) as a social condition that renders racism itself inevitable. Consequently, racial difference and tensions are seen as something to be managed through state multiculturalism or race relations training.

Rather, as the previous chapter attests, such racial thinking is best unpacked when traced back through the routes of Empire, particularly during the eighteenth and nineteenth centuries, when imperial cultures and discourses were popularised through media that included government reports, journalism, fiction and philosophy. We shall now see how race and racism, rather than being fixed, are a process which is constantly shifting across time and space. As Britain rose to become the greatest slave-trading nation in modern history, ideas about gender and race became fundamental to justifying the trade and the brutality which underpinned it. Black people in drama and novels were stereotyped through a number of different caricatures. These cultural phenomena served as the mass media of their day, complete with recurrent characters and memes which both reflected and helped produce 'common-sense' assumptions of racial Others. Some, such as *Oroonoko: or, The Royal Slave* by Aphra Behn, published in 1688, portrayed enslaved Black people as violent, lustful and vengeful, reinforcing the images made familiar in the justification of chattel slavery in the Americas. Later, theatrical productions such as *The Padlock*, by Charles Dibdin and Isaac Bickerstaffe, first performed in London's Drury Lane Theatre in 1768, deployed tragically comic Black servants, objects of ridicule whose infantile existence made them dependent on the institution of slavery and their masters' love.[9]

As moves towards abolition gained in popularity, this anti-Black racism became more reactionary. Edward Long's 1772 reflections on the 'Negro Cause' to abolish the trade, reported an alleged 'sloth and pride' among Jamaica's enslaved population. Describing Blacks as 'lazy and lawless', Long justified both the value of enslaved, as opposed to waged, labour, and the necessity of disciplinary violence, given their allegedly deviant predisposition. Robert Norris's 1789 account from the slave-trading coast of Guinea in West Africa argued that, owing to 'a continual state of war … many innocent lives are spared'[10] by the trafficking of Africans to Caribbean slave plantations. Bryan Edwards' 1801 history of the British West Indies informed readers of the benefits of colonial slavery, given that 'the negro … when unconverted, are particularly given to an unbounded gratification of every sensual lust'.[11] Edwards' account reproduced myths of Black men as sexual predators who lacked the restraint of a more civilised masculinity. John Stewart, however, reporting in 1823, claimed that the Blacks were not lawless, but simply lived by a moral code which ran counter to that of the slave colony:

> They [negroes] are in general crafty, artful, and plausible, little ashamed of falsehood, and strangely addicted to theft: to pilfer from their masters they consider as no crime, though to rob a fellow slave is accounted heinous: when a slave makes free with his master's property, he thus ingeniously argues, 'What I take from my master, being for my use, who am his slave, or property, he loses nothing by its transfer.'[12]

Stewart demonstrates how, in the years leading up to the abolition of chattel slavery in the British Caribbean, many images of Blacks depicted a playful childishness, requiring the guidance, and at times firm discipline, of British governance. Importantly, as arbitrary violence is done away with as Europe emerges from the medieval period, such insights are not extended to enslaved Africans, for whom ever-changing justifications for violent coercion remains routine.[13] As scholars such as Lisa Lowe argue, slavery and imperialism created the conditions for modern Europe and its liberal ideals to emerge. On the one hand colonialism created the material conditions for liberalism, through the economic development and the freedoms of a new capitalist class. Simultaneously, the enslaved and colonised symbolised the Other, which required despotic rule or imperial control. The 'ideal human' of Europe, with its freedoms and liberties, found identity through what it was not – the unhuman or not-quite-human colonised subject.[14]

One of the most celebrated abolitionists was William Wilberforce, who saw Britain's role in the world as that of the civiliser. He envisioned a civilised future for Blacks across the Empire, but in 1807 claimed that a 'reign of law and of civil order must be first established'[15] before social improvement from barbarism to civility could begin. Later in the century, John Stuart Mill published *On Liberty*, a seminal text on nineteenth-century British liberalism, in which he states that 'despotism is a legitimate mode of government in dealing with barbarians, provided that the end be their improvement, and the means justified by actually effecting that end'.[16] Mill demonstrates how this liberal turn was still premised on a white supremacy over 'barbarians', to which the liberal ideals of Enlightenment Europe could not be applied. Deploying a perverse logic, Mill claims that it is the despotism of colonial rule which will improve colonised peoples.

However, it remains unclear whether such an improvement-through-despotism could (or should) ever lead to colonised nations progressing into polities with the liberal rights and freedoms of civilised nations. This ambiguity is important because, while the discourse of imperialism had changed to moral and intellectual improvement, these positions did not envisage an end point whereby imperial power relations would no longer be necessary. In other words, the colonised might well show improvement if guided and disciplined by 'civilised' powers, but would never reach a level of equivalence with their masters. This conceptual sleight of hand simultaneously paints civilisation as constantly progressing and ensures that racial hierarchies and the essential differences between the races remain fixed. While colonised peoples were certainly not regarded as equal to whites, slavery, it was argued, should be considered a shameful chapter in Britain's past, and the future was one in which Britain would lead the world with a more enlightened vision of Empire.

By the middle of the nineteenth century, the abolition of slavery had led to debates about the merits of a civilising mission that relied more on the Bible than the gun. Philosopher Thomas Carlyle opposed free-market liberalism, arguing that this led to exploitation of English workers at home, while providing waged labour for lazy, undeserving Blacks. While Carlyle favoured Africans over the indigenous peoples of the Americas, arguing that the former were able to live among Europeans, his 1853 'Occasional Discourse on the Negro Question' affirmed a specific place for

Blacks: 'if the Black gentleman is born to be a servant, and in fact, is useful in God's creation only as a servant, then let him hire not by the month, but by a very much longer term'.[17] Campaigning for the reintroduction of chattel slavery, Carlyle argued that Blacks were people who, at the very least, required serfdom and 'the beneficial whip' from white landowners and masters.[18]

While Carlyle drew on philosophy and religion, a different approach was taken by one of the fiercest critics of liberal, progressive imperialism, the anatomist Robert Knox. Reproducing some of the earlier, pre-Darwinian arguments for scientific racism (before the emergence of eugenics towards the end of the nineteenth century), Knox published *The Races of Men* in 1850 and toured Britain delivering public lectures that warned against the freedoms being sought by enslaved and formerly enslaved peoples in the Americas. Knox used medical science, geography and interpretations of culture and history to argue that distinct human 'races' were in fact different species, suited to the environment in which they lived. In effect, he argued against settler colonialism, as he believed that whites did not have the physiological capacity to survive in tropical climates, and that long-term interbreeding between the races was impossible. A key element was the essential differences between the races of people he identified, attributed to a perhaps unfortunate, but nonetheless natural, hierarchy of human species.

In Jamaica, British colonialism was also responding to the end of chattel slavery with a renewed despotism. From abolition in 1834, records demonstrate a steady increase in prosecutions of Black men for sexual offences, including sodomy, bestiality and rape.[19] Peaking in 1853, when a third of all court cases involved Black men accused of sexual crimes, this rapid increase is unlikely to reflect an actual increase in such incidents. Rather, white Jamaica framed abolition as heralding the return of Black people to their natural barbarism, awakening the hyper-sexuality of Black men which had been controlled by plantation slavery.[20] This 'moral panic' enabled colonial Jamaica to increase the use of corporal and capital punishment, while racial borders and hierarchies were retrenched.[21] Racist paranoia about Black male sexuality will be revisited in the next section, focusing on Black migration to Britain in the twentieth century.

This reaction to abolition and liberal imperialism also provoked responses from cultural and social influencers rarely identified as advocates of violent racism. In an opinion piece ironically titled *The Noble Savage*, published in 1853, Charles Dickens laments the sentimental Christians and anthropologists who show an interest in the lives, livelihoods, languages and customs of indigenous peoples in the Americas, Africa and Australia. Indirectly critiquing liberals such as Wilberforce, he furiously opposes the notion that such 'savages' could ever be noble, attacking the colonised man as 'cruel, false, thievish, murderous; addicted more or less to grease, entrails, and beastly customs; a wild animal with the questionable gift of boasting; a conceited, tiresome, bloodthirsty, monotonous humbug'. Dickens pours yet more vitriol on the leaders among the colonised savages, recounting that they are so inherently violent that one of their monarchs, 'after killing incessantly, is in his turn killed by his relations and friends' – framing their lives as a relentless scramble for power through a pathological, unthinking violence.[22]

The civilising project afforded to the colonised, Dickens concludes, should be 'to be civilised off the face of the earth'. This genocidal position was controversial among liberals in Britain, but gained traction later in the century, as social Darwinism envisaged the replacement of indigenous peoples in the Americas by those of superior European stock. It was also taken seriously in Australia where Aborigines, by the mid-nineteenth century, were considered a 'doomed race', fit for neither civilised life nor survival alongside whites.[23]

Dickens was uninterested in the specificities of different colonised people. His polemics jump between accounts of Zulus in southern Africa and Ojibbeway Indians in North America. Dickens is angered by how the attention given to these peoples distracts the public from the plight of the poor in London. Echoing Thomas Carlyle's appraisal, Dickens articulates a sympathy for the white working class conveyed in the novels that made him famous, reinforcing an emergent narrative of deserving and undeserving poor. During this same period, campaigners arguing for improved conditions for English workers and the poor often used enslaved or formerly enslaved negroes as a reference point. Figures such as Samuel Roberts, who advocated on behalf of child chimney sweeps, and William Cobbett, who was concerned with the plight of rural labourers, consistently contrasted the noble and deserving white worker with the 'fat and lazy and dancing' Blacks of the Caribbean.[24] Dickens, of course, was most successful in popularising images of the deserving poor with characters such as Oliver Twist, using racial Others such as the figure of the Jew (Fagan) to symbolise a criminal underclass.

Dickens' genocidal posturing articulated the extreme end of British imperial culture, yet the more moderate Victorian colonialists still drew on assumptions posited by commentators such as Dickens when it served specific interests. The propensity for violence was an ascribed racial trait that became increasingly useful in justifying the corporal and capital punishments deployed to repress anticolonial dissent. The Sepoy 'Mutiny' in 1857, in which Indians rebelled against the British, was framed as a conflict to which Britain could not apply conventional rules of engagement. While respectable soldiers would recognise the division between the private sphere of the home, occupied by women and children, and the public terrain of the nation, over which men fought their disputes, the violence of the colonised was seen to deviate from such convention.[25] As well as accounts of the murder of British women and children, there were reports of the rape of British women in their homes by rebelling Indians. So popular were these shocking stories of white women – the symbols of purity for the British nation – being violated in this way, that novels, poems and even children's stories were published on the topic.[26]

Like the gendered racial tropes outlined in the previous chapter, the essential characteristics projected onto colonised men were uneven. British army officers waging war against the Zulu in southern Africa described them both as courageous warriors who could 'run like horses' and as 'murderous savages' or 'Black devils'.[27] In the Caribbean context, Black men were contrasted as more European and therefore more civilised than their African counterparts, given their prolonged proximity to white Europeans. The formerly enslaved were portrayed as independent yet at the same time well suited to the hard labour of agricultural production. While the mid-1800s saw Indian men portrayed as sexually violent, later colonial discourses framed Hindu men as weak and effeminate. What remains consistent in these uneven and continually shifting images of colonised Others, is the ideal norm of white Europe with which they were compared.[28] Even poor whites in Europe, while sometimes described with language similar to the peoples of the Americas, Africa, Asia or Australia, were never considered to be the equivalent of darker peoples.[29]

It is the apparent fixity, but constantly changing nature, of racialisation, which gives racism its power. Race is presented as being natural, yet is constantly being remade by human thought and action. 'This is true for the contemptible Black', Cedric Robinson argues, 'at one and the same time the most natural of beings, and the most intensely manufactured subject'.[30] These colonial histories demonstrate the ways in which Black and other racialised subjects are continually (re)manufactured across time and space. Being able to change the stereotypes and tropes of a given population to suit the needs of a given colonial context is made all the more effective if those tropes are believed to be natural or fixed within the limits of the civilising mission.

Across British colonies, the racial myths that framed colonised men as violent, often sexual, predators aided the justification for

97

mass imprisonment, torture and massacres through which the colonial administration would respond to any violation, from petty crime to armed uprising. Flogging was common in Britain's colonies in southern and eastern Africa until well into the twentieth century, justified by an epidemic of petty crime, which settlers did not have the resources to punish through any other means. For more serious accusations, imprisonment without trial and execution became the norm. Only Black men ever received the death penalty for rape after it was introduced in Rhodesia in 1902,[31] and the alleged rape of white women during anti-colonial uprisings in East Africa helped justify Britain's gulags in Kenya, in which hundreds of thousands of Kikuyu people were imprisoned and tortured in the 1950s.[32]

While detailing the racial violence of British colonial governance is always shocking, it may not come as a surprise to readers familiar with recent work on how colonial policing helped to form racist thinking and practices.[33] This section has demonstrated that the criminalisation of colonised men relied on ideas based on a dangerous masculinity – a masculinity committed to violence, sexual depravity and greed. This framing serves two important purposes. First, it acts as a useful contrast to Britain's view of itself, which incorporated a noble, white masculinity that effected a just and upright governance. Secondly, and of equal importance, the attribution of a violent, predatory and ungovernable Black masculinity deflects the very coercion, theft and sexual aggression by which colonial governance had wielded its power since its inception. In other words white, civilised, European masculinity holds within itself the savage attributes that it projects onto the colonised.

Through the images, discourses and practices continually reproduced throughout European colonialism which framed colonised men as pathologically violent and uniquely repressive towards women (both white women and 'their own'), colonised men became the contrasting image through which white men could define themselves. In the normative image of the European man, the head of the properly ordered, respectable nuclear family was well-mannered and sexually restrained. The public sphere was dominated by respectable men – courageous and morally righteous gentlemen, defending the institution of marriage and their patriotic duty to the nation, performing a hegemonic masculinity.[34] Through institutions such as the armed forces and justice systems, both at home and in the colonies, the violence of the state became legitimised through the framing of the men who ran it as respectable, and the men subjected to its force as their opposite. In what follows, we shall see how these contrasting masculinities, of the powerful and the oppressed, the hegemonic and the subordinate, continue to shape ideas around race and crime in twentieth- and twenty-first-century Britain, and how this racial thinking legitimises police violence.

Family values, respectability and Black masculinity

Black sexuality was one of the lenses through which racist paranoia about 'coloured' immigrants became apparent as they migrated to Britain in significant numbers throughout the twentieth century. As early as 1919, Cardiff erupted into violence, as 'coloured' men were attacked for allegedly propositioning a white woman.[35] Racial myths about the sexual appetites and desires of Black people proliferated further in the 1950s. Attacks on Black people in Notting Hill in 1958 escalated into a riot following an alleged argument between a Black man and white woman outside a pub.[36] Chamion Caballero and Peter Aspinall detail how much public concern centred on the prospect of white women being seduced by 'coloured' men who had migrated from the colonies to the mother country. When a 'vice squad' was set up in 1950s Newcastle to police the alleged drugging of white girls by 'coloured' men at parties (despite police and hospitals having zero reports of such incidents), journalists assured readers that 'the only white women some young coloured lads are likely to get near enough to desire are those [women] quaintly called undesirable'.[37] Tainted by their proximity to Blackness, white women suspected of having relations with Black men were the target of both intrigue and contempt.

Investigative reporters crossed the country posing the question 'would you let your daughter marry a Black man?' – giving rise to concerns about what the neighbours might think, how 'coloured' offspring might be dealt with and, importantly, how the honour of the white woman's father might be tarnished by such relations. Miscegenation threatened the sanctity of the respectable British home, with the prospect of Black hyper-sexuality interfering with the order and civility of 'traditional' family values.[38] This racial threat was most famously exploited by Enoch Powell in his Rivers of Blood speech, which warned of elderly white women facing robbery and violence from Black immigrants.[39] This perceived degeneracy – biological as well as moral – infecting British society from the colonies formed much of the basis for the racist attacks and state criminalisation in the post-war period. But while Black men were considered threats to white women and the white family in the twentieth century, by the twenty-first century, moral concern became focused on the danger Black men posed to each other.

Politicians and journalists reporting on Black communities as violent in a manner new and alien to Britain are connected to the racist thinking of the colonial era. And while such imagery was based on more recognisably explicit articulations of Black degeneracy, in the twenty-first century more subtle stereotypes are enthusiastically reproduced by a growing cohort of Black conservatives occupying positions in policy, academia and journalism. Like the work of Tony Sewell outlined in the Chapter 2 these twenty-first-century iterations of the 'native informant' play a pivotal role in lending an effective post-racial alibi to these reheated imperial racisms.

Shaun Bailey grew up on a council estate in west London, entering youth work and politics in his late twenties. In 2006 he founded a youth charity which provided outreach to young people affected by violence and drugs. In his book *No Man's Land*, about growing up in a working-class Caribbean household and becoming a youth worker and politician, Bailey lays out his political vision for Britain. First, he explains how, despite his upbringing in an area with high levels of recorded crime, he avoided a life of violence and incarceration:

> [My mother] made sure that I never went to a school in our locality – she didn't want me to be too friendly with the boys here. A deliberate ploy not to leave me among too many Black children. She had seen how Black people interact with Black people – what they say to other Black people – that means you can't go forward. That you're trapped in your own poor community.[40]

Explicit in Bailey's analysis is the need for Black people from low-income communities to leave, and spend as much time as possible with more affluent non-Black people. The apparently innate deviance among Black people, exacerbated by their lack of contact with people who live by a more moral code, offers sinister echoes of missionary projects during colonialism.[41] The tired circulation here of a 'culture of poverty' motif is made all the more powerful because it comes from a man identifying firmly as Black.

Bailey went on to became advisor on youth and crime to Conservative Prime Minister David Cameron, and was the Conservative Party's candidate for London Mayor in 2021. In keeping with the Conservative tradition, Bailey does not critique racism and the class system, or even the chauvinistic identities that can lead to violence and other criminalised behaviour. Instead, his analysis reproduces a hegemonic masculinity. Hegemonic masculinity implies that male identity is attained by men 'who received the benefits of patriarchy without enacting a strong version of masculine dominance'.[42]

Bailey finds solace in these forms of masculinity as a politician, a spokesman for his community and an alumnus of the army cadets. He embodies the myth that Britain is a meritocracy, and those 'trapped in [their] own poor community' generally have only themselves to blame. These forms of material wealth, social status and legitimate violence are used by Bailey to set himself apart from the Black people who 'can't go forward' and who attempt to attain wealth and status through the criminalised avenues that emerge out of Black people's interactions with one another. In other words, Bailey presents himself as the respectable face of Black masculinity, well-integrated into the institutions of power, which enable him to perform a hegemonic masculinity. Bailey is the 'good Black', who can exist only by first being closer to a white ideal and norm, and secondly by being juxtaposed with the 'bad Blacks' it is his mission to rescue.[43] As a representative of the Conservative Party and the British army, his claim to power and violence is legitimate, in contrast with that of the Black gang, which must be stopped and its members disciplined and transformed by the civilising institutions of the state.

During the period of Empire, hegemonic masculinity was demonstrated through being a gentleman, defending the family and the nation and its colonies from invasion and disorder. In the postcolonial world, it continues to be defined by the accumulation of capitalist wealth, intellectual superiority and/or wielding physical or psychological power. This is done through an influential role in the coercive arms of the state (police, prisons and armed forces) and/or the nuclear family unit. A complex and contradictory coding of masculine virtue is being staged here, wherein material ambition, male valour and martial prowess are foregrounded as admirable aims, but quickly become vulgar, uncouth and degenerate when wielded by the 'wrong' body – wrong in both classed and racialised terms. Internalising the assumption that physical and material power, both in the home and in the nation, should be pursued by men through the means available to them, contributes to their near-monopoly over violence – from state warfare to street fights, and from prison expansion to domestic violence. Yet, rather than seeing these different types of violence as connected, hegemonic masculinity frames the violence of war and prisons as legitimate, with criminalised forms of violence remaining the only cause for concern. It is worth returning to Shaun Bailey, who illustrates well this division of violent masculinities:

> When the whole smoking and carrying knives thing came about I could have been one of them … I was unique in that I was cool but I wasn't having to be carrying out the crime to be seen in that way. What it was, Army Cadets made me confident … My connection with the Army Cadets gave me an understanding of Britishness and that made my life much easier. I felt much less separated. I didn't feel the whole racism thing.[44]

Here, Bailey reveals two important features of hegemonic masculinity. First, he demonstrates how manifestations of Black masculinity (drug use and carrying knives) are delegitimised and criminalised, while institutionalised forms of hegemonic masculinity (the armed forces) provide individual confidence and social assimilation, as well as a collective sense of patriotism. Second, this hegemonic masculinity legitimises the structural racism that produces both the social conditions in which Bailey grew up and the role of the British armed forces in carrying out acts of violence in the Global South (e.g. Libya or Afghanistan).

The ironic logic of the social mobility that Bailey advances here is consequently revealing about the ideals of masculinity that engender today's anxieties about the self-gain and violence of 'gangs'. More specifically, Bailey's social conservatism claims that hard work within the parameters of capitalist and state institutions is the route to overcoming poverty, crime, prison and other manifestations of 'the whole racism thing'. Bailey's logic runs counter to the radical anti-racist thought that identifies capitalism and the state as producing and enforcing racism, offering crumbs of success to a small number of individuals. The myth of meritocracy and the hope of social mobility and integration help to maintain the legitimacy of racism and the class system, a legitimacy further entrenched when its 'successful' Black advocates are afforded influential political platforms. Importantly, this is not simply part of a

Black conservative agenda, but a wider modern 'civilising' project in which the state seeks to instil values on racialised minorities.[45]

Policing patriarchy, Black masculinity and community resistance

One morning in March 2014, around a dozen people from the LCAPSV came to protest outside a south London magistrates' court. The campaign was headed by the mother of a young Black man who had been assaulted by police officers and subsequently charged with obstruction. Most people entered the court when the proceedings began; a small group, including myself, remained outside collecting signatures for a petition and handing out flyers. A young Black man, Malcolm (not his real name), had just left the court having received a community service order. He was drinking a beer and talking to us about his life. When homeless he had been befriended by gypsy travellers and had since lived at their campsite, which he had found a positive experience. He spoke emotionally about losing his parents, his recent suicidal feelings, and his anger and frustration with the political system.

A female lawyer walked past, telling someone on the phone that she was on her way to meet her client. Malcolm commented loudly, 'I'd like to be *her* client!' The group responded with silent disapproval; an already tense atmosphere became awkward as we went from listening to Malcolm's deeply personal and painful story, to feeling he should be challenged. Doing so sensitively, in a way that would not escalate the situation, was not going to be easy, but fortunately Malcolm took his cue from the wall of silence, and continued with his life story. What kind of power is gained, even momentarily, for someone who is clearly depressed, suicidal and vulnerable, but in the same breath publicly harasses a woman? It would perhaps be better, I thought, for someone to take Malcolm aside later, for a private conversation about his behaviour.

A few minutes later, a male security guard approached Malcolm and challenged him about his comment to the lawyer. However, he did this in an aggressive manner, invading Malcolm's personal space and wagging his finger in his face. Malcolm responded badly and lost his temper. He took off his coat and challenged the security guard to a fight. After an exchange of angry words, with onlookers trying to defuse the situation, the court police were called. From an encounter lasting around fifteen minutes, two comments used by the male police officer stand out:

Trust me mate, page 3 is my favourite bit of the *Sun*.
Do you wanna be arrested? Do you wanna get locked up?

Here, we see two contrasting performances of patriarchal power. First, the street harassment of a woman by Malcolm – sexual power, and the proposition of a fist-fight – physical power. Secondly, the assertion by an arm of the British state that they 'love page 3 of the *Sun*' (which then showcased topless female models) – sexual power, and the proposition of arrest and detention – physical power. We don't know whether the police officer actually liked the *Sun* newspaper's page 3 or whether he seriously intended to arrest Malcolm. What is clear, however, is that his sexual and physical performances of patriarchal power are regarded as legitimate, whereas those exhibited by Malcolm are not. This power difference was clear for Malcolm, the officer, and everyone around – it was an unspoken truth that Malcolm's chauvinism was a crime, whereas that of the police officer was not. This separation of patriarchal power, subordinate and state-sanctioned, is refined by racial logics. Malcolm's Blackness confirms his criminal intent via a 'common-sense' racism; in order to understand this better, it is worth returning to colonial history.

Cultures of racism in the eighteenth and nineteenth centuries depicted colonised men as sexually promiscuous (during the period of enslavement or settler-colonial incursion), and sexually violent (particularly during anticolonial uprisings). Equivalent forms of sexual power and violence on the part of the colonial state or its actors remained unspoken or legitimised. It is this dichotomy between different types of patriarchal violence which criminalises many oppressed, particularly Black, men in the post-colonial context, further legitimising the hegemonic patriarchal violence of the state. Rather than enacting patriarchal power through, for example, police and prisons, pornography or access to capital, the avenues accessible to subordinated masculinities are more likely to be criminalised. Racism, therefore, leads to manifestations of patriarchy that not only legitimise the violence of hegemonic masculinity, but which also obscure racial violence. One female activist who attended the TDC meetings described in the next chapter, talked about the problem of doing anti-racist work which confronts both of these types of patriarchal power. She echoed the Black feminist critiques of masculinity established by bell hooks,[46] Beth Richie[47] and others:

> Under white supremacist patriarchy, capitalist patriarchy, men are victimised because they are forced to try to aspire to or emulate models of manhood and masculinity which are based on subjugation and are based on dominance, which is based on a fear ... They are denied the space to be able to truly feel and be sentient beings. To be beings that are able to reflect and analyse their own role and their position and their own contribution – and also challenge the notions of what masculinity is, and what manhood is, and what it means to be powerful. And so within this type of society manhood gets attributed to an external notion, such as how much money people have or what status they have ... and this in a way is actually quite disempowering to our men. They too often end up trying to live up to all this, that is ultimately dehumanising. And in the process they not only dehumanise themselves, they dehumanise people who are meant to be their loved ones.[48]

Here, this Black feminist approach names racism as 'white supremacy' – not simply the violence of groups like the Ku Klux Klan, but a racist system which empowers people, spaces and ideas racialised as white. This system is connected to the masculine power of patriarchy and the material power of capitalism. As Black feminists critical of policing and prisons also affirm, state institutions are not only ineffective in protecting women from being dehumanised by the men in their lives, but they also often exacerbate the problem by bringing the violence of arrest and imprisonment into an already harmful situation.[49] It is important to note that the police officer in the above-mentioned incident outside the courthouse did not intervene on behalf of the female solicitor but on behalf of the male security guard, who had had his physical power challenged by Malcolm. All of this is worth bearing in mind as we discover the outcome of the incident.

The case that had sparked the protest ended and the defendant's mother left the court; having been apprised of the situation, she took Malcolm aside, spoke to him calmly, and was able to defuse the conflict between him and the police officer. This woman clearly had no intention of defending street harassment in general or Malcolm's behaviour in particular. What she recognised, however, was that the power of state violence far outweighed Malcolm's power as an individual Black, working-class, criminalised man with mental health issues. Importantly, her response to Malcolm's violence was not an escalation of violence – the threat of a greater violence had not dealt with the situation. It was an intervention of care which brought an immediate end to the violence. Nonetheless, a longer-term process would be needed to transform Malcolm's chauvinism, temper and trauma as well as the poverty and racism which shaped his interactions with the police. This example helps to illustrate the difficulty in engaging in resistance to policing, in a context where men subjected to carceral violence can also engage in behaviour and gendered power which is harmful to themselves and to others. The final chapter of this book will think through community-led transformative approaches to justice more broadly.

The above story reaffirms the necessity of a Black feminist analysis for effectively understanding racist criminalisation. Such an approach provides the necessary political position to reject state violence in all its forms, while also identifying and challenging the gender-based and other forms of violence that occur on the interpersonal level. Countering the violence of oppressed people *and* the violence of state institutions is a difficult task in a context in which the latter is often considered the antidote to the former. Furthermore, these Black feminist critiques of violence demonstrate how the patriarchal pursuit of power is damaging for people of all genders in different yet interconnected ways. The harassment experienced by the woman heckled by Malcolm is connected to the harassment he himself later received from the security guard and the police officer. Each of these incidents caused distress both for the woman subjected to the initial harm and for the Black mother who eventually de-escalated the situation.

Malcolm experienced violence from the state both through his pre-existing criminal record and through the threat of arrest he received following the above incident. These multiple harms demonstrate the urgency for activists of all genders to incorporate a feminist analysis into their anti-racist work. As JJ Bola[50] has recently argued, this is the only route for Black men to understand and unlearn the harm they do to women *and* themselves which does not overburden women with political work. This approach can also avoid slipping into the damaging and ultimately racist tropes re-popularised by Black conservative spokesmen. The urgency of this political transformation is underlined not only by the gendered nature of racism and resistance to it highlighted here and in the previous chapters, but also by the chauvinistic impunity with which the police continue to criminalise Black men.

Conclusion

The racist outcomes produced by the normal functioning of policing in Britain, through Black people being stopped and searched, identified as gangsters or imprisoned, are some of the ways in which institutional racism affects the everyday. This function of policing does not produce such racist outcomes simply because racism has been entrenched in policing over the years, decades or generations since Black people came to Britain in significant numbers after World War II. Rather, we must understand British institutions and their racist functionality by looking at British histories which go beyond the borders of the mainland. Britain's policing of colonised peoples, both in the conventional sense and in the pre-police security used during enslavement and early colonial projects, has always relied on racist logic. Framing colonised men as a violent threat that can be controlled only by deploying the most punitive forms of justice, has continued to inform the law-and-order policing of the twentieth and twenty-first centuries. The clear material differences between the plantations of the Caribbean and the streets of British cities should not obscure the ideological and discursive continuities between these different spaces of British governance.

Imperial discourses of respectability and nationalism are fundamental to understanding the ways in which Black men are criminalised in the twenty-first century. The white, bourgeois, colonising man embodied the legitimate institutions of power such as the police, the military and the penal system. Both these individuals and the institutions they represented were considered to be respectable, rational and honourable mediators of control and justice. They performed a hegemonic masculinity which rendered colonised men the antithesis of this patriarchal status. The subordinated masculinities of the savages framed as violent, unthinking and sexually unrestrained, does not simply contextualise the criminalisation of Black men today, but provides us with the analytical tools to better understand racism itself, and the power it continues to serve. Attempting to replace a subordinate set of patriarchal norms, such as carrying knives or smoking, with hegemonic masculinities through joining the army or capitalist wealth accumulation, obscures how these different forms of oppressive power are linked. While patriarchy is often understood as a system of power which oppresses women, understanding how imperial discourses of masculinity and state control institutionalise masculine power illustrates how patriarchy is also dehumanising for men.

The racist mythology of Black-on-Black violence, often considered a relatively new phenomenon, is actually rooted in some of the most reactionary imperial discourses of previous centuries, as Charles Dickens's diatribe against the 'noble savage' exemplifies. Presenting Black men as a category of people who do not value their own or each other's lives is an effective prelude to a penal system that treats them as disposable. The police exploit the prevalent Black folk devils and the racial mythologies of criminality and deviance that are rooted in the cultures of slavery and colonialism. Framing young Black boys as in need of discipline empowers conservatives such as Shaun Bailey and the over-policing of Black communities. Operation Blunt 2, which swamped London's lower-income, multi-ethnic communities with stops and searches, took place in the three years leading up to the civil unrest of August 2011. Many of the young people who participated in these actions cited police stop and search as a key reason for their involvement.[51] The next chapter looks in some detail at the Black resistance to British policing which took place in 2011, sparked by the police shooting of Mark Duggan but connected to an interconnected web of racisms which spanned policing, the press and political rhetoric.

4

2011:
revolt and community defence

In 2011, Black communities in Britain were galvanised into mass mobilisation following three high-profile Black deaths at the hands of police. On 15 March, reggae artist Smiley Culture died during a police raid on his home in Warlingham, Surrey. Officers claimed that during the raid, he went to the kitchen to make a cup of tea alone, where he allegedly died by suicide after putting a kitchen knife through his chest. Smiley's 1984 hit 'Cockney Translation' conveyed how the identities of people of Caribbean heritage and other working-class Londoners converged, yet remained separate.[1] One of the first British reggae artists to gain television airplay, his hit single 'Police Officer' helped make him famous among reggae-listeners across the country. Smiley's popularity and anti-establishment stance meant that, after his death, over a thousand people marched from Vauxhall (south London) where Smiley had performed regularly, to Scotland Yard, the headquarters of London's Metropolitan Police, in protest. It was one of the biggest Black-led protests since the Stephen Lawrence Campaign in the 1990s.

Later in the same month, Kingsley Burrell died in custody in Birmingham. This resulted in one of the largest Black community protests the city had seen in a decade. Kingsley, a student with a history of mental health issues, called the police because he feared he was being followed. He was detained and held down with leg restraints, handcuffs and a towel over his head, on the floor of a mental health unit – he eventually died of a cardiac arrest.[2]

Most significantly, on 4 August 2011, twenty-nine-year-old Mark Duggan, from Broadwater Farm in Tottenham, north London, was shot dead by police on nearby Ferry Lane. Duggan's family were not informed; they found out about the killing when it was reported on the evening news. The police and the Independent Police Complaints Commission claimed that Duggan had fired shots at officers, a story widely reproduced by the press. However, it emerged that Duggan was in fact unarmed when killed – an officer had accidently shot a colleague, discovered when a police-issue bullet was recovered lodged in the injured officer's radio. However, it was too late, or indeed not expedient, to correct the stories parroted by newsrooms – reports of a shootout that never occurred filled headlines and were broadcast into homes throughout the country, shaping the narrative of Duggan as a gangster. Organising a march to Tottenham Police Station, the local community demanded answers from a senior officer.

As nightfall approached, the protesters outside the police station became agitated as their requests were ignored. A group of women led the demonstration into the station itself, confronting the police directly. When one of the women was allegedly struck by an officer, an unattended police vehicle had a brick thrown through its window, and the area erupted into civil unrest.[3] For five days, towns and cities across the country saw thousands of people take to the streets, attacking police stations and commercial outlets, clashing with officers in riot gear and appropriating high-value goods.

The rebellions resulted in nearly three thousand arrests[4] and countless raids, stops, searches and other instances of police violence and harassment. The anger at the police killing of Mark Duggan and the dismissal of his family, friends and community by officers at the local police station was perhaps unsurprising. However, few would have predicted the speed and scope with which the disturbances advanced. The rebellion began in London, with occurrences in twenty-two of its thirty-two boroughs, and quickly spread to other cities and towns across England. Sixty-six separate locations reported civil disturbances over those four days in August, with an estimated fifteen thousand people participating in the unrest. In Nottingham (East Midlands), police stations in Canning Circus, The Meadows, Oxclose, Bulwell and St Ann's were all attacked, some with petrol bombs.[5] Nationwide, research suggests that over 90 per cent of the damage was inflicted on chain stores or state institutions, and that much of the violence was directed towards the police. However, the press focused on the relatively small number of independent local shops damaged in the disturbances.[6] As the disturbances spread across mainly working-class, multi-ethnic communities, people from a range of backgrounds participated in the unrest. Yet it remains significant that the spark was the police killing of a young Black man, and racism played a role in shaping the context of the sixty-six localities which saw unrest in the August of that year.[7]

This chapter focuses on Black resistance to British policing in the aftermath of the 2011 'riots'. The historical section of this chapter offers an account of a very recent history – the media reports, police and political rhetoric which began in the twenty-first century, concerned with 'gang crime'. This provides some context for an analysis of the 2011 civil unrest and of three community-led defence campaigns. The first of these campaigns, the Tottenham Defence Campaign (TDC), is one of the many local initiatives which sprang up to challenge the increase in arrests, raids and imprisonment following the 2011 revolts. The second campaign concerns Mauro Demetrio, a young Black man violently assaulted by police in the aftermath of the 2011 unrest.[8] Finally, we turn to the inquiry into the police killing of Mark Duggan, and how his family-led campaign challenged racism from the media, politicians and the criminal justice system. These forms of Black community defence echo similar campaigns in previous decades and, like those outlined in Chapters 1 and 2, also draw on histories of anti-colonial struggle.

A recent history of a moral panic: the gang

Twenty-first-century moral panics are purportedly crises of criminality and disorder. Like their predecessors, they can be best understood as a way for governments to deal with very different crises. The financial crisis of 2007–8, which resulted in governments across Europe introducing austerity reforms, cutting jobs and public services, caused misery and hardship for millions of people. This formed part of a wider pattern of late capitalism, in which employment was becoming less secure and states struggled to make the promises of improving the livelihood of their constituencies.[9] Creating a moral panic over forms of violent criminality, or over immigration or terrorism, enables governments to better secure their legitimacy in the eyes of the public. The use of violent crime as a 'crisis' in society has led to an unprecedented expansion in police and prison power as we enter the third decade of the twenty-first century – this will be discussed in more detail in Chapter 5. For now, we will briefly examine the rise of the moral panic around 'gang crime' with a specific focus on the police shooting of Mark Duggan, and the civil unrest that ensued.

While the killing of Mark Duggan sparked an initial revolt, there can be little doubt that the wider context of police harassment and violence fuelled the resentment which led to young people across the capital joining the rebellions. The image cultivated of the gangster framed Black men like Duggan as violent and unthinking, justifying over-policing and punitive forms of justice. In the wake of the unrest, a refreshed moral panic was opportunistically exploited by the government and the media. Historian David Starkey's comments went viral after he explained white involvement in the unrest as a result of the whites of England 'becoming Black'. He alleged that the widespread use of Jamaican *patois* had left many Brits feeling as if they lived in a foreign country, and that this had led to a 'nihilistic gangster culture' among the working classes. David Cameron[10] echoed Starkey's sentiments, albeit in less bigoted language, as he declared an all-out war on 'gangs and gang culture'.

Those directly affected by such racism remain acutely aware of the dangers of this profiling: interviews with those involved in the 2011 civil unrest found that many rejected or challenged the term 'gang', highlighting its manufactured and racist connotations.[11] A number of investigations were carried out to ascertain precisely how the police and policy-makers define a 'gang'. In Manchester, Patrick Williams and Becky Clarke became interested in the moral panic around 'gangs' when the term gained popularity in the mid-2000s.[12] They were told by Greater Manchester Police and London's Metropolitan Police that they assigned groups of young people to their gang databases based on their involvement, or suspected involvement, in Serious Youth Violence (SYV). This covers a broad range of offences involving young people, and the researchers asked for the gang database to be broken down by ethnicity. They then requested the data on all the people identified as being involved in SYV, again broken down by ethnicity. What they found reaffirmed the racist imagery used by the press, commentators and politicians.

While the majority of people on Greater Manchester Police's gang database were Black, Asian or Minority Ethnic (BAME), the majority of those involved in SYV were white. In London, the majority of alleged gangsters were also BAME, but the SYV was split fifty-fifty between BAME and whites, roughly proportionate to London's youth population. Williams and Clarke could only conclude that the stated criteria for inclusion in a gang database do not align with the police's definition of SYV. What emerges as the most consistent factor in the gang databases of these two major English police forces is that race is the most salient signifier that determines a young person's status as gang-involved. The police currently distinguish 'gang members' from other criminal-ised people by characterising them as 'a noticeable group'.[13] What their databases indicate is that racialised minorities, particularly Black people, are considerably more 'noticeable' than their white counterparts. We will look in more detail at the new ways in which 'gangs' are policed in the next chapter, but for now, it is worth turning our attention to the role played by the media in reproduc-ing the moral panic around 'gangs'.

Reporters utilise nebulous definitions of 'gangsters' in a form of pseudo-empiricism. They often rely on piecemeal and anecdo-tal police data when they warn their readership that '[t]urf wars among London's 250 gangs account for half of all shootings and a fifth of stabbings and have fuelled this epidemic of violence'.[14] Like the police's gang databases, newspaper headlines, stories and photographs obscure our understanding of violence, and repro-duce racist mythologies. As is apparent to anyone who has ever attempted to define 'gang' (including the police themselves), the term lacks consistency – so much so that the attribution of spe-cific incidents to a gang is slippery. But these headlines serve a more instructive purpose. They signify a devaluing of Black life through the racial connotations of the 'gang', with similarly racial-ised images accompanying the reports. As with their predecessors, the Black men here are shadowy, menacing creatures, emotionally numb from their own pathological violence. And in a manner reminiscent of the reports (described in Chapter 3) of the 'negro cause' in Britain's Caribbean slave colonies, or the justifications for corporal punishment, mass imprisonment and massacres in Africa and South Asia, race remained the key to decoding the social abnormalities and disorder of 'revolting' subjects.

In the months and years following the disturbances, tales of the gangster proliferated. Aided by David Cameron's declaration of war against gangs, Britain's mainstream press latched on to this narrative. For example, the *Guardian* uncritically quoted the Press Association: 'The police had been authorised to use Section

60 powers, which allow random searches, in the Haringey area because of gangland violence'.[15] This reflects the Metropolitan Police website, which explains that 'use of the power to tackle gangs' results in Black and Asian people being disproportionately stopped and searched.[16] There was little coverage of the proven inefficacy of this power in reducing violence, although there was the occasional mention of the racially discriminatory way in which officers use the power. As part of its 'Gangs of London' campaign, London's *Evening Standard* ran a series of headlines claiming: 'These young gangsters have lost so many friends they've stopped going to their funerals … With thousands more caught up in this culture of "easy dying", we attend a secret summit of "soldiers" to hear them talk about weapons, jail and life in the "hood".'[17] A tone reminiscent of nineteenth-century anthropologists stumbling across 'primitive rituals' in Africa's 'dark heart' is reproduced without irony, with 'gangs' portrayed as luridly as any of the Black folk-devils of previous centuries.

It is the moral panic around gangs which enables these resource-intensive, violently racist and wholly ineffective police operations used by officers and championed by politicians under the guise of improving public safety. While increasing numbers of these young people were made to fit the profile of 'gangster', what is perhaps underappreciated is the effect of these orthodoxies of contemporary policing on the collective consciousness of those on whom it is enacted. The thousands of, predominantly Black, young people subjected to the escalation in stops and searches resulted in a popular resistance that contributed to the rebellions which took place in 2011. As has been the case in previous decades, such policing produces an antagonism against state power which can galvanise collective resistance. Unsurprisingly, the rebellions gifted the state with the opportunity to further escalate public panic around gangs, justifying the escalation of arrests, raids and incarceration which followed the disturbances. In the next section, we will look more closely at how Black-led community organisations created defence campaigns against the police response to the 2011 'riots'.

Youth in revolt and community defence

As with urban rebellions in previous decades (Chapter 1), the 'riots' of 2011 were dismissed by right-wing politicians and commentators as being devoid of politics – despite them being sparked by a state-sanctioned killing.[18] My own experience of working with young people has always pointed to their antagonism towards the police as something inherently political, but even commentators on the left disagreed. David Harvey saw 'mindless rioters' participating in 'feral capitalism';[19] A. Sivanandan claimed that they were 'neither community-based nor politically oriented', dismissing them as 'riots mobilised on a Blackberry'.[20] Such analyses are confusing, since working-class people appropriating high-value goods is nothing new – the main difference was that the availability of portable high-value goods on local high streets in 2011 was far greater than in previous decades and centuries. Furthermore, organising a rebellion on a Blackberry requires prior contact-sharing – this suggests community links rather than an impersonal summoning from the internet. One key difference between the rebellions in August 2011 and those in previous decades is the lack of involvement in 2011 by Black organisations, which had been a major feature of uprisings in the 1960s, 1970s and 1980s (see Chapter 1). However, the relative absence of Black social movements in 2011 to interact with and interpret the unrest, does not negate the political efficacy of the rebellions.

Another indication of the political nature of the unrest was the state's response. Nearly three thousand people were arrested in the months that followed the disturbances, two-thirds of whom were in London. Raids on homes escalated dramatically in a desperate search for stolen goods, and community groups reported young people badly beaten and subjected to racial abuse. Members of the judiciary had been instructed by politicians to deliver the harshest possible punishments for riot-related offences, and they openly declared their commitment to passing 'deterrent' sentences. This led to a mother receiving a custodial sentence for handling goods appropriated in the unrest, suspects as young as eleven appearing in court, and a man with a history of mental health issues dying in prison while he awaited sentencing for stealing a gingerbread man.[21]

Sweeping up suspects *en masse* and expounding collective punishment as a necessary response, echoes the response of British colonial administrations to anticolonial uprisings in colonies such as Kenya and India. Associating the 2011 unrest with Black communities through the language of the gangster and other imagery further entrenched the racial mythology that the state was dealing with an unthinking pathological violence that could be dealt with only through the harshest punitive measures. Suspect faces captured on CCTV covered billboards across London; the Mayor of London, Boris Johnson, purchased unlawful water cannons for the Metropolitan Police; and social media celebrities and media pundits asked whether a return to corporal punishment was the answer the nation needed.

It is worth remembering that regardless of the popular vilification in the wake of the 2011 unrest, Black communities quickly mobilised to challenge the state's response, providing legal and civil defence against the stops, searches, arrests, raids, imprisonments and naked violence licensed to the police in a desperate attempt to re-impose order. At a packed public meeting I attended in Tottenham in October 2011, attendees fiercely debated the issues and strategies they considered necessary for challenging police violence. Someone at the back identified herself as 'a Black woman' and demanded to be heard. Wearing a baseball cap low on her face, and a long dark green anorak, she stood up and exclaimed 'We're always on the back foot, we're always firefighting, it's like we just keep going from one crisis to the next'. Echoing these sentiments, similar opinions were often shared by older activists at public meetings about police violence in Tottenham. Fatal instances of police violence often recur in a specific geographical location, and the rest of this section examines in closer detail why Tottenham's history and ongoing issues with the police make space and place central to our understanding of both racism and anti-racist struggle.

The meeting in question was led by former organisers of the Broadwater Farm Defence Campaign, which formed part of a wider Black social movement against police racism in the 1980s (Chapter 1). This history of struggle, and Tottenham's large Black population, have led to the area being closely associated with Black politics and culture. Present at the 2011 meeting was a mixture of community elders, Pan-Africanists, Rastas, youth workers, parents, Haringey residents and some local white trade unionists, socialists and anarchists. Despite their broad range of political and cultural backgrounds, attendees were discouraged from engaging in theoretical political discussions once inside the meeting. Speeches and debates over long-term strategies for policy proposals or electoral change, aimed at overthrowing racism or capitalism, were thus absent from the discussion. Instead, over two hundred people gathered, anxious to learn from the newly formed TDC how they could best deal with the increasing intensity of police stops, searches, interrogations, arrests, raids, incarceration and acts of brutality and racism. It was quickly established that providing free legal advice for Haringey residents was a priority of TDC. One of the key resources was 'bust cards' containing information helping people utilise legal tools. This included access to police action lawyers who do not encourage guilty pleas, together with evidence collecting during raids and other civilian strategies (Figure 4.1). These A6-size leaflets were distributed across every housing estate in the borough in the aftermath of the 2011 unrest. Underneath the TDC heading is written 'Tottenham Defence Campaign ... For Us! By Us!'

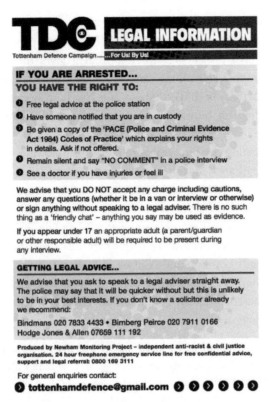

Figure 4.1 Tottenham Defence Campaign flier/bustcard

Tottenham is a racialised place, generally associated with its large Black community,[22] and it also has a strong history of Black resistance to policing (Chapter 1). The leaflet reaffirms a sense of place, with the first-person-plural pronoun 'us' used to invoke a collective sense of self in the local community. The bust card encourages residents to resist the police: 'DO NOT accept any charge including cautions, answer any questions (whether it be in a van or interview or otherwise), or sign anything without speaking to a legal advisor. There is no such thing as a "friendly chat".' This implicitly communicates to residents that the police may use deception in order to incriminate an individual. At the bottom, the small print explains that it has been produced by the Newham Monitoring Project (NMP), an 'independent anti-racist and civil justice organisation', and it gives their twenty-four-hour support telephone number. NMP worked closely with TDC in 2011–12; both Tottenham and Newham became places that exhibited an outward-looking anti-racist solidarity against policing.

This meeting in 2011 mirrored events following the 1985 Broadwater Farm uprisings in Tottenham. Police violence twenty-six years earlier had compelled the Black community of Tottenham to form a defence campaign (Chapter 1). During this period, Tottenham became part of the 'front line' in the battle against police violence, along with other Black communities in Brixton (south London) and Notting Hill (west London).[23] Long-standing community organiser Stafford Scott was part of both the 1985 and 2011 defence campaigns in Tottenham. He is worth quoting at length here:

> When I say Tottenham's a front line, I don't mean Tottenham's a place where people come to sell drugs and do things like that. When I say it's the front line, I mean it's at the fore of a battle against this onslaught of this militaristic, racist police force. And the reason we're at the fore of that battle, is because we had to set up a defence campaign, because we had to rise up, because the police took the life of a Black woman in Tottenham, and we stood up to them … It's the place where they want to get but they can't. It's the place where PC Blakelock lost his life … And ever since then, they've ensured that it remains a symbolic location.[24]

While Black resistance and policing are associated with what both Scott and the British press refer to as the 'front line',[25] Tottenham and Broadwater Farm are places racialised as Black, a 'symbolic location'. Scott says they are 'a place where they want to get, but can't'. In saying this he does not necessarily mean that the police cannot enter the physical place that is Tottenham. What remains clear, however, is that the police, and the state in general, cannot quell the spirit of rebellion felt by those on the 'front line'. The dual nature of the front line became clear one chilly October evening in 2011 when around a dozen members of TDC were distributing leaflets on a Tottenham council housing estate. When we reassembled, we noticed a number of police vans and some teenagers who had just been searched. The young locals hadn't been given an adequate reason for the search, and were told they would need to go to the police station if they wanted a receipt, which they declined. Speaking to the teenagers, we heard from them about the increase in searches and raids since the unrest in August. As the police vans doubled back, creeping past us slowly, the faces staring out at us from the moving vehicles felt like part of an occupation rather than a routine patrol. The experiences of such policing can thus mark places with a racial stamp, continually reproduced through state violence and resistance to it.

In the direct aftermath of the civil disturbances in August 2011, twenty-one-year-old Mauro Demetrio was stopped by the police in east London for alleged erratic driving and then arrested for an unrelated incident. He was handcuffed and detained in the back of a police van. PC Alex MacFarlane, one of the officers present, turned to him and said, 'The problem with you is you'll always be a n****r. You will always have Black skin colour … That's your problem.' What the officers didn't know is that Demetrio had set his phone to record audio of the incident. Another officer also assaulted Demetrio, putting his hands round his neck in a police cell. In the recording, an officer can be heard calling Demetrio a 'scumbag', to which Demetrio retorts, 'You tried to strangle me like a mug'. The officer immediately responds, 'No, I *did* strangle you'. When Demetrio asks the officer 'Why did you strangle me?', he replies, 'Because you're a c**t'. Despite what many would see as incontrovertible evidence of racism, the case was initially dismissed by the Crown Prosecution Service (CPS) as insufficiently strong to bring a charge of racial abuse.

Following this decision, Demetrio spoke publicly of his ordeal and released the audio to the media with the support of NMP. While complaints of racism by police are commonplace, NMP found that the majority of complainants do not attempt to press criminal charges or even report the complaint, lacking faith in the apparatus of accountability and justice. Ordinarily the press would have little interest in such an allegation; however, the presence of the audio and the potential insight into police racism, already under scrutiny because of the riots, altered this. The voice of the 'victim' can awaken a strong sympathetic public reaction, just as stories of people who were scared or whose property had been damaged during the unrest were prominently centred in news reports. Stuart Hall *et al*[26] acknowledge the victim's presence among the 'voices of authority', recognising the emotive value of the 'real experience' of victims of violent crime, even if it is often used by those in power to shore up a political agenda intent on extending police powers. However, when used to convey the trauma of police violence, this voice can provide a valuable counterbalance to the dominant narrative of those in power.

Bringing the incident to public attention allowed a unique scrutiny of police behaviour 'behind closed doors' and of how challenges to this behaviour are dealt with by the CPS. Following a public outcry, the CPS reversed their decision and the case came before the courts. The accused officer claimed Demetrio had racially abused the white officers and then described himself as a 'n****r'. MacFarlane had repeated the term, owing to the stress and fatigue of long working hours after the disturbances. He effectively argued that the intensity of the external environment had caused him to make an uncharacteristic and isolated professional mistake. He went on to claim:

> I had formed an impression in my mind that he had low self-esteem ... I wanted him to reconsider his lifestyle, to not view his skin colour as the reason behind the problems he had, not to blame the police, not to blame other people.[27]

His defence team took an unexpected turn to brazen gaslighting, suggesting that this approach was in fact 'in the spirit of the Black Panther Party'. Furthermore, PC MacFarlane's defence team argued that Demetrio's use of the word 'mug' was in fact a synonym of the term 'motherf****r'. In common UK parlance the term 'mug' means something quite innocuous, akin to 'fool'; however, the Urban Dictionary website suggests that in the US it can in fact mean 'motherf****r'. The sheer confidence exhibited by PC MacFarlane's defence team in redefining commonly used words to malign a young Black man is just one example of the self-assurance of the police in court, even when faced with evidence of violently assaulting a young Black man. It is unclear how the defence arrived at this argument, but it was in all likelihood exploiting the stereotype of a mouthy and offensive young Black man, who, of his own volition, used profane, racially charged language to describe both himself and abuse his arresting officers.

The case against PC MacFarlane was eventually dismissed, after two juries were unable to reach a unanimous decision. The semantic acrobatics by which such an acquittal was ultimately obtained warrant some examination in the context of wider colonial continuities. While the material circumstances which existed in Britain's colonies are certainly very different from the experiences of Black communities in twenty-first-century Britain, the political cultures and processes indicate important similarities. The assumption of Black deviance on the one hand, and state institutional innocence on the other, remains the order of the day. The subtext of the police defence was that they were dealing with a childish, rude and violent young Black man in need of the perhaps harsh, but ultimately fair, discipline of the state. Consequently, any act of violence on the part of the police is excused as an unfortunate, unusual aberration, arising necessarily from interaction with the chaos and criminality of the 'subject' population.

This case was one of many taken up by the community defence campaigns that mobilised during and after the unrest of 2011. It shows how, despite community-led organising, well-resourced legal campaigns and public outrage at the racism and impunity of the police, in the eyes of the law a young Black man is excluded from the presumption of innocence, let alone permitted access to victimhood. It also highlights the discrepancy between public opinion and the formal administration of justice in the courts. PC MacFarlane was subsequently dismissed from the force for gross misconduct, which in the eyes of the public is likely to be seen as an acknowledgement of serious wrongdoing on behalf of the police, or at least a desire by the police to avoid any further reputational damage and subsequent scrutiny.

For the TDC, it was insufficient to draw links between the racial violence of policing in the twenty-first century and that of previous decades; the organisers also connected it with colonial slavery. These theoretical links were brought to life during exchanges at a public meeting organised by TDC and The Monitoring Group called 'The enduring effects of slavery and institutional racism'.[28] The event took place in October 2013, and the organisers said they had been planning it since the 2011 unrest. They hoped it would better contextualise how Black communities in Tottenham and beyond experienced racial violence. Nearly four hundred people attended the day-long meeting. Attendees included 'cultural nationalists' in African and African-style dress, representing organisations such as the interim National Afrikan People's Parliament (iNAPP), and members of the Nation of Islam, recognisable by their slick suits, sharp hairstyles and bowties for men, with dresses and headscarves worn by the women. About thirty young people attended, ranging in age from around fourteen to twenty-five, who were allocated reserved seating at the front of the room. The few white people may have been there by invitation; they included radical lawyers and activists who had supported TDC and similar organisations in the past.

The visiting speaker, Joy Degruy, discussed the links between experiences of violence under colonisation and racial violence in Britain today. A formal response to Degruy's work is beyond the scope of this book, but what was made clear at the meeting was that the collective experience of racial violence endured by Tottenham's Black community constitutes part of a collective memory of colonialism and slavery shared by members of other Black communities in Britain. This was illustrated by contributors from Brixton and Newham, who drew parallels with the histories and experiences in the areas in which they lived. Reference was made to plantations in the colonial Caribbean, with activists likening police brutality today to the brutality of chattel enslavement.

These overlapping networks of social relations were recalled to illustrate symbolic, collective memories of colonisation and slavery, reawakened by contemporary experiences of racial violence. Despite the large geographical and temporal disjuncture between Britain and its former slave colonies, cultures of imperial racism were continually highlighted at the meeting. The organisers urged those visiting to return to Tottenham in order to support their struggles, promising that they would respond in kind. While the racism experienced by Black communities across London is constructed through both colonial histories and recent experiences of police brutality, these interconnections are also used to articulate Black solidarities across communities. Systems of racial violence which manifest across different times and spaces are conceptualised in relation to each other. This leads to articulations of resistance which extend beyond localities and national borders. Identifying the links between the colonial Caribbean and postcolonial Britain is not simply an intellectual exercise which provides historical context, but a tool for Black organisers to both make sense of the enduring nature of state racism and build the communities of resistance equipped for this challenge.

Resisting criminalisation

In 2013, there was an inquest at the Royal Courts of Justice into the death of Mark Duggan. The packed public gallery heard how Mark was shot dead by one of the Metropolitan Police's gang units, the 'Trident Gang Crime Command', which focused 'primarily on gun crime and homicide within the Black community'.[29] Like the paramilitary policing of Northern Ireland, Trident deployed armed units upon 'suspect communities'. Explicitly articulating a causal relationship between race and crime also echoed the policing of colonies in previous decades and centuries, outlined earlier in the chapter. For the Metropolitan Police in the twenty-first century, linking race and crime remained uncontroversial. Those representing the police generally referred to the findings of the Macpherson Report, which branded them institutionally racist, in the past tense – as if the racism endemic within policing had been definitively eliminated. When Tony Blair was prime minister, he made speeches about violent crime in which he maintained that it is 'young Black kids doing it'. The Conservatives who followed him seamlessly inherited and entrenched the rhetoric and policies of this racist moral panic. This left the police comfortable in dealing with the purportedly objective relationality between Blackness and violence.

The inquest was told that the failure of the police to engage with Duggan's family after the killing led to widespread civil unrest,[30] at which point officers went to great lengths to communicate closely with the press. In the aftermath, the police propagated much misinformation, including that Duggan was a violent gangster linked to numerous murders[31] even in the total absence of supporting evidence. The reports of the mythical 'exchange of fire' between Duggan and the police shaped public perceptions of Duggan in the days following his death. Compounding this, London's *Evening Standard* newspaper launched the aforementioned high-profile 'Gangs of London' series in the same week as the 2013 inquest.

Thus, while the truth behind this police killing was being exposed in court, newspapers carried images and descriptions of young Black men as gangsters. Despite the public scrutiny surrounding the inquest into Mark Duggan's death, officers in the dock appeared relaxed. The activists and Tottenham residents in the public gallery were keen to see those responsible for the killing face public scrutiny. During cross-examination, a police witness was asked to expand on the lessons learnt from what had gone wrong on the day of Mark's death. The officer paused, looked slightly confused, then shook his head and said:

> Gone wrong? Well, from my understanding, the – it depends on how you see that because the operation was planned as expected.[32]

Here, the police witness confidently asserts that he considered the killing of a Black suspect to be a legitimate outcome. Even in court, the lack of evidence that the suspect was armed or otherwise dangerous did not concern him. Rather than apprehending, questioning and charging Mark Duggan, with the courts deciding his fate, the police unashamedly designated themselves judge, jury and executioner. This killing of a Black man must be contextualised, not just in the disproportionate use of force used by police against Black people,[33] but also in its historical context.

As Chapter 3 argued, Black men were racialised through discourses that framed them as violent threats to safety and public order during periods of slavery and colonialism. Indeed, the state racism of a police unit whose explicit function is targeting violent Blacks, evidently considers the fatal use of force to be a predictable necessity in the maintenance of law and order. The violence of these and other police officers is not just shrugged off as morally defensible, but considered a necessary 'burden' on the police. This reproduces the colonial logic of punitive power as the only means by which the implicit pathology of Black criminality can be contained. It is within this logic that we must place the assertion that 'nothing went wrong' in the extrajudicial killing of Mark Duggan.

The recovery of a firearm was based on an eye-witness account by a police officer, which mobile phone footage from a member of the public later proved to be false. The gun that was recovered from a bush five metres from the scene did not have Duggan's fingerprints or DNA, and no witnesses could explain how it got there. Other police witness accounts were described by the coroner as 'contradictory', including a sergeant 'directing officers to go and secure a gun which hadn't yet been found'. The coroner added: 'It is not a question of anybody being mistaken. It is something which is a direct contradiction here'.[34] This is particularly surprising given that, unlike civilians who are investigated for a suspicious death, police officers are permitted to write their witness statements together, conferring and colluding with each other, with senior officers and with their legal team to ensure one cogent police voice. Many of those involved in the campaign against the police found the discrepancies between police accounts and the physical evidence of the case startling, and some maintained that the litany of contradictions suggested that the gun might have been planted. The police's apparent nonchalance in expounding their view that Duggan's death was an appropriate outcome says little for the inquest process and its ability to hold the police to account for acts of violence.

The gendered and racialised framing of Black men like Mark Duggan as violent was reproduced by the national press beneath headlines such as 'Mark Duggan, the man who lived by the gun' in the *Daily Mail*.[35] Figure 4.2 shows the photograph of Mark Duggan commonly used in the press – a man staring malevolently into the camera.[36] The physical image of this stony expression is contextualised only by the descriptions of Duggan as a 'gangster' and 'senior member of notorious Tottenham Man Dem'.[37] This framing was challenged by Justice4Mark, the family- and community-led campaign which emerged as a response to the shooting. Figure 4.3 is their flier showing the uncropped photograph of Duggan taken in the same place, which explains his solemn expression – he is standing next to the grave of his daughter, who died as a baby. He is

Figure 4.2 Photograph of Mark Duggan commonly used in the press

holding a heart-shaped memorial plaque which reads 'Daughter. Always in Our Hearts'. Campaigners were compelled to reclaim the conceptual and physical images of Mark Duggan, both of which were subjected to racialised misrepresentation.

This new image disrupts the stereotypes of Black masculinity projected onto Duggan by the police and the press. In order to counter this narrative, Justice4Mark displays an image of a young Black man living through the crushing emotions of mourning and loss. Rather than bowing to the whims of hegemonic masculinity, Justice4Mark campaigners, led by women, raise their fists and employ the slogan 'No Justice, No Peace'. At the same time, they are reframing the narrative of Black masculinity, portraying the caring, loving family and community member they dearly miss and for whom they seek justice. The reclaiming of Mark Duggan's conceptual and physical image helped the campaign attain national headlines while refusing to compromise with a system that seeks to dehumanise victims of police violence.

Figure 4.3 Flier produced by Justice4Mark

From Duggan to Demetrio, the attempt to seek justice and counter the authority of the police is – with the total complicity of the British tabloid press – presented as a threat to a state engaged in a 'total war on crime'[38] and an 'all-out war on gangs and gang culture'.[39] But amidst the hard, reactionary power of racial violence on the part of the police, there was also a softer, more liberal racism on the part of politicians, aided by academics and the charity sector. The leaders of the three main political parties in the UK backed the London *Evening Standard*'s new paternalistic campaign to help former gang members transform their lives. This campaign was, in part, based on a University College London study[40] of 105 children who were being helped by the since-discredited charity Kids Company; government and press employed the charity sector and academia to lend legitimacy to their skewed and alarmist statistics. Following a familiar pattern of conservative paternalism, the proposal was made to employ these young men in the service sector. Referring to jobs in removal services, the *Evening Standard* ran the headline 'The Ex-Cons Who'll Take Away Your Stuff ... But Only if You Pay Them!'[41] This light-hearted conclusion to the paper's 'Gangs of London' series attempted to demonstrate how integration into the market economy is the solution to the problems posed by gangs. David Cameron commended the *Standard* for its 'bold lead', Labour leader Ed Miliband hailed the 'fantastic initiative', and Liberal Democrat Nick Clegg paid tribute to the 'great campaign'.[42] Rather than simply identifying an apparent social problem, this campaign manufactured solutions which used work as a disciplinary and civilising force for alleged former gang members. This echoes not just the Dickensian workhouse but the positing of slavery and colonial exploitation as a civilising and cleansing endeavour (Chapter 3). This logic not only echoes the civilising missions of previous centuries outlined in the previous chapter; it also informed a policy which garnered a jingoistic consensus among twenty-first-century politicians.

Conclusion

Since 1990, on average more than one person a week has died at the hands of police, prisons and border authorities in Britain. In 2011, the figure for Black people was well over double that of previous years. It is difficult to identify the factors that led to this rise. However, for a few years after the 2011 riots, Black deaths in police custody decreased dramatically despite the increased police powers in the aftermath of the rebellion. This decrease could be a result of the response of young people to the fatal use of force, which appears to have temporarily tempered the confidence of officers to act with violent disregard, or to make premeditated decisions over the life or death of a Black suspect. This trend did not last, and it was not long until more Black people were dying at the hands of officers than in 2011. Indeed the years 2016–17 saw a further increase in Black people losing their lives in such circumstances.[43]

While sporadic instances of civil unrest can erupt in response to police violence, and public meetings are frequently called to address immediate concerns, it is the organised resistance (for example by TDC) in these moments of crisis that speaks to the everyday violence and indignity of police racism. Further to this, the Black community campaigns outlined in this chapter draw on both the histories of Black British resistance in previous decades and histories of resistance to slavery and colonialism in the British Empire. The rage expressed by the family and friends of a person who has died at the hands of the police can become the focus of a wider movement of people angered by police harassment – stops, questionings, searches – which, to an unaffected onlooker, can appear isolated or mundane.

Rather than representing specific crimes such as murder or theft, Black people come to represent whole categories of crime such as 'gang crime'. These categories have inconsistent and often ambivalent definitions on paper (further developed in Chapter 5), while signifying a coherently racist formulation in the popular imagination. At the sharp end of police racism, victims experience two types of violence – the initial physical assault and the subsequent character assassination. So Mauro Demetrio is subjected to both physical and psychological violence, and Mark Duggan is killed twice over.

The next chapter extrapolates from these two case studies to illustrate the countless examples of young Black people framed as gangsters and subjected to the full extent of police and prison power. As in previous chapters, I also analyse colonial policing and colonial propaganda campaigns, this time in the dying days of Empire, to illustrate how they are connected to the cutting-edge policing of Black communities in twenty-first-century Britain.

5

All-out war: surveillance, collective punishment and the cutting edge of police power

It is a major criminal disease that has infected streets and estates across our country ... We will fight back against gangs, crime and the thugs who make people's lives hell and we will fight back hard ... The last front in that fight is proper punishment. (David Cameron, Prime Minister's speech on the fightback after the riots, 2011)

Politician, hush don't make a sound
Been oppressin' us couple centuries now. (Kane 'Kano' Robinson, *Trouble*, 2019)

In 2012, after nearly two decades of protest, lobbying and legal struggles, two people were found guilty of the racist murder of Stephen Lawrence. The convictions of Gary Dobson and David Norris, who received fifteen and fourteen years in prison respectively, were welcomed by the Lawrence family and their supporters. Of the group of racist youths that attacked Stephen in 1993, prosecutors were no longer able to ascertain who delivered the fatal blow; they were able to win the case using a legal doctrine known as Joint Enterprise (JE). A conviction under JE requires proof of common purpose among individuals not always present at a crime, often accompanied with evidence of 'bad character'. Hidden cameras placed in the homes of the suspects recorded them recounting their desire to violently attack Black people.

The racist language and aggressive footage shocked the court. For the campaign, it provided the evidence which confirmed a shared racially motivated intent to kill Stephen Lawrence the night they and their friends attacked him. This was not the first time JE had been used to convict more than one person of a serious offence. Importantly, it popularised JE as a tool of anti-racism. Yet few of the people who had campaigned for justice following Stephen's murder were aware that the power of JE to convict and hand out lengthy prison sentences to violent racists was quietly having profound consequences for young Black men across the country.

In the years leading up to the high-profile convictions for the killing of Stephen Lawrence, hundreds of young people were being given lengthy prison sentences under the JE doctrine. While the media and anti-racists celebrated the courts' and prison system's capacity to lock away two violent racists through JE, it was young Black men who were disproportionately the target of these powers. Despite only constituting 3.3 per cent of the general population, Black people received over a third of JE convictions between 2005 and 2013. Those who defended JE claimed Black overrepresentation in 'knife crime' could explain the Black conviction rate. However, it is often the racist narratives about 'gangs' (outlined in Chapter 4) that prove crucial in securing JE convictions.[1] Convincing a court that a group of individuals are all part of the same gang has proven hugely effective in the government and police's campaign against 'gangs'. It is not uncommon for the police to play footage from rap videos and social media posts which show the defendants together. This is used to 'prove' they are part of the same gang and therefore demonstrating a shared 'belief and contemplation'. Consequently, whoever the principal 'offender' in the group may have been, those in their 'gang' are equally guilty of the offence.

The racist nature of how gangs and gang members are defined, identified and monitored means that when police reveal to the court that the defendants all appear on their gangs database, it is more than likely that the defendants will be young Black or Asian men. The police held conferences in London's City Hall to discuss the need for new approaches, weapons and powers to police those identified as gang members. One example includes a £1 million annual fund to provide, among other judicial powers, 'dedicated gang prosecutors'[2] in order to ensure that those accused of 'gang-related' offences were more likely to be convicted. Young people linked to gangs form part of a 'suspect community' for which JE is a powerful form of collective punishment. The monitoring of social media and surveillance technologies enables police to collect ever-increasing 'evidence' of 'gang' associations. A 'proven' gang member does not have friends, close family members or acquaintances, but 'gang affiliates' and accomplices, who should be similarly monitored, harassed and, if necessary, convicted and imprisoned under JE.[3]

JENGbA (Joint Enterprise Not Guilty by Association) is a campaign group set up to challenge JE convictions, mainly made up of the mothers and family members of young Black and Asian people incarcerated under the doctrine.[4] It is worth noting that many of the JENGbA organisers are white parents whose 'mixed-race' child has been incarcerated. As in the case of Mark Duggan detailed in the previous two chapters, the state uses racist policing against these young people in the same way as people with two Black parents. Supporting over a thousand prisoners, the group campaigns against JE through awareness raising, protest and legal campaigns. Given that most of the cases involve murder convictions and assume gang membership, convincing the public and the courts that the law is unfairly harsh can be an uphill battle.

JENGbA raises awareness about the flimsy evidence against a young person, and assumptions made about those who are present when a crime take place. The activists affirm that people are always shocked when they learn about JE, exclaiming 'That happens in the UK?!'[5] The cruel irony, of course, is that while this legal doctrine is used in Britain, its most visible targets are not people who fully belong to the nation – they are racialised outsiders. The 'gangs' who are subjected to incarceration through JE are disproportionately Black and Asian, with these racialised criminal categories serving as the popular justification for the collective punishment served to young working-class people from a range of backgrounds. JENGbA activists are clear about the racist nature of JE, but also see their struggles connected to earlier campaigns against British policing beyond the mainland. One formerly incarcerated JENGbA activist compares their struggle to the one in Northern Ireland: 'The last catastrophe to happen for the judiciary occurred in 1989 when the supporters of the Birmingham Six, Maguire Seven, Guildford Four held the judiciary to book'.[6]

This chapter explores the ways in which new powers are reproducing racism in British policing. There will be further analysis of the development of the 'all-out war on gangs and gang culture' announced by David Cameron in 2011, and discussed in the previous chapter. I also detail the ways in which new technologies, surveillance and injunctions are used to criminalise Black communities and expand the use of prisons and other forms of punishment. We begin, however, by stepping back in time to explore the ideas, cultures and practices of state racism and policing during decolonisation. This counterinsurgency policing in the dying days of Empire used surveillance, mass incarceration, forced migration and coercive violence against 'suspect communities'. Interestingly, this colonial policing also used the language of 'gangs' to depict the targets of state violence. This power of distortion, to portray groups of people as criminal, influences racist stereotypes in the postcolonial period. This racist 'grammar', argues Hortense Spillers, finds its way into our present 'from the semantic and iconic folds buried deep in the collective past'.[7] Consequently, racial governance in both the colonies and modern Britain enables these forms of collective punishment to be planned, implemented and justified by state institutions, aided by popular racist cultures. While there was little attempt to distinguish between police and military operations in colonial contexts, racist policing in Britain since the 1980s has slowly introduced counterinsurgency tactics, a trend which has accelerated in the twenty-first century.

Counter-gangs, anti-terror and 'hearts and minds' policing at the end of Empire

Between 1945 and 1971, the British army was involved in at least thirty-seven conflicts across a rapidly decolonising world, from tiny islands such as Anguilla and strategic sites such as Cyprus or Suez, to the jungles of Ceylon (now Sri Lanka) and the deserts of Aden and Oman. These military operations involved a war of ideas as much as a military conflict, argued Sir Frank Kitson, now a distinguished former general and military writer who played a key role in directing operations against anti-colonial insurgents in Malaya (now Malaysia), Kenya and Northern Ireland. Kitson's insight will inform the analysis of these three case studies in this section. He claimed that the role of the British was to win over 'hearts and minds' using minimal force. I would argue that British colonial propaganda sought to obscure the violent nature of British policing in the dying days of Empire. Kitson is particularly useful in understanding both colonial and contemporary policing, as his entire combat management experience emerges in the colonies and then Northern Ireland, after which it is applied in the domestic context.

Kitson and other British military strategists used violent strategies of coercion and control against anti-colonial movements. So how was British colonial policing rewritten in order to propagate the myth of the 'hearts and minds' approach to governance? First, the many acts of rebellion against British power would suggest that violent confrontation was not an unusual feature of decolonisation and anti-imperialism. Despite the frequency of these revolts, each time the British army was deployed it was generally described as an exceptional case, an 'emergency'.

Secondly, while military tactics were being used in each case, opponents of the British were rarely described as an army themselves. It was important that those resisting British rule were not considered legitimate, organised and state-like. Indeed, during the Malaya 'Emergency', even referring to anticolonial forces as an 'insurgency' was considered too legitimising. Rejecting the possibility that they were operating with the consent of the wider colonised population, those resisting British power were often instead called 'gangsters', 'terrorists' or 'thugs'[8] – the same racist categories used to identify and label 'criminals' in Britain today. This helped to justify collectively punishing suspect populations, including the use of mass arrest, imprisonment and forced resettlement.

Thirdly, the 'hearts and minds' approach purportedly used relatively little violence, both when compared with that used by their adversaries and that used by other European colonial powers. Echoing the popular mantra of British policing 'by consent', clear evidence of abuse could be dismissed as the misguided actions of the proverbial 'bad apples'. Kitson argued that winning 'hearts and minds' simply required a colonised people, with the help of the army, to properly understand and appreciate the benefits of British influence or rule. He maintained that mass arrest, detention and resettlement were necessary for general surveillance, identifying criminals hiding in the suspect population, or keeping civilians safe.[9]

Often held up as the best of example of a British 'hearts and minds' counterinsurgency operation is the Malaya 'Emergency' between 1948 and 1960. Military strategists such as Sir Frank Kitson used this war in South East Asia to cement the notion that the UK was a nation that could oversee a 'peaceful' transition to independence while at the same time defeating communism, all without the scandals of the French in Algeria or the US in Vietnam. When communist-inspired workers, mainly from Malaya's Chinese population, began to agitate against colonial rule, the British could not afford to let the territory fall into China's or the USSR's sphere of influence. Malaya produced 45 per cent of the world's rubber, a vital commodity. As of 1947, it was also Britain's largest dollar earner, bringing in $200 million every year, more than all exports from the British mainland combined.[10]

Britain's intended plan was for a client government to be handed power following a transition period which would take at least twenty-five years. Following a series of industrial actions, including a general strike in 1946, the British began targeting suspected communists. In the first days of the Emergency, six hundred trade unionists were detained and, in a matter of months, over six thousand arrests had been made. Later that year, S. A. Ganapathy, a former president of the Pan Malayan Federation of Trade Unions, was hanged by British authorities for possession of a firearm. By 1949, trade union membership in the colony had fallen by nearly 80 per cent.[11] When the resistance progressed into a guerilla movement, targeting white settler plantation managers, Britain scaled up the counter-offensive. The rebels retreated into Malaya's dense rainforest, forming the Malayan National Liberation Army (MNLA). They were often simply referred to as 'Communist Terrorists' by Britain's representatives, such as colonial civil servant in Malaya Sir Robert Thompson.[12]

For the first two years of the Emergency, the British engaged in a counter-terror operation in which they made sweeps of rural villages, burning the homes of those suspected of supporting the resistance. High Commissioner Sir Henry Gurney told the Legislative Council in 1948: 'There are bound to be cases in which hardship will be caused to innocent people who do not feel that they have a duty to distinguish themselves from the guilty. I say this in no way as a threat but as a plain statement of fact'.[13] The 'hardship' which caused the most controversy back in Britain came to be known as the Batang Kali Massacre, in which twenty-four unarmed Malay Chinese villagers were killed by British forces.[14] A Scotland Yard investigation into the massacre began in the 1960s, but was dropped in 1970 owing to an alleged lack of evidence. Survivors of the massacre and their descendants petitioned the British government in the early 1990s to hold those responsible to account. It took until 2015 for the UK Supreme Court to rule that Britain was not obliged to hold a public inquiry into the massacre as it had taken place so long ago. The decision was challenged in the European Court of Human Rights, but upheld in 2018.

In 1950, British General Sir Harold Briggs took over operations in the Malay Emergency. By 1953, the so-called Briggs Plan led to over twenty thousand Chinese Malayans being deported to China (a country most had never visited and where they had no family), with around eleven thousand imprisoned at any given time, often without trial. Half a million of the remaining Chinese-heritage population, mainly smallhold farmers, were subjected to resettlement. They were forcibly removed from their homes and placed in heavily controlled 'New Villages' surrounded by fences with guarded entrances.[15] Han Suyin, a Chinese-Belgian author who was married to a British Special Branch officer, described the 'New Villages' in her memoirs:

> at the edge of a fetid mangrove swamp … behind … the barbed wire manned by a police post … four hundred beings, including children, huddled there … I shall never forget their pale and puffy faces: beriberi, or the ulcers on their legs. Their skin was the hue of the swamp. They stank. There was no clean water.[16]

Perhaps unsurprisingly, the Chinese Malay called the New Villages 'concentration camps'.[17] In an attempt to limit support for the MNLA, those not subjected to resettlement or imprisonment instead experienced British control of food, censorship, curfews, fines, mass arrests and the death penalty for carrying arms.[18]

The British considered these tactics a success and the last five years of the conflict, according to Sir Robert Thompson, simply involved the 'mopping-up of the remaining communist terrorist gangs'.[19] The tactics better remembered by the British were those used in the later years of the conflict. Wage increases, political representation and softening military control in the 'White Areas' from which the MNLA had been cleared constituted the 'hearts and minds' approach which the British used to whitewash the conflict. Indeed, it enabled the British field marshal in Malaya, Sir Gerald Templer, to claim that victory was won by gaining the consent of the colonised population, and that '[t]he shooting side of this business is only 25% of the trouble and the other 75% lies in getting the people of this country behind us'.[20] Senior military figures like Sir Frank Kitson[21] claimed that their sophisticated hearts and minds approach was able to effectively discriminate between innocent and insurgent. Yet what is clear from the historical record is that a suspect community, the Chinese Malay, was subjected to what amounted to ethnic cleansing. While the British considered the conflict a victory, MNLA resistance meant that independence for the colony arrived in 1960, far sooner than the projected twenty-five years.

Constructing an ethnic or racialised relationship to criminal violence was as important to the policing of decolonisation as the establishment and maintenance of colonial rule itself. While the Chinese Malay were the suspect population of Malaya, in Kenya it was the Kikuyu people who were the primary targets of mass arrest, imprisonment, forced resettlement and other abuses.

The Kenya 'Emergency' between 1952 and 1960 was one of the most violent anti-colonial conflicts of the twentieth century. In this settler colony, which by 1950 had a white population numbering over 23,000,[22] racist laws regulated every aspect of Kenyan society under British rule. White people purchased land in highly fertile 'White Highlands' and grew profitable crops such as coffee, which Africans were not permitted to cultivate. Working on white-owned plantations, Africans toiled for low wages and were barred from practising skilled trades. Flogging was a common disciplinary tool, used both informally in the workplace by settlers and as a punishment handed down by the colonial courts. Like other apartheid states, Africans did not have the right to vote or to trial by a jury of their peers, and were barred from many hotels, restaurants, sporting events and other public spaces.[23]

Sir Frank Kitson, whom we have already seen in Malaya, also played a key role in the Kenyan Emergency. He described the counterinsurgency operation in a memoir of this posting titled *Gangs and Counter-Gangs*.[24] The 'gang' activity first arose in attacks on white plantation owners, often in their homes, suggesting that the 'gangsters' had support from plantation workers. Reflecting the horror felt by white settlers and the British public back home, Kitson writes of gangs 'betraying and murdering their white employers'. He continues romantically: 'Many of these Africans had lived all their lives with European families and occupied positions of trust and friendship'.[25]

The movement grew quickly into an organised insurgency, with Kitson distinguishing between two different types of gang. First, there was the 'Militant Wing' known as the Mau Mau, who lived in the forests and carried out guerilla attacks on white settlers, their property and Kenyans loyal to Britain. Supporting them was the 'Passive Wing', which provided information, supplies and shelter for the militants, while continuing their everyday lives. Fighting a guerilla war against enemy combatants who were difficult to distinguish from civilians proved tricky. One white Kenyan typified the racism of the settler population, demanding: 'Why the hell can't we fight these apes and worry about the survivors later?'[26] However, the British officers flown in to deal with the Emergency needed a more systematic approach.

Given the widespread support among Kenyans for the uprising and the large number of combatants, which Kitson estimated to be up to fifteen thousand by 1953, a plan was devised for sifting through the large Kukuyu population. This involved identifying, interrogating and punishing suspected Mau Mau members and their supporters. A series of prison camps was to be established, where Kukuyu would be processed, and then detained, questioned and charged if necessary. Kitson recalls how the idea first came to him:

> This decision took a firm hold of my imagination while I lay on
> the beach at Malindi. I could actually see the camps in my mind's
> eye: little clusters of mud huts with wire round them, and Africans
> [soldiers loyal to Britain] pedalling in and out on bicycles.[27]

The ease with which Kitson introduces the idea of camps makes
the horrors that unfolded within them all the more disturbing.
Over the course of the Emergency, hundreds of thousands of
Kenyans, mainly Kukuyu, were imprisoned in appalling conditions and tortured. In Nairobi, the African population was summoned for screening – those who did not comply were arrested
in their homes or workplaces, or simply kidnapped on the street.[28]
Kenyans loyal to Britain would look at each detainee and decide
there and then whether they were an enemy who would remain
in detention. Detainees were shipped to Mageta Island in Lake
Victoria in the cargo hold of a boat, shackled like slaves in the
Middle Passage. But there was no camp on the island – the captured were forced to spend days uncoiling barbed wire and digging
the isolation pits in which they themselves were to be confined.
They then had to build the watch towers and trenches which
would secure their capture.[29]

Forced labour was common in the overcrowded prisons, riddled with disease and death. While hundreds were sentenced to
hang, many more died slowly in the camps without charge or trial.
For those Kukuyu who were not formally detained, over a million
were forcibly removed from their homes and resettled in 'villages'
where curfews and other controls meant effective imprisonment.[30]
Frank Kitson's only critical reflection on the mass imprisonment
was to concede that: 'It was of course contrary to the principles
of British justice' but maintained that 'it was merciful', given that
the camps 'probably saved many Mau Mau lives by locking up
people who would otherwise have joined the gangs and been killed
by the Security Forces'.[31]

British racism against Kenya's Black population was clear and
direct, even among those claiming liberal, progressive values.

Missionaries and humanitarians saw the violent uprising as a mass psychosis, generated by the African mind coming into contact with modernity too rapidly. This 'ethnopsychology', cemented in a study for the World Health Organization by Dr J. C. Carothers, argued that anti-colonial resistance 'reflects a condition of mass hysteria or mass anxiety neurosis'.[32] This indicated that the rebellion against British rule could not be rationalised as a response to exploitation and injustice, or a desire for self-determination.

This liberal colonialism, with its connotations of pity for the Black population, found favour in the British press, with the *Manchester Guardian* interpreting the resistance to British rule for its readers in 1952: 'Such an attitude, known to psychologists as "regressive", is not infrequent in primitive societies confronted with an advanced society'.[33] Yet, rather than rolling back the policies which attempted to replace African religious, spiritual and social systems with European ones, the proposed remedy included Christian education, teaching profitable crafts to landless men, or hygiene and childcare to African women. British personnel formed 'moral rearmament' teams and internment became 'rehabilitation camps'. Christian values were enlisted to fight the 'mass pyschosis' from which apparently helpless and confused Africans were deemed to be suffering. This psychological diagnosis both depoliticised the uprising and masked the abuses that took place throughout Kenya during the Emergency. In this way the British response became another 'hearts and minds' mission.

Both Kitson and Thompson, in their reflections on policing anti-colonial insurgencies, maintained that it was fundamental that the British were seen as a legitimate power in the eyes of the local population. Criminalisation, shaping who and what is considered criminal, is therefore fundamental to the colonial project.[34] Policing 'by consent' meant that the British had to be seen to be operating within the law. As Thompson explained during a posting in Vietnam, 'when I heard of a case of a peasant suing the government for a buffalo killed by the army during operations and being paid compensation, we would be winning the war'.[35] The appearance of accountable, transparent policing is seen here as a sign of strength for control of insurgent populations.

This appearance of accountability became even more important during the Troubles in Northern Ireland. Here, the military and the police converged to fight an insurgency taking place within the UK, against a white population, with an international audience following the conflict on television and in print. Kitson was also in charge of military operations in Northern Ireland in the 1970s, personifying the continuities between this and the policing of Britain's former Empire. It should come as little surprise that mass arrest, imprisonment and other forms of collective punishment were as important to his operations in Northern Ireland as they were in his previous operations.[36]

Northern Ireland's geographical and political situation as part of the UK did not just mean that the principles of accountability and consent (or perceived consent) were more fundamental than ever. It also meant that the tactics and tools of counterinsurgency policing could be more easily transferred to the UK mainland. As Chapter 1 illustrated, it was the 1980 uprising in multicultural St Pauls in Bristol, followed by rebellions against racism across urban areas in 1980s England, that paved the way for the policing of anti-colonialism to be used against Britain's Black populations. These included militarised forms of policing initially used in Northern Ireland (CS spray, armour and baton rounds), coupled with colonial-style collective punishment of racialised 'suspect communities'.[37]

This process continued in the twenty-first century, as counter-terror policing in Britain continued to be shaped by counterinsurgency operations in Northern Ireland. Forming part of a global circulation of counter-terrorism policing tactics (also involving the US and Israel), this kind of policing rejects the presumption of innocence, 'policing by consent' and 'minimum force'. As in colonial policing, Britain's armed counter-terror police focus on discriminating between civilian and enemy combatant, aiming to neutralise the latter with immediacy.

The racism of policing, both in former colonies and in Britain today, means that all people in racialised suspect communities come under threat from state violence. One example is that of Jean Charles de Menezes, a Brazilian plumber shot dead in a south London train station by undercover counter-terror police in 2005. He was described by officers as having similar 'Mongolian eyes' to the suspect of Arab heritage he was mistaken for. In counterinsurgency operations, such 'mistakes' may form part of a broader tactic to deter, intimidate or collectively punish a suspect community or perceived enemy.[38]

The decision was taken not to prosecute any of the officers involved in the killing. Cressida Dick, who was in charge of the operation, was promoted to Commissioner of the Metropolitan Police in 2017. In 2019 she became a Dame Commander of the British Empire (DBE), symbolising the state's commitment to honouring the most violent forms of policing in twenty-first-century Britain, as well as harking back to the imperial past to which the logic and tactics of that policing remain intimately connected.

In what follows, we explore how colonial, counterinsurgency policing tactics continue to inform the policing of Black communities in twenty-first-century Britain, and look at some examples of resistance to state racism. Importantly, these histories do not signify a straight line from colonial policing to twenty-first-century racism, but instead illustrate how the routes of racial power from the colonies to the mainland have shaped present-day police racism. In other words, while the term 'gangs' is used in both colonial and contemporary domestic policing, it does not point to the genesis of these racist ideas, or their exact reproduction, but rather creates echoes of the past. The racist identification of 'suspect communities' in modern Britain is Black youth, framed as 'gangs'. Like the suspect communities of the colonial period, these contemporary 'gangs' are subjected to surveillance, collective punishment and violence, justified by a racism which links these racialised Others with violent criminality.

Gangs and anti-gang policing in twenty-first-century Britain

In Chapter 1, we saw how paramilitary policing from Northern Ireland and Hong Kong was incorporated into the policing of working-class, multi-ethnic, inner-city areas of England in the 1980s. This intensification of violent policing was coupled with a greater reliance on the prison system. It was Margaret Thatcher, following her election victory in 1979, who elevated crime and punishment as a key area of media interest and public concern. For example, she used televised debates to disagree with the decisions of specific judges, calling for harsher sentences.[39] Moral panics around foreign criminals from Ireland or the West Indies, or simply migrants with a foreign culture 'swamping' British natives, reaffirmed the association of crime and deviance with ethnicity, nation and 'race'. This tough approach to law and order formed a central part of a new authoritarian populism in British politics.[40] Cultures of white British superiority that were formed during the colonial period became fundamental to the performance of a resurgent nationalism.[41]

By the time the Conservatives lost power in 1997, law-and-order policing had gained so much popular appeal that it was adopted by New Labour through their 'tough on crime, tough on the causes of crime' slogan.[42] Racialised crimes such as terrorism,[43] drug dealing[44] and 'Black-on-Black crime'[45] contributed to the introduction of over three thousand new criminal offences by Blair's government, a new crime for each day he was in office (compared to around five hundred under the previous Conservative governments over the same timescale).[46]

Between 1993 and 2019, the prison population in Britain almost doubled, with almost half of incarcerated adults being reconvicted less than a year after their release. Like the policing that precedes it, prison sentencing is institutionally racist. Black men are 228 per cent more likely than their white counterparts to be arrested, and over 50 per cent more likely to be given a custodial sentence. Over a quarter of the people incarcerated in Britain are defined as Black (13%), Asian (8%) or another racialised minority (7%).[47] The disproportionate imprisonment of Black people in Britain is greater than that of the US. Perhaps unsurprisingly, given the long history of racist criminalisation by the British (at home and abroad), every juncture of the criminal justice system produces institutionally racist outcomes.

The number of imprisoned people categorised as 'foreign nationals' has doubled over the last thirty years. This is part of a Europe-wide trend – a number of governments have created special punishments for non-citizens, including surveillance,[48] harsher sentencing and prison segregation.[49] The British government has also increased the use of deportations as an additional punishment for people found guilty in court. Between 2005 and 2008, the number of foreign nationals deported as a result of criminal convictions increased fivefold, from around 1,000 to 5,400. This increase is partly attributable to a moral panic led by the right-wing press in 2006 about 'foreign criminals' being released from prison.[50] In response, the government introduced the 2007 UK Borders Act, which provided for the 'automatic deportation' for any non-UK citizen who had been convicted to over a year in prison. The government went on to reduce rights of appeal against deportations and to cut legal aid in this area. It also introduced a 'deport first, appeal later' policy, so transparently draconian that it was eventually repealed in 2017. Nonetheless, deportation of 'foreign criminals' has not reduced significantly, with between five and six thousand people deported following imprisonment every year.[51]

Maintaining popular concern about criminals and public order requires the inventive construction of new threats. These threats often arise through the emergence of new categories of crime or criminal. 'Terrorist' and 'gangster' were terms used in British policing during the period of decolonisation in order to create divisions between ethnic or racialised groups by categorising them as either 'criminals' or 'law abiding'. These distinctions helped to perpetuate the idea that the actions of insurgents are illegitimate, immoral and criminal, whereas any violence used by the colonial state is necessary, fair and within the law.

Categories of racialised crime in Britain today do not work in the same way as counterinsurgency policing in the former colonies, but some clear continuities exist. Like the moral panic around 'mugging' in the 1970s outlined in previous chapters, creating novel categories of crime in modern Britain brings together a number of existing crimes, creating the impression that these types of social problems are different from any that existed before. It is this purported newness and difference which enables these categories of crime to be associated with communities that are 'new' to Britain, or not British at all. This creates fear and panic towards racialised minorities, migrants and perceived migrants, justifying a punitive response from the state in order to make them more like, or keep them away from, the respectable, law-abiding national majority.

Two categories of crime soliciting a great deal of attention from police, politicians and the press in the twenty-first century are 'gang crime' and 'knife crime'. Like 'mugging', neither of these types of crime are crimes at all, but categories of crime. They both incorporate a large and often ambiguous collection of both violent and non-violent offences – in fact, 'knife crime' data are collected differently by different police forces in Britain. The problem of recording 'knife crime' is not just geographical; it is also difficult to be sure how much it is increasing long-term, as it only emerged as a category of crime in the early 2000s.

A survey of every national newspaper found only one mention of 'knife crime' in 2000 and twenty-four in 2003, peaking in 2008 with over two thousand mentions.[52] Interestingly, hospital admissions involving a knife injury have been decreasing since 2007, with a slight upward trend in 2015.[53] Cautions and convictions for knife-related offences also started to increase in 2015, but by 2018 they had still not come close to 2009 levels.[54] But the statistics are slippery, and these fluctuating figures fail to give us an accurate picture of incidents or injuries involving knives in Britain. What remains important, however, is the impression that these social problems are new, and thus attributable to 'new' people or communities – in this case, young Black men.

Moral panic around 'knife crime' has led to politicians on the right of the Conservative Party calling for the army to be brought in to deal with the issue, a demand for paramilitary policing which echoes the governance of Northern Ireland and other counter-insurgency conflicts.[55] While this has not (so far) happened, other forms of policing which are similar to those in the colonial era have been developed. Knife Crime Prevention Orders (KCPOs) are a provision of the Offensive Weapons Act 2019. They empower police to criminalise 'suspect communities', imposing controls on them based on 'intelligence' – often little more than suspicion.

KCPOs enable the police to impose injunctions on people as young as twelve if they identify them as being 'more likely than not' to carry a knife. Without requiring a criminal conviction or any concrete evidence, the police can impose such an order on any child or young person their intelligence indicates is 'at risk'. KCPOs can prevent a young person from going to a specific area (including routes to work or study), seeing specific people (including family members), or using social media. Breaking these orders can lead to a custodial sentence, potentially making prison a first, rather than last, resort punishment for a child or young person who has not committed a serious offence.[56] At the time of writing, KCPOs are being piloted in London for fourteen months, from April 2020.

The Metropolitan Police's Gangs Matrix was established in 2012. In 2018 this comprised 70 per cent young Black men.

Chapter 3 detailed how this database targets Black people, but what follows will elaborate on how gang affiliation goes beyond the police powers to stop, search and arrest. People need not be convicted of a serious offence to be added to the Matrix – social media usage or the music they listen to is sufficient 'intelligence' for the police to connect them with gang activity. Young people can also be added to the Matrix if they are identified as 'gang associated', which may simply mean they have family members or friends identified as gang members, or live on a housing estate which police have identified as being a site of gang activity.

People added to the Gangs Matrix can have their data shared with other agencies, with Amnesty International finding that one young person lost his place in further education after police informed the college of his alleged gang affiliations. Housing officers regularly serve eviction notices on homes occupied by people on the Gangs Matrix. In one case, a family received a letter saying that they would be evicted if their son did not leave the gang he was in; the son in question had been dead for over a year.[57] The police themselves acknowledge that education and secure housing are important for those at risk of coming into contact with the criminal justice system, but these are thrown out of the window in the above examples. The policing of 'gangs' is a way of criminalising lives and livelihoods, as the police gain additional powers to control and surveil suspect communities in an increasingly invasive, draconian and militarised way.

Public agencies have also been brought into the policing of 'gangs' through the so-called public health approach to serious youth violence. A public health approach saw violence among young people reduced significantly when it was used in Glasgow. According to a 2007 United Nations report, Glasgow was one of the most dangerous cities in western Europe. The Glasgow model used familiar tactics of increased policing, but also made large investments into youth services, mental health provision, addiction services and other targeted interventions from non-police service providers. The Scottish government also drastically reduced school exclusions, seeing this as a policy which socially excluded young people from their friends, community and trusted adults.

Glasgow went from being one of the most violent cities in Britain to a model for crime reduction in the rest of the UK.[58] However, the public health approach adopted for English cities was very different. Relatively little money was invested in youth projects – at the time of writing over a hundred youth centres in London have closed since 2011. In Manchester, more police were stationed in schools, purportedly to tackle youth violence, but this often led to criminalisation, particularly of Black students.[59] This has led to anti-racist campaign groups such as the Northern Police Monitoring Project (NPMP) in Manchester campaigning against the increase of police in schools.[60] The flagship public health policy for England was the proposal to make it a statutory duty for healthcare workers, housing officers, social workers and teachers to report young people to the police who displayed 'signs of violence'. The policy mirrors the anti-terror programme Prevent and the Hostile Environment, which task public sector workers with reporting signs of 'extremism' or undocumented status among their service users.[61]

While there are likely to be a number of reasons why the public health approach in English cities is so different from that used in Glasgow, one glaring difference is the way in which racism was used to explain the problem of young people affected by violence. While the likelihood of young Black men being affected by specific types of youth violence is regularly referred to or implied by politicians and the press, Glasgow, one of the whitest major cities in Britain, never sees race used as an explanation for its very similar social problems. With race being the subtext for explaining the problems of 'knife crime' and 'gang crime' in multicultural English cities, a principally punitive approach could be adopted.

Specifically, the racialisation of the 'Black gang' makes a punitive approach appear natural, necessary and unavoidable. Rather than attempting to investigate and address the complex social problems that can lead to a young person being affected by violence, 'race' became the implicit explanation for this social problem. Consequently, forms of surveillance, control and punishment for young people which went far beyond the Glasgow model were proposed. In England, attempting to police the everyday lives of young people suspected to be involved in 'knife crime' or 'gang crime' went beyond monitoring their interactions with public agencies. The government and police have also gone to great lengths to police the social, cultural and personal lives of these young Black suspect communities.

New technology, collective punishment and the criminalisation of Black culture

The pursuit of greater 'efficiency' in policing has led to police and politicians pushing for greater use of biometrics. This involves unique biological data (e.g. fingerprints or a person's facial features) being used to monitor large sections of the population and identify suspects. Shaun Bailey (see Chapter 3), Conservative candidate for the 2021 London mayoral election, has made 'stop and scan' one of his flagship policies. Bailey's campaign seeks to increase the use of CCTV; celebrating London as one of the most surveilled cities in the world, he claims: 'There are computer programs that mean you can get much better evidence off that and save police time and money to reinvest in better local policing'. Specifically, he wanted more facial recognition technology: 'Stop and search is a bit hit and miss and sometimes very antagonistic … But when you do scan and search, the technology there means you can stop many hundreds of people and accurately find criminals'.[62] Bailey's policies are part of a wider trend. Aware of the ways in which stop and search was being resisted, including its role in the civil unrest of 2011, police and politicians, supported by the press, explored a range of more covert forms of population control. While cutting-edge facial recognition technology is lauded as the future of policing, the less-sophisticated monitoring of social media or phone data has also been used to criminalise Black young people.

Since 2011, the police have been imposing injunctions using Criminal Behaviour Orders (CBOs) to punish drill rappers for covering specific themes in their lyrics.[63] In 2019, Rico Racks, a young Black rapper from London, was sent to prison for possession of criminalised drugs. Like other young people whose limited employment options lead to involvement in drug distribution, he was using drill music to express, recount and reflect on life on the streets. Yet rather than seeing music as a way out of criminalised sources of income, the police and the courts put measures in place to limit his ability to write, record and perform. They issued a list of words which, on his release from prison, he was banned from using in his lyrics. Most of the words were associated with drugs, but also included other words such as 'whipping', slang for driving a vehicle.[64] The presumption here was that any reference to driving a vehicle in his lyrics must relate to the distribution of drugs, or some other criminal behaviour.

In a similar case, Valentini, a rapper from Thurrock in Essex, had an injunction imposed in 2018 which prevented him from wearing hoodies or face coverings, and from producing 'any audio or video online that is threatening, abusive, insulting, incites violence, promotes criminal activity, shows weapons or makes reference to gang affiliations'.[65] Using a 'rap translator' (native informer?) the police were able to convince a court that Valentini had breached the injunction by rapping about weapons in a newly released song.

Valentini received a prison sentence for this, with a police spokesperson telling the press 'The C17 gang thought they could get away with selling drugs ... and committing violent crime in Thurrock – we proved them wrong and secured an injunction'.[66] What is important here is that the police were not able to present evidence of Valentini committing violent crime or selling drugs, but considered the music which depicts these themes as an attempt to 'get away' with these offences. In other words, rap music never simply describes or glamourises violence, it also incites violence and confirms actual criminality beyond reasonable doubt. This erosion of civil liberties is one example of how (Black) music is seen not as a form of expression but rather as an occupation or pastime carried out by criminals, whose activities should be heavily policed and regulated on that basis. By censoring these artists, not only is drug distribution criminalised, but merely speaking of it is considered, for some, a crime worthy of imprisonment.

Civil liberties constitute little more than an inconvenience when proposing ways to ban Black popular cultures like drill music. But other sections of criminal law are also disregarded and treated with disdain when targeting Black young people in this way. Two drill rappers from Brixton (south London), Skengdo and AM, were targeted by police and vilified by sections of the media. The police ran into problems when they were unable to convince a judge that their lyrics incited violence – mainly because they did not. But, via the summary imposition of a gang injunction, the police labelled the duo as part of a group of people responsible for violence in south London, presenting them to the court as such. The court then banned the rappers from referring to any specific people, places or events, as this would be interpreted as inciting violence. This interpretation of incitement hinged upon the police categorising these young people as being part of a gang.[67] Detective Inspector Luke Williams of the Lambeth and Southwark Gangs Unit confirmed: 'The court found that violence in drill music can, and did in this case, amount to gang-related violence'.[68]

Here we see the police unequivocally conflate racialised 'gang' crime with nebulous interpretations of violence to punish young Black artists. The statement asserts that the 'violence in drill [lyrics]' is akin to actual violence, rather than the artistic recounting or evoking of violent experiences as afforded to other genres including operas about rape or in a myriad film or TV offerings. The police interpretation of these lyrics goes even further by categorising this violence as 'gang-related', which does significant heavy lifting in an already primed public's imagination.

Researchers, policy-makers, journalists and campaigners all follow differing and sometimes conflicting definitions of 'gangs'.[69] The gang is such a vague concept that the police can designate almost any group of people to a gang, even in the absence of evidence of criminal activity or criminal record.[70] As a result, 'gang-related violence' enables police to connect otherwise unrelated people to a general set of violent incidents, presenting this to courts from the outset. By constructing categories of crime, the police are able to widen the net of young Black people they can punish for involvement in them. Not only can people identified as being involved in the same 'gang' be punished via JE for an offence that they themselves did not commit, but artists can be punished for any offences arising out of descriptions of possibly fictional violence and criminality in their music, as interpreted by police officers.

One of the ways in which Black people are being swept up, almost *en masse*, into the police's gang databases is through new policing technologies. Patrick Williams and Eric Kind's work for the European Network Against Racism provides some insight into how these technologies are being used across the continent to criminalise Black communities.[71] Biometric data collection is one of the ways in which the police can accurately identify individual people; as of 2005, the UK government had the largest known DNA database in the world. The DNA of everyone arrested is kept on record, even if they are the victim of mistaken identity or other form of wrongful arrest. Three-quarters of the database consists of young Black men between the ages of eighteen and thirty-five.[72]

Being part of a mass arrest of anti-racist protesters (described in Chapter 6) for charges eventually dropped by the Metropolitan Police has put this author onto the police's biometric directory of possible suspects. More recently, the police have trawled social media, creating 'profiles' of suspects, including where they study, work and socialise. They can find out who their friends and close relatives are and, if they make music, who they collaborate with. This has led to whole families, groups of friends, neighbours or college students being categorised as part of the same gang.[73] This trawling of social media can be used as the basis for imposing the aforementioned CBOs and KCPOs on young people.

Automated technologies that can identify people, leading to inferences about who they associate with, when and where, are also being rolled out by police in England and Wales in ways which reproduce racism. Facial recognition technology was first trialled at Notting Hill Carnival, Britain's biggest Caribbean street festival.[74] In the north of England, facial recognition cameras were installed on high streets, with members of the public who attempted to shield their faces from these unwarranted and contested intrusions often stopped by police for 'suspicious behaviour'. At the time of writing, civil liberties groups are challenging proposals to place permanent facial recognition cameras across cities such as London. Along with concerns for the civil liberties of all people, one of the criticisms is that these cameras will be concentrated in 'suspect communities' – in other words, focused disproportionately on Black people. Police forces in the north of England have also been trialling fingerprint collection when carrying out 'routine' stops and searches, regardless of the outcome of the search. While there is no obligation to consent to this, such a refusal is likely to be treated with suspicion by police, as are attempts to avoid facial recognition.

The huge volume of personal data carried on our mobile phones has led to the police purchasing technologies that can extract data from any phone they confiscate. Even when the police have not officially seized a mobile phone, they are sometimes able to use IMSI-catchers (international mobile subscriber identity) to access call data from mobile providers. This enables police to determine where a mobile phone user has been and with whom they have been in contact. This type of evidence gathering was used during the civil unrest in August 2011, with some people convicted of riot-related offences and given significant custodial sentences in cases where this formed the primary evidence.[75]

Vehicles that have been 'marked' by police as being used by potential suspects such as alleged gang members can be quickly identified by Automated Number Plate Recognition (ANPR) technology. Simply being pulled over by the police can result in your vehicle being added to the database, regardless of whether unlawful activity is uncovered. While ANPR can be used to track specific suspect people (including those on gangs databases), they have also been used in more covert ways. Areas of Birmingham with large Muslim populations were treated as suspect communities by police, when ANPR and other CCTV cameras were placed on local roads. The West Midlands Counter Terrorism Unit sub-contracted the maintenance of the cameras to Olive Group, who carry out surveillance operations in Iraq and Afghanistan, suggesting a paramilitary element to the operation.

The local community were not consulted about these cameras, and when they questioned West Midlands Police, they were told that they were being used to improve community safety and reduce crimes such as theft and anti-social behaviour. After a prolonged grass-roots campaign for greater transparency and accountability, it was revealed that the data captured by these cameras were not even sent to West Midlands Police, but went straight to the counter-terrorism unit. These revelations demonstrated that the police were fully aware that profiling Muslim residents as suspected terrorists, while their community safety concerns were neglected, would solicit a great deal of criticism.[76] The racialising of violent crime, and the bending of the law in terms of surveillance and collective punishments, echoes colonial penal systems and counter-gangs policing in the dying throes of Empire.[77]

Given the scale of state surveillance that a generation of young people have grown up with, it is unsurprising that a great number of them take precautions about anonymity more seriously than many older people. Using 'burner' phones is very popular among young people, making use of service providers that do not require registration. Making calls and texts on basic mobile technology means that they are not using social media or taking photographs on their phone, and cannot be monitored by other forms of data surveillance. The police have urged the government to crack down on the use of mobile phones that cannot be tracked, claiming that it prevents them from investigating the possession and sale of drugs.[78] The police, the government and some journalists are also increasingly concerned by the use of masks by rappers when performing or recording music videos. But given the ways in which musicians, and anyone who may appear in a video or on social media, have been criminalised, it should be unsurprising that they choose to wear masks as a precaution.

The rolling-out of facial recognition technology simply increases the likelihood of young Black men, in particular, finding ways to avoid surveillance. Rapper M Huncho, who wears a mask for public appearances, explained in one interview that he wears it because he values his privacy, adding that the average UK citizen is monitored by at least two CCTV cameras every time they leave their home.[79] Skengdo and AM, mentioned above, even attended a debate in Parliament about the criminalisation of drill, during which AM wore the mask he uses for other public events.[80] Young people avoiding surveillance may simply be engaging in an individual act of self-preservation, avoiding criminalisation and maintaining a degree of personal privacy. Yet the widespread use of untraceable phones and masks is also a commentary on a nation with one of the highest number of CCTV cameras in the world. This kind of everyday resistance is often born from a (sometimes inexplicit or even unconscious) collective agreement that these technologies of control are not simply unhelpful and unjust, but that they are functional only with our consent. Normalising the use of barriers to surveillance should be seen as a form of collective resistance, with important messages for both proponents and critics of this form of state power.

Conclusion

While racist ideas shape popular conceptions of criminalisation, the police and prison system produce racist outcomes at every juncture. Racialised minorities make up a quarter of the prison population, as the image of the 'Black', 'Muslim' and/or 'foreign national' spawns new kinds of criminality, purportedly heralding the nation's moral decline. It is through these racialised crimes that more police power and imprisonment are justified, perpetuating state-sanctioned violence that affects all working-class communities.

What is generally misunderstood about this kind of institutional racism, is that it is not the product of a critical mass of police or bureaucrats holding bigoted or prejudiced views. While canteen and locker-room cultures are often racist, chauvinistic spaces in which these stereotypes are nourished, this bigotry is the outcome, rather than the source, of racism. Black people are not categorised as gangsters because senior police officers sit in dimly lit rooms consciously inventing new racialised crimes. Rather it is the normal functioning of the police as an institution, following every procedure and policy, that produces racist outcomes. Importantly, state racism is embedded in policing because racism has been fundamental to British governance for centuries rather than just decades. Racism did not arrive in Britain with colonial migrants; it was exported by Britain to its colonies over centuries of expansion, control and conflict. Reaching back into Britain's colonial past is therefore vital to understanding the production of today's 'common sense', which racialises crime as a seemingly natural reflex.

As we enter the third decade of the twenty-first century, new technologies of policing are intensifying the criminalisation of

Black communities. The monitoring of digital communication and social media is being used to deem friends, neighbours and family members 'gang affiliates' and consequently guilty by association. These forms of collective punishment echo counterinsurgency tactics, yet operate in a manner which is far more covert and invasive. These powers expand carceral control by limiting the freedom of people outside prison walls, affecting housing, education and social life. The moral panic around Black cultural forms, in particular drill music, has appealed to racist cultures within politics and the media, and has resulted in substantive changes to the law and sentencing policy.

Masks and burner phones are forms of resistance to the expansion of police surveillance. But in order to understand these struggles against policing, we have to disrupt the division between innocence and guilt, good and bad, organised and spontaneous. In the next chapter, I look at how organised rebellions such as those led by BLM activists demand an erosion of police and prison power, envisioning a world in which these forms of state control are obsolete. These radical political visions disrupt the ways in which the state frames criminalised people as morally degenerate, separate and different from 'mainstream' society. Similarly, forms of resistance to policing including spontaneous rebellions are also often framed as criminal and deviant. We must, I argue, also resist pressures to separate 'legitimate, peaceful' protest from forms of resistance characterised as 'violent', which, rather than being an immoral aberration, are the predictable offspring of state violence.

6

Futures of Black resistance: disruption, rebellion, abolition

Staring up, shivering on a cold, hard, blue bed, I kept reading the words glaring at me from the ceiling: 'Do you have information about a crime? If so, call Crimestoppers anonymously'. I imagined how I might feel if I had witnessed a crime, and how reading those words might affect me. The silent interrogation, positioned to catch the eye as it opens from the bed of the custody cell, implied a criminal association and a guilty secret. The message lingered: the situation you're in can be resolved only by consenting to and colluding with the power of the police – the same powers used to forcibly detain you. I was one of over a hundred people arrested and charged with offences including violent disorder at BLM direct actions that disrupted transport hubs and shopping centres across England between 2014 and 2016. Transnational connections with activists in Europe and North America were bolstered by a far-reaching social media campaign. This wave of militant protest led by young Black activists catapulted Black resistance to policing back into a national conversation that few could ignore.

Angered by the failure of the courts to acknowledge the injustice of police killings, particularly that of Mark Duggan (Chapter 3), younger activists upped the ante. Building links of solidarity with the emergent BLM movement in the US, UK-based branches of the campaign, many led by young Black feminist and Black queer activists, emerged in cities across England. Using direct action, they protested a range of issues including the indefinite incarceration of undocumented people, deportations, deaths in police custody, racist criminalisation, deaths of migrants attempting to cross Europe's borders,[1] and the penal system more generally. These campaigns of Black solidarity attempted to make connections between police violence, border controls and other forms of state racism. Like the radical youth of previous generations, they experimented with ideas and concepts that produced new forms of resistance, unfamiliar political alliances and, for many, counter-intuitive political targets. But it is via this process of learning through practical action and prolonged, often critical, reflection that new ways of understanding state racism and organising to resist it are often forged.

As in Chapter 4, what follows focuses on Black resistance to policing in twenty-first-century Britain. Here, I want to push the boundaries of how policing can be resisted, and what demands can be made for radical change. It begins with the newer waves of protests and rebellion against police racism. Shutting down shopping centres, roads and transport hubs engenders fresh ways of thinking about protest. Shopping centres are spaces familiar to young people, and blocking roads or transport hubs forces the media and government to pay attention to protests which would otherwise be ignored. Crucially, however, these protests also disrupt critical capital flows – the profit-making of commercial spaces or the transport of goods, disrupting capitalism in ways that echo strike action. These radical forms of protest reflect radical demands made by BLM activists, who argue that the police are beyond reform.

Whereas the previous chapter outlined the recent growth of policing and prisons, this chapter details how activists are demanding the erosion of police and prison power, alongside the provision of alternative social policies and community-led solutions to reducing violence and harm. This requires a radical vision for a world in which police and prisons are abolished. This movement rejects the assumption that 'bad' people are sent to prison, but instead illuminates the ways in which prison punishes working-class people and attempts to lock away social problems, rather than addressing them at their root.

The final section connects this emergent form of Black organising against policing to more spontaneous rebellion against police violence. Here, I argue against the distinction made between peaceful, legitimate protest and the revolts which respond to an instance of police brutality. What may appear as merely reactive is, I argue, connected to young people's knowledge and lived experience of police racism, and should not be dismissed as apolitical, illegitimate or misguided forms of Black resistance. It is through this wider understanding that we can see Black resistance to policing beyond organised campaigns and protests, and into the everyday and the spontaneous, among people who are often not identified as political or activists. Thus, while protest can arise in spaces that feel unfamiliar, political resistance also emerges from people too often dismissed as unconnected to movements for change.

The breaking down of the barriers between different forms of resistance coincides with the dismantling of the categories from which police and prisons draw their legitimacy and power: a good or bad person, peaceful or violent, innocent or guilty. Rather than seeing criminalised people as simply bad and guilty, we need a more radical vision which views them as people who are oppressed, harmed by a deeply unjust society. In fact, the prison system caters mainly to some of the most marginalised and vulnerable people in society. Rather than prisons being used to provide safety on principles of morality and justice, I argue that their primary targets are among the most oppressed and neglected people in society. It is with this in mind that we must understand the police and prison system as causing more violence to people experiencing social problems, rather than addressing the root causes – inequality, exploitation and harm. Specifically, I argue that Black resistance to British policing must not only use radical forms of resistance; it must also provide a radical vision for a future in which police and prisons are no longer how we solve social problems.

Disrupting transport, commerce and business-as-usual: Black Lives Matter in the UK

One of the first targets in this wave of BLM solidarity action was Westfield in Shepherd's Bush (west London), the largest indoor shopping centre in London. On 10 December 2014, I was one of hundreds of protesters who gathered in and outside the enormous building, while an outsized Westfield security presence attempted to regulate the premises. It was clear that Westfield was determined to keep shops open and continue turning a profit for itself and its franchisees in the run-up to Christmas. Crucially, however, it was near-impossible to tell protesters apart from other members of the public. While some activists staged a die-in inside, covering the wide corridors with their bodies, others blocked the busy roads outside. When different parts of the protest eventually converged outside Westfield, they were addressed by Black campaigners, such as Marcia Rigg, sister of Sean Rigg, who died in 2008 (see Chapter 2). Older activists used the space to educate younger protesters about police killings in the UK, since it was police racism in the US that dominated mainstream news coverage in Britain. Eric Garner had been killed by police in New York, with footage of him being strangled by officers going viral. 'You've all heard of Eric Garner, but how many of you have heard of Joy *Gardner?*' one speaker asked the crowd. They went on to talk about the death of Joy following an immigration raid at her home in Haringey in 1993, and the ongoing campaign for justice led by her mother (Chapter 2).

The protest had become more than an expression of anger at police racism, or a social disruption to amplify demands for justice. The gathering was also a space of learning, in which people were able to absorb and take away testimony of struggles hitherto sidelined. This would aid young protestors better to understand the histories of racism in Britain which often remain underreported and underappreciated. Following the speeches, protesters moved back into Westfield, past the security guards who were standing powerless in front of the main entrance, and proceeded to chant, occupy and block the spaces where people were attempting to shop. Westfield was completely shut down for the evening, losing customers, revenue and profit. Although the protest had been peaceful, many of us were eventually surrounded and kettled by police vans and officers in riot gear. After a long standoff in the freezing cold, I was among the seventy-six arrested.[2]

Speaking to older activists sometime later, there was confusion about why Westfield Shopping Centre was targeted as part of resistance to police violence. When they were younger, they had protested police racism and injustices outside institutions of power such as government buildings, police stations or the courts. What is the connection between a shopping centre and racist policing? Why target a commercial hub like Westfield, if you want to stop Black people dying at the hands of the state? These straightforward questions were surprisingly difficult to answer. Yet the targets appeared to make perfect sense to the hundreds of young people who attended the Westfield protest, as well as those who had attended similar actions in North America, where for instance, Macy's and other department stores were shut down by BLM protestors.

Subsequent UK BLM protests in 2016 extended to transport networks. In Nottingham (East Midlands), activists bound their arms together across a busy tramline in the city centre during rush hour. Thousands marched in Manchester, bringing the Oxford Road shopping district to a standstill. A road near Birmingham City Airport and the M4 motorway near London's Heathrow Airport were also blocked by activists, drawing attention to the detention and deportation of migrants.[3] The hundreds of people who supported and participated in these coordinated actions, risking arrest in the process, will have had different understandings of why these targets were identified. But below, I give three broad explanations for why I think shopping centres and transport hubs were the chosen targets of these direct actions.

First, over successive decades, in both Britain and the US, many public spaces have been privatised. Places where people gather, meet and trade goods were once public high streets, markets and squares, but increasingly they are private or semi-private shopping centres,[4] and these have become the focal points of many cities. These easily identifiable yet privately owned spaces are often more familiar to young people than the government buildings traditionally targeted within earlier campaigns against police racism. Shopping malls are often the spaces where young people congregate, and although they are heavily policed and surveilled, they are generally warm, dry, large spaces in which to socialise.[5] In short, demonstrations in shopping centres such as Westfield were popular partly owing to their familiarity and accessibility – spaces young people felt confident to navigate.

Secondly, in a society where public spaces are being decimated, and shopping and transport have become central to public life, shutting them down is likely to attract far more public and media attention than other forms of protest. Traditional demonstrations, typically outside public institutions – even, for example, Downing Street – often barely receive a mention, but novel political actions that differ from the usual A-to-B march catch the eye of the press. Furthermore, occupying the town square has a long protest tradition, and the centrality of the shopping centre in social and commercial life means that the shopping centre is a modern version of the square. While shutting down motorways near airports formed a coherent narrative about resistance to deportations, the other shutdowns also offered a fresh angle that attracted wide attention from both mainstream and social media.

The third possible explanation reads the protest as more creative and experimental. Shutting down commercial spaces and transport hubs disrupts the normal functioning of capitalism and is, in that sense, comparable to industrial action. For previous generations of activists, the strike was one of the most effective ways to bring about political change. As widely documented elsewhere, under capitalism, big business and industry always influence political decision-making.[6] Therefore, disrupting profit-making by halting production until management or politicians agreed to negotiate workers' demands is an important part of working-class, as well as anti-colonial and anti-racist, history.

At the start of this book, we saw examples of this in the Caribbean during the 1930s, when widespread strike action brought about massive social improvements for poor Black people across the region. Britain, of course, is no different – previous generations of activists regularly used the strike as a powerful political tool. The Grunwick photo processers' strike in Willesden, north London during the 1970s saw South Asian women battle police on the picket line to challenge racial discrimination and have their union recognised.[7] The decision to host the Black People's Day of Action in 1981 (see Chapter 1) on a Monday forced the tens of thousands in attendance to withhold their labour or skip school. This involved a march and protest on Fleet Street, then London's newspaper quarter, to challenge the racist coverage of the New Cross Fire. It disrupted the functioning of the City of London on a busy working day.[8]

Following the defeat of the Miners' Strike in the mid-1980s, widespread reforms eroded the power of unions, reducing both their political influence and eventually their membership, thereby making strike action more difficult.[9] Trade union membership for people aged under thirty in Britain is dramatically lower than that of their parents' generation, and it is not uncommon for younger people to have little or no understanding of the nature and purpose of trade unions. This is compounded by the disappearance of lower-wage jobs in large factories, as they are replaced with a rise in precarious jobs in the service sector such as catering or call-centres, where it is more difficult to organise workers.[10]

The power of ordinary people in Britain to pursue political demands through industrial action has thus been severely eroded. Of course, Black and other racialised minorities have often struggled to bring anti-racist demands to trade union actions. However, the barriers to shutting down capital flows at the point of production does not mean that they cannot be disrupted elsewhere. Indeed, some political theorists have indicated that shutting down cities can be an effective political tool, particularly following observations in the Global South.[11] In these actions, revenue streams are not disrupted by workers withdrawing their labour, but by activists using their bodies to occupy spaces of consumption and transit.

This new iteration of the strike does not require formalised links of solidarity between workers in different industries to fight against capital. In the instances I have cited, it mobilises Black and anti-racist solidarities in order to fight against racial violence by bringing people to one or more key commercial spaces or transit hubs. Like the anti-colonial and Black Power movement of the twentieth century, these actions treat state power and the power of capital as connected – disrupting commerce or transit is recognised to be as effective as shutting down government agencies. In other words, as one potential form of action became inaccessible, a new one emerged: the rise of consumerism made shopping centres and transport hubs symbols of power, easily identifiable and effective political targets.

Of the seventy-six people arrested at Westfield that evening in 2014, all but one of the charges of violent disorder were dropped; one teenager (a young Black man on his first protest) was found guilty of assault, and given a non-custodial sentence. Since then however, many other young anti-racist activists have faced serious charges and prolonged court battles in similar actions. The response of the state illustrates the threat that disruptions at points of consumption and transit pose to the maintenance of social order. The panicked response of the government and police to comparable disruptions to the City of London and its profitability, such as Occupy in 2011 (occupiers were forcibly moved from the London Stock Exchange to St Paul's Cathedral) or Extinction Rebellion (XR) in 2019 (all XR protests in the City were banned by the police), demonstrates the authorities' focus on the prevention of disruption in such places.

It is noteworthy, however, that the mass arrests during Occupy and XR followed a prolonged occupation, whereas the shutting down of Westfield resulted in mass arrests within a matter of hours. While this form of collective punishment is not unprecedented, the police response to the Westfield demonstration was reflected in the policing of subsequent BLM actions. It is therefore impossible to ignore the intensity of violence that the police use when responding to Black youth in protest.[12] Using direct action to grab public attention and force those in power to listen, even if for only a short period of time, was certainly not new for the anti-racist activists in 2014. What was new were the targets they identified, and how these actions communicated a connection between different institutions of power. The radical creativity and risk taken by these young, Black, often feminist and/or queer, activists re-centred the city as not simply a space of power, work and consumption, but a site of radical resistance and protest. This wave of protest marked another important development for a generation of anti-racist activists resisting policing, as it reaffirmed the interconnections between racist police violence and the penal system more generally.

Beyond reform: against policing and prisons

In May 2020, in response to the police killing of George Floyd in Minneapolis, some of the largest protests in US history took place. The harrowing footage of Floyd with a knee on his neck for nearly nine minutes struck a chord with activists across the globe, and demonstrations in solidarity began in the UK the following month. These would become the largest anti-racist protests in

British history, with hundreds of thousands of people taking to the streets in cities, towns and villages across the country. While many of these protests used familiar tactics of congregating in town centres and outside government buildings, their sheer scale made them impossible to ignore.

These mobilisations took place over consecutive weekends for nearly two months. The predominantly younger people who organised them protested against racism in British policing, education, healthcare and work. Boris Johnson's Conservative government paid lip service to the demonstrations, setting up a commission led by Tony Sewell, a highly divisive academic with a long history of disavowing the existence of institutional racism (Chapter 2). Sir Keir Starmer, the leader of the Labour Party, was criticised for describing BLM as a 'moment' rather than a movement, and their demands for criminal justice reform as 'nonsense'. He was forced to qualify his statements, saying that he would receive unconscious bias training, a popular but futile liberal remedy for racism.[13]

This more radical aspect of the movement criticizes, first, the abject failure of policing in improving public safety and second, the fact that prisons are filled with working-class and racialised people who have often experienced harm or violence themselves. The final critique is that prisons bring more trauma and harm to such people, exacerbating rather than ameliorating the social problems that lead to them being imprisoned in the first place. Abolitionists therefore argue for constructive alternatives to these ineffective attempts to 'police away' social problems. It is worth restating that calls for the abolition of the police and prison system do not argue that every prison should close tomorrow and every officer be sacked the day after; they argue that social problems can be resolved only through social responses.

Chapter 4 detailed how the state has continually expanded the power of the police and prison system. The creation of hundreds of criminal offences, surveillance technologies and powers such as injunctions has inevitably led to an extraordinary expansion in the use of prisons. The assumption that prison – locking a human being in a cage for a set period of time – is the best way to solve a social problem such as drug possession, theft or violence, has become 'common sense'. It is erroneously assumed, much as it used to be for capital punishment, that the fear of imprisonment deters people from committing crimes, and that actual imprisonment consequently deters them from reoffending. But the continual growth of prisons, with no long-term reduction in violence within low-income communities, indicates that they are by no means a deterrent. The levels of recidivism add further weight to the failures of the purported benefit of prisons.

People with a history of mental health problems, special educational needs, problematic drug use, trauma, homelessness, precarious legal status, school exclusion, child abuse and domestic violence are grossly overrepresented in prisons.[14] But rather than decriminalising drugs and investing in the social and other services that could address these social problems, the police and prison system is used to problematise the people rather than the issues they face. As Angela Davis argues,

> Prisons do not disappear social problems, they disappear human beings. Homelessness, unemployment, drug addiction, mental illness, and illiteracy are only a few of the problems that disappear from public view when the human beings contending with them are relegated to cages.[15]

Prisons also cause long-term social, emotional and physical harm to the people they incarcerate. In other words, policing and prisons are forms of state violence which add more violence to the problems they claim to solve.[16] The state uses a range of tools and tropes to create divisions in society between people whom we should consider innocent or guilty, or who should be thought of as law-abiding or criminal. These dichotomies are necessary as state power is premised on the assumption that the police, courts and prisons are fair and just, and those subjected to punishment are morally degenerate individuals who deserve or need to be locked away from the rest of society. This was clearly demonstrated during colonial policing against the Kukuyu 'gangs' in Kenya and the Chinese Malay 'communist terrorist gangs' in Malaya. It is just as clear for those identified as 'gangsters', 'extremists' or 'foreign nationals' today (Chapter 5).

One of the more radical demands of the BLM protests was therefore based on a vision of police and prison abolition. This is not a demand for the abolition of the penal system tomorrow, in the way that historical campaigns called for an immediate end to slavery. Police and prison abolition argues for abolitionist reforms. Such reforms would erode society's reliance on the police and prison systems, and instead empower community-led and social solutions to the inequalities which lead to violence and harm in the first place. Abolitionist reforms are therefore part of a strategy which works towards a future without policing. Thus, while BLM protests were sparked by police brutality and racism, their critique of policing goes beyond these stark kinds of injustice.

British governance in the twenty-first century has claimed that young 'offenders cope poorly with life because they exhibit various cognitive deficits'[17] – in other words, they are unable to think in a way which is considered 'normal'. Citing an academic study from the 1980s, the Home Office claims that offenders aged between fifteen and twenty-five lack impulse control, are poor at controlling their emotions, are poor problem solvers, exhibit rigid and inflexible thinking, do not recognise the consequences of their behaviour and cannot see another person's perspective.[18] Those of us who know young people, or remember being young ourselves, might well recognise such traits in many who are still maturing socially and emotionally. But what the government is doing here is important. They are listing the unique character faults, pitched as a static fact of their existence, in those it imprisons – distinguishing them from the rest of society and proposing ways in which they should be moulded by the criminal justice system to normalise their personalities.

Assuming that state institutions are fair and just always renders their use of force as falling outside the parameters of immorality or criminality. While historically this has been used to justify imperial violence, in the post-colonial period we see the notion evolving. Decisions of the state: those to bomb foreign civilians,[19] execute domestic civilians[20] or criminalise drugs used by the poor or racialised minorities,[21] are not held to account or scrutinised by the criminal justice system as they would be had they been made by individuals. The politicians, military commanders and CEOs responsible for war, mass exploitation or the destruction of the planet, are not targets of the law. The prison system is not designed for them, rather it is designed for working-class people (disproportionately Black and racialised minorities) that make up the vast majority of the imprisoned population. Thus, the prison system not only seeks to control people considered disorderly, it also serves to afford the state a total monopoly on the legitimate use of violence. As Derecka Purnell states:

> Police manage inequality by keeping the dispossessed from the owners, the Black from the white, the homeless from the housed, the beggars from the employed. Reforms make police polite managers of inequality. Abolition makes police and inequality obsolete.[22]

Prison abolition, popularised by activists such as Angela Davis in the 1970s and 1980s, helped the American radical left to envision a future in which prisons are no longer needed. Premised on the simple observation that police and prisons have done little to make life safer and have little effect on reducing violence or harm, prison abolition activists demonstrate how the prison, rather than being an institution which is moral and just, serves to provide the state with a violent tool that can be used to control the masses.

The abolition of prisons has been a popular demand among radical activists for decades, especially in the US, but is becoming increasingly influential among a new generation of anti-racists in Britain. Prison abolition is not simply about closing prisons and reducing police power; it is about reducing society's reliance on police and prisons. The movement argues that community social problems are better solved with community-led social solutions which address their root causes. For instance, provision of secure housing, free education, creating gainful employment with strong democratic trade unions to represent worker rights, are a more salutary and effective means of reducing criminal activity such as theft. Teaching young men to dismantle sexist assumptions while building restorative and transformative justice mechanisms is one of the ways we can work towards reducing gender-based violence.[23] Decriminalising drugs and providing social care and emotional support for people with addiction problems is better than locking them up for drug offences. Prison abolition involves working towards a more humane society which is less exploitative, while always envisaging an end point in which prisons are no longer how society deals with social problems.[24]

Importantly, these abolitionist reforms should not be misinterpreted as a liberal appeal for a return to the welfare state. As Chapter 1 outlined, Britain's post-war consensus was still a place in which Black and working-class life was criminalised, with police and prisons still playing a central role in disciplining exploited workers, controlling populations and imposing violence. Rather, abolitionist reforms work towards a vision of a world which is free from capitalist exploitation, racism, patriarchy and the violent control of the state. It enables activists and communities to develop incremental changes in their own lives and their localities, as well as making demands on the government for progressive reform, while simultaneously working towards dismantling the existing institutions of power and building community-led alternatives. This resistance to policing seeks to break down the barriers between reform and revolution, by showing how reforms can bring us closer to more systemic changes, by empowering communities and eroding their reliance on the police and prison system. Therefore, trade union organising, campaigns for better housing, youth work, community-led mental health provision, domestic violence services, educational initiatives and many other forms of grass-roots organising, can and should be considered part of a movement for abolition. These initiatives can all move us closer to a world in which relationships to work, power and each other are revolutionised. The politics of abolition provides a vision for Black resistance to policing in the twenty-first century which allows for a continuity with older anti-colonial and anti-capitalist struggles. Abolition provides a politics which, like the Black Power movements of the past, is grassroots-oriented and internationalist. Vitally, it offers new strategies and demands, and a vision to revolutionise social relations across the world – the job of abolitionists is to identify where the possibilities of a different world arise, and develop a collective understanding of what can bring us closer to it.

Resistance everywhere

The BLM mobilisations are just one example of how police and prisons are resisted by international networks, large organised protests and popular campaigns. But importantly, breaking down the distinction between 'innocent' victims of police brutality and people prosecuted for crimes can also be found among smaller campaigns and sporadic uprisings. In July 2017, Rashan Charles was killed as a police officer kneeled on his back during an arrest in Hackney (east London). Protesters demonstrating in Hackney's Kingsland High Street after Rashan's death were met by riot police. Predictably, this led to a confrontation, as protesters from the local area resisted the riot shields and batons laying siege to a community in mourning.

While it was revealed that no illegal items were found on Rashan Charles, the police press releases had already been reproduced across the media: images of a young Black man in a baseball cap, smoking, accompanied headlines that claimed Rashan boasted on social media of 'drug dealing' and that he was 'hard to kill'.[25] The criminalisation of Rashan Charles demonstrates the limitations of 'innocence' as an argument against policing and prisons. Would the actions of the officers who were present at his death be more legitimate if drugs or weapons had been found on Rashan's body? Are people who are found in possession of prohibited items less worthy of civil liberties, humanity, forgiveness or life? The press and police fabricated a narrative around Rashan Charles that portrayed him as a violent drug dealer (much like Mark Duggan in Chapter 4). But it is not enough simply to prove that these accusations were false – what abolitionists call the 'problem of innocence'[26] requires us to dismantle the divisions between 'guilty' and 'innocent' people.

No doubt there is violence which precedes the criminalisation of certain drugs. There are economic environments which lead to people selling criminalised drugs. There are psychosocial conditions which lead people into taking such drugs problematically. But these cannot be solved by policing. Instead, policing exacerbates risk and harm by bringing more violence and harassment through searches, raids, imprisonment and, in the case of Rashan Charles, death. The social problems which lead people to break laws or harm others cannot be addressed by police and prisons. If Rashan Charles, or anyone else, is suspected of breaking the law or causing harm, it is vital that solutions minimising our reliance on the police and prison system are prioritised, with criminal justice always the last resort. This is not simply due to its ineffectiveness in reducing harm and improving safety long-term, but also because these institutions compound and increase violence and harm. Resistance to policing and the 'problem of innocence' can also be seen in spontaneous responses to policing, as in the case that follows.

In August 2018, police followed a young Black man into a McDonalds restaurant in Kingsland Road, Hackney, a stone's throw from where Rashan Charles was killed the previous year. Officers wrestled him to the ground, restraining him and striking him. But unlike the newsagents where Rashan was killed, this McDonalds was full of young, predominantly Black, people. While some of the young people recorded the incident on their mobile phones, others intervened physically, attempting to stop the assault with their bodies. In the recorded footage one officer can be heard swearing at the young people, while another draws his taser and points it at the crowd.

The police and media led a public campaign claiming the incident to be a 'breakdown in society', calling for people to stop recording officers on their phones and for harsher sentences for those who intervene in arrests.[27] The killing of another Black man, under similar circumstances just over a year before, seems to have escaped their attention. If such a 'hostile crowd' had been present during the restraining of Rashan Charles, might he still be alive today? And to what extent did that event influence the reaction of the young people in McDonalds? It is impossible to say. What is clear, however, is that direct action by onlookers and other spontaneous forms of protest are the predictable consequence of a system of racist policing which stops, searches, detains, arrests and kills.

For these young Black people, violence from the police does not constitute a 'breakdown in society'; it is the state functioning as normal. The police violence in the above two incidents was unquestioned by the press; on the contrary, the police were provided a platform to state their own, unproven, case. The young people of Hackney who took action against the police in both these cases did not wait to determine the extent to which Rashan Charles or the young man assaulted by officers in McDonalds was 'innocent'. The police were not recognised as the solution to whatever problem led to them arriving on the scene. The experience of policing had developed a racialised and class consciousness which led to collective action that did not require formal coordination or planning.

The young people in that moment identified a threat, and collectively saw an opportunity to resist. The violent power of the police was considered illegitimate *per se* by the local community and spontaneously resisted. They knew what was at stake for intervening in an arrest, yet put themselves at risk in solidarity with someone facing police violence. Abolition is not just an alternative to policing, it is a practice of care against police violence which is embedded in the everyday. Abolition is not just a long-term vision for dismantling prisons and borders, it is a lived practice of collective resistance and protection. While protests are met with riot squads, and direct action is criminalised, preventing possible harm or death is something some young people are clearly willing to take into their own hands. These snapshots of how organised campaigns against deaths at the hands of police and spontaneous responses to criminalisation can converge, help to give us a better understanding of state violence and the range of responses to it.

Conclusion

The constantly shifting nature of suspect communities, harbouring 'terrorists', 'gangsters' or 'foreign nationals', reveals the futility of searching for an ideal category of 'innocent' deserving of protection. The growth of prisons on the British mainland follows the growth of these suspect communities, often drawn from those associated with former colonies. The fight against police racism necessitates the fight against police and prisons themselves, and the logic they rely on, which delineates society into the respectable and the deviant, criminal and law-abiding, citizen and non-citizen – shifting dichotomies to which racialisation is always an element. Colonialism and racism don't simply punish 'criminals', they actually produce criminality through the oppressions they perpetuate and the state violence on which their power relies. But it is by casting the net so wide that they engulf entire communities, threaten the freedom of a generation, and bring criminalisation so close, that collectivity, solidarity and common cause are formed. This chapter, like the others, has offered just a few snapshots of the ways in which racism's rapidly evolving pursuit of power and control can motivate a multitude of dissenters.

The wave of anti-racist direct actions against policing between 2014 and 2016, and again in 2020, began in the US, where campaigns against prisons and police violence are often one and the same. Transnational connections led to visits to the UK from Black organisations challenging policing and incarceration in the US, sharing political ideas that ranged from Black feminist and Black queer politics, to analyses of problems such as racist criminalisation and the prison industrial complex. These transnational links of solidarity under the banner of BLM helped a new generation of anti-racists in Britain to incorporate abolitionist thought into their work. Rather than arguing that 'innocent' people are being targeted by police and prisons, prison abolitionists show how we can re-organise society to erode the power of police and prisons, and empower community-led organisations which can provide safety and harm-reduction in ways that don't rely on state violence.

Vitally, Black resistance to British policing takes a range of forms. First, many of these are well-organised, involving legal campaigns, mass demonstrations and international networks of solidarity. Shut-downs and protests at sites of commerce and transit are connected to organised mobilisations outside government buildings and police stations. Secondly, spontaneous rebellions against policing are as important as more formalised resistance. When England's Black and other youths in urban areas passionately articulate a rejection of racism and state violence, they cannot be dismissed as mindless criminals (Chapter 3) or contrasted with 'legitimate' peaceful protesters. Thirdly, everyday forms of resistance to surveillance and the policing of everyday life are a vital component of Black resistance to policing. Non-compliance among young people who witness police violence or harassment is also a vital form of resistance. These are also rarely considered to be political acts, but they are based on the collective assumption that policing can only continue the way it is if we stand by and allow it. Dismantling the boundaries between the organised and the everyday, the formal and the spontaneous, reveals the scale and frequency with which people are rejecting the control, policing and punishment which constantly loom as a threat to those the state deems deviant.

Conclusion

The time is now ripe for HM Government to think how the Africans should be governed, and we are not fed up with British laws at all ... But we really pray for well instructed Government officials who understand the Queen's Government Laws. (Petition from the detainees of Embakasi Camp, Kenya, 1957)[1]

The above passage is from a petition letter sent by a group of Kikuyu detainees who were among hundreds of thousands held in prison camps by British colonial authorities in 1950s Kenya. While the petitioners awaited their fate in the camps, the British colonial authorities spread propaganda warning British citizens against the dangerous Africans intent on attacking innocent British settlers. Reading it today, the petition by these Kenyan detainees to Britain's Commissioner of Prisons, with its earnest appeal to British law in the hope it could be enforced and thus bring the death camps to an end, appears, to us, futile in the extreme. And yet, when looking at the racism of the British courts over a half a century later, investing faith in the British justice system, with its labyrinthine, opaque complaints systems, inquiries and formal investigations, seems to be as futile an act of misplaced faith as it was for the Kikuyu petitioners.

We now know from the historical record that the British state was wholly complicit in what was taking place in Kenya, actively producing propaganda and fuelling misinformation to sustain public support. But the petition of those accused of being Mau Mau insurgents was just one component of a multitude of manifestations of resistance, which eventually led to the British withdrawal from Kenya and, half a century later, a partial admission of guilt for some of the crimes committed during the Emergency. In addition to the armed uprisings and protests, these legal petitions attempted to articulate the humanity of imprisoned Africans: those denounced as terrorist gangsters by native informers, diagnosed as psychotic by European doctors, and reduced to identification numbers by British administrators.

Like the Africans imprisoned in Kenya, dark bodies to be processed, punished and civilised, colonial governance across the Empire relied on cultures of respectability and racial hierarchy. Specifically, the disciplinary power of labour could teach colonised men the value of work, while loyalty to the mother country could elevate them from their state of disorderly tribalism. But colonised men were never 'honourable' soldiers, and when rebellion erupted, Europeans could not be expected to apply the normative rules of law or warfare. Colonised women lacked the domestic capacities to reproduce a respectable family. Hyper-sexuality condemned the colonised household to languish in chaos, justifying violence and exploitative labour on the part of the colonisers, together with the soft touch of the Christian civilising mission. Indeed, during the drawn-out battles against colonial order, it was hyper-sexuality which formed a compelling justification for the calculated brutality of colonial governance – defending white women from the savage rapists of Delhi or Nairobi.

The power of these imperial discourses lies in their fluidity, their ability to draw on an embedded stereotype in one colonial jurisdiction and to make use of it in another, very different, colonial context. It is the slippery nature of racialisation which enables the colonised simultaneously to be infantilised, in need of care from an imperial patriarch, and dangerous, untamed beasts who must be subjected to violence and coercion. Racist definitions, descriptions and imagery are never fixed – as the priorities and circumstances shaping colonial rule changed over time and across different colonies, imperial cultures and discourses shifted accordingly. Colonial governance could at once be the mission of liberal reformers bringing enlightenment to the dark corners of the earth and the vessel from which totalitarian control, brutality and exploitation flowed so inexorably.

These facets of colonial power are of course two ends of the same stick used to cajole or coerce the colonised. Rule through direction, with 'hearts and minds' and 'minimum force', is a display of power wielded through discourses, cultures and diplomacy. When colonial governance resorts to naked violence in an attempt to maintain order in the face of popular resistance, the mask of just laws, respectability and being a gentlemanly 'good sport' slips. It is worth repeating Sir Robert Thompson's appraisal that when a peasant farmer successfully sues the colonial army for shooting a cow, then the counterinsurgency will know that the army is winning the war. What Thompson is saying is that curating the appearance of legitimacy, fairness and civility, courting the consent of the subject population, is far more powerful than resorting to the ghastly business of the whip, the gun or the prison camp.

Britain, once the world's largest slave-trading nation, nowadays feels more comfortable being remembered as the nation that abolished the trade. Its 'hearts and minds' counterinsurgency and its bobbies who police by consent set it apart from and above the crass neo-imperialism of the US. In twenty-first-century Britain, racialised minorities are permitted to be the people who staff our health and social care system, celebrated at the Olympic opening ceremony, publicly thanked by politicians and commentators during the coronavirus pandemic. Yet, when necessary, particularly when challenging exploitation or control, they become racialised outsiders of a different nature – criminals who require discipline, order and punishment.

Conclusion

In typically British fashion, former Prime Minister David Cameron declared UK policing 'the envy of the world',[2] just a month before the 2011 'riots'. The police shooting which sparked the revolt, and the ensuing stops, searches, raids and mass imprisonment, were justified as the necessary response to an emergency. Declaring an 'all-out war' on the 'gangs and gang culture' held responsible for the 'riots', Cameron drew a sharp distinction between the respectable majority and a suspect community. But Cameron's war was not a brief suspension of the policing by consent so envied globally. It was part of a prolonged operation which used racialised folk devils, from the drug dealer, mugger or illegal immigrant, to the terrorist or gangster, to expand the power of the police and the prison system in Britain.

The slippery nature of colonial-era racisms and systems of control makes it both impossible and undesirable to draw a neat line from the plantation, the conflict-zone and the prison camp to the factory, the street and the detention centre. Such an oversimplification fails to acknowledge new forms of political economy, xeno-racism towards eastern Europeans or travelling communities, and the influence of American racisms. Thus, rather than thinking about anti-Black racism as being a distinct form of racism which can be clearly defined, we must understand that it is not only constantly changing, but intrinsically linked with a multitude of racisms which overlap, interact and converge across different social contexts. Racism never moves in straight lines or fixes itself in a clearly defined way – it is not a clean, mathematical science with boundaries and rules. Racism's enduring power lies partly in its incoherence. Racialisation never produces a finished product, but requires constant reinvention to deal with the changing backdrop against which it operates. The constantly shifting social relations that shape how racist thinking becomes common sense, and how racial power is deployed, are partly moulded by capitalism's quest for new markets and more wealth. But the developments which most influence racism's evolutions are the multitude of resistances that push back against its cultures and practices wherever they are found.

Uprisings in former slave colonies such as Trinidad exemplify how, after centuries of racial slavery, indentured labour and colonial governance, Caribbean populations refused to succumb to the British Empire's seemingly insurmountable power. The urban uprisings in England in the 1980s and in 2011 emerged from Black experiences of racism in multicultural communities, articulating a complex set of discontents which included racism, class struggle and the sharp end of state power. By 2020, BLM protests brought the largest anti-racist mobilisation onto the streets of Britain. The demands from the hundreds of thousands who marched through multicultural cities, or rallied in small towns and villages, ensured that BLM gained national renown and even corporate appeal. The success of state co-optation of radical Black politics went into overdrive in 2020, cleaving anti-racism from its antagonism against the state, capitalism and imperialism. Brands such as Nike and the Premier League adopted the language of Black politics, resulting in a market competition in which individuals and groups compete with each other to be the most Black, the most oppressed and the most deserving of a slice of the corporate social responsibility budget. But the elastic nature of racism and class struggle means that few, if any, of the radical Black political grassroots campaigns against state violence were made up exclusively of Black people.

The Black struggles led by women in campaigns such as UFFC (Chapter 2) are part of a multi-ethnic campaign of families and friends of those who have died at the hands of the state. The local police monitoring projects and defence campaigns, although militantly anti-racist, were often led by Black people, but never exclusively (e.g. LCAPSV in Chapter 3, TDC and NMP in Chapter 4, NPMP in Chapter 5). The survivors of the 2017 Grenfell Tower fire, many of whom articulated a militant anti-racism, also constituted a campaign made up of people from a range of backgrounds (including South Asians and Arabs, many of whom were Muslim, and some of whom had precarious immigration status).[3] Thus, the movements which emerge out of struggles against racist state violence are organically multi-ethnic, and not without messiness, contradictions and conflict. Black resistance to British policing does not exist in a vacuum, separate from other people, but is intimately bound with the many racisms and class antagonisms that are experienced every day and resisted through non-compliance, rebellion, protest and organising.

Race presents itself as natural, but in reality it does not operate in fixed categories[4] – when we try to argue that it does, we reproduce the racial categories that need to be dismantled in order for racism to be defeated. We must push against the narrow, blinkered politics that treats different racisms as distinct and separate from each other, and Black resistance to policing as necessarily distinct from other struggles. As Chapter 1 argued, this does not reflect the realities in which Black politics was formed in Britain or its colonies. This is not a call to ignore or deny the prejudices and inequalities that exist between people of differing ethnicities or nationalities, or racialised people from different classed, gendered, sexual or abled groups. Rather, like the Black Power and anti-colonial movements of the twentieth century, it recognises both a political and strategic requirement for working through difference in order to develop and maintain the movements of solidarity needed to resist racism. Into the twenty-first century, organising with other oppressed people does not simply remain a practical necessity, it is a moral imperative and, I would argue, urgently needed for any future for Black radicalism. It is only through links of solidarity with all oppressed peoples that Black liberation becomes possible. These are well illustrated by Elma Francois' 1937 speech, quoted in Chapter 1, where she compared the oppression of African-Caribbean and South Asian workers in Trinidad with working-class protests in Germany and Britain, and with the uprisings of colonised people in Nigeria and Kenya. We have seen how these links have been exemplified more recently by alliances between radical Black, Asian and other working-class communities in post-war Britain and, crucially, the British Black Power movements which linked anti-racism to the anti-colonial struggles across the planet.

The vision of prison and police abolition popularised by the radical voices of the BLM movement in 2020 is testimony to Black radicalism's commitment to solidarity. Envisioning a world in which prisons are obsolete compels us to visualise a world free from all oppression. It is a world which dismantles capitalist exploitation of people and the planet, a society which undoes patriarchal social relations. It requires us to reimagine how we interact with differently abled people, and how we understand health and wellbeing. Among all of this, of course, is the overthrow of racism and capitalism as modes of governance and reproducers of state power. This revolutionary vision is not a moment in time, but a process which requires collective and continued movement. Eroding the power, resources and legitimacy of the criminal justice system, which entrusts the police and the prison system with the social problems of a deeply unjust world, can be achieved through incremental reforms. The best way we can resist policing itself is through replacing punishment with community-led social initiatives that provide care, health and wellbeing, supporting livelihoods which can prevent people from coming into contact with the police. Vitally, abolitionist reforms are not simply about welfare reform, replacing state policing with the softer power of state provision. Abolitionist reforms must be about people, part of a process which erodes the power of police and prisons while empowering communities to provide for and support themselves and each other.

Black resistance to policing is all around us. It can be found in the community care which keeps the police and prison system away from people who have experienced trauma, harm or exploitation. Resistance to policing is in the everyday non-compliance of young people with being monitored by CCTV or digital communications tracking, or the cultures of resistance to the everyday antagonisms with the criminal justice system. Resistance is in the willingness to challenge police harassment, recording videos to shame and expose, or using direct action when state violence is imminent. It can be found in our spaces of learning, where histories of slavery and colonialism are connected to contemporary racisms, and where the anti-colonial struggles of previous decades are understood as the precursors of twenty-first-century anti-racism. This book has focused on just a few of the urban rebellions and organised campaigns that have articulated the sentiment behind the widespread quotidian antagonism to policing in Britain. They are just part of a larger mosaic of Black struggles in Britain and worldwide, which are wresting a better world for all oppressed people from violence, exploitation and harm.

Notes

Introduction

1 Aamna Mohdin and Glenn Swann, 'How George Floyd's death sparked a wave of UK anti-racism protests', *Guardian* (2020), www.theguardian.com/uk-news/2020/jul/29/george-floyd-death-fuelled-anti-racism-protests-britain (accessed 12 October 2020).

2 For the variety of forms which racialisation takes, see Karim Murji and John Solomos (eds), *Racialization: Studies in Theory and Practice* (Oxford: Oxford University Press, 2005).

3 For more on the centrality of racism in the development of modern Britain, see Catherine Hall, *Macaulay and Son: Architects of Imperial Britain* (New Haven: Yale University Press, 2012); Gurminder Bhambra, *Rethinking Modernity: Postcolonialism and the Sociological Imagination* (Basingstoke: Palgrave Macmillan, 2007).

4 Hazel Carby, *Imperial Intimacies: A Tale of Two Islands* (London: Verso, 2019).

5 Black Panther Movement Newsletter, quoted in Rob Waters, *Thinking Black: Britain, 1964–1985* (California: University of California Press, 2018), 103.

6 bell hooks, *We Real Cool: Black Men and Masculinity* (New York: Routledge, 2004).

7 Julia Chinyere Oparah, *'Other Kinds of Dreams': Black Women's Organisations and the Politics of Transformation* (London: Routledge, 1998).

8 Niki Adams, *Chronology of Injustice: The Case for Winston Silcott's Conviction to be Overturned* (London: Crossroads Books, 1994).

9 Natalie Thomlinson, *Race, Ethnicity, and the Women's Movement in England, 1968–1993* (London: Routledge, 2016).

10 Paul Gilroy, 'Police and thieves', in Centre for Contemporary Cultural Studies (eds), *The Empire Strikes Back: Race and Racism in 70s Britain* (London: Routledge, 1982).

Notes

11 Ann Phoenix, 'Theories of gender and Black families', in Heidi Safia
Mirza (ed.), *Black British Feminism: A Reader* (London: Routledge, 1997);
Tracey Reynolds, '(Mis)representing the Black (super)woman', in Mirza
(ed.), *Black British Feminism*.

12 Annecka Marshall, 'From sexual denigration to self-respect: resisting
images of Black female sexuality', in Delia Jarrett-Macauley, *Reconstructing
Womanhood, Reconstructing Feminism: Writings on Black Women* (London:
Routledge, 2005).

13 Avtar Brah and Ann Phoenix, 'Ain't I a woman? Revisiting intersectionality', *Journal of International Women's Studies* 5:3 (2004), 75–86; bell hooks,
Ain't I a Woman? Black Women and Feminism (London: Pluto Press, 1987).

14 Floya Anthias and Nira Yuval-Davis, *Racialized Boundaries: Race, Nation,
Gender, Colour and Class and the Anti-Racist Struggle* (London: Routledge,
1992); Beverley Bryan, Stella Dadzie and Suzanne Scafe, *The Heart of
the Race: Black Women's Lives in Britain* (London: Virago, 1985); Akwugo
Emejulu, *Minority, Women and Austerity: Survival and Resistance in France and
Britain* (Cambridge: Polity, 2017); Yasmin Gunaratnam and Gail Lewis,
'Racialising emotional labour and emotionalising racialised labour:
anger, fear, and shame in social welfare', *Journal of Social Work Practice* 15:2
(2001), 125–142.

15 Amina Mama, 'Woman abuse in London's Black communities', in Clive
Harris and Winston James (eds), *Inside Babylon: The Caribbean Diaspora
in Britain* (London: Verso, 1993); Amina Mama, 'Black women and the
police: a place where law is not upheld', in Harris and James (eds), *Inside
Babylon*.

16 Amnesty International, 'Death in Police Custody of Joy Gardner' (1995),
www.amnesty.org/download/Documents/172000/eur450051995en.pdf
(accessed 29 January 2018).

17 Amelia Gentleman and Damien Gayle, 'Interview: Sarah Reed's mother:
"My daughter was failed by many and I was ignored"', *Guardian* (2016),
www.theguardian.com/society/2016/feb/17/sarah-reeds-mother-deaths-
in-custody-holloway-prison-mental-health (accessed 11 September 2020).

18 Rachel Nurse, 'Online Petition Aims to Keep Cardiff Woman Out of
Prison', *InterCardiff* (2 March 2020), www.jomec.co.uk/intercardiff/pol
itics-social-justice/social-justice-petition-for-south-wales-local?fbclid=I
wAR3pW7hFloR6ARSqAgVwPVUduiqNEDXYH4dZMKfiOCRcV6
xxYQBkN163fZA (accessed 11 September 2020).

19 Linda Moore and Phil Scraton, *The Incarceration of Women: Punishing Bodies,
Breaking Spirits* (London: Routledge, 2014).

20 Patrick Woolfe, *Traces of History: Elementary Structures of Race* (London:
Verso 2016), 2.

21 Cedric Robinson, *Forgeries of Memory and Meaning: Blacks and the Regimes of*

Race in American Theater and Film before World War II (Carolina: University North Carolina Press, 2007), 4.

22 Homi Bhabha, *The Location of Culture* (London: Routledge, 1994).

23 Catherine Hall, *Civilising Subjects: Metropole and Colony in the English Imagination, 1830–1867* (Cambridge: Polity, 2002).

24 George Moss, *Nationalism and Sexuality: Middle Class Morality and Sexual Norms in Modern Europe* (Madison: University of Wisconsin Press, 1985).

25 Anne McClintock, *Imperial Leather: Race, Gender, and Sexuality in the Colonial Contest* (New York: Routledge, 1995).

26 George Moss, *Nationalism and Sexuality: Middle Class Morality and Sexual Norms in Modern Europe* (Madison: University of Wisconsin Press, 1985), 16.

27 *Ibid.*

28 Robbie Shilliam, *'Race' and the Undeserving Poor: From Abolition to Brexit* (London: Agenda Publishing, 2018).

29 Caroline Elkins, *Britain's Gulag: The Brutal End of Empire in Kenya* (London: Pimlico 2005), 3.

30 Remi Joseph-Salisbury, 'Race and Racism in English Secondary Schools', *Runnymede Trust* (2020), www.runnymedetrust.org/projects-and-publications/education/racism-in-secondary-schools.html (accessed 12 October 2020); Katy Pal Sian, 'Spies, surveillance and stakeouts: monitoring Muslim moves in British state schools', *Race Ethnicity and Education*, 18:2 (2015), 183–201; Institute of Race Relations (2016), 'Interview with Schools ABC', https://irr.org.uk/article/interview-with-schools-abc (accessed 12 October 2020).

31 Aviah Sarah Day and Aisha Gill, 'Applying intersectionality to partnerships between women's organizations and the criminal justice system in relation to domestic violence', *The British Journal of Criminology*, 60:4 (2020), 830–850.

32 Nadine El-Enany, *Bordering Britain: Law, Race and Empire* (Manchester: Manchester University Press, 2019); Gracie Mae Bradley, 'A Prevent-style plan for knife crime is not just misguided, it's dangerous', *Guardian* (2019), www.theguardian.com/commentisfree/2019/apr/02/knife-crime-prevent-teachers-doctors-youth-violence (accessed 1 October 2020).

33 Amnesty International, 'Trapped in the Matrix: Secrecy, Stigma, and Bias in the Met's Gangs Database' (2018), www.amnesty.org.uk/files/reports/Trapped%20in%20the%20Matrix%20Amnesty%20report.pdf (accessed 13 October 2020); El-Enany, *Bordering Britain*.

34 Unison, 'Youth Services at Breaking Point' (2019), www.unison.org.uk/content/uploads/2019/04/Youth-services-report-04-2019.pdf (accessed 11 September 2019).

35 Barnor Hesse, 'Racialized modernity: an analytics of white mythologies', *Ethnic and Racial Studies*, 30:4 (2007), 643–663.

Notes

36   Cedric Robinson, *Black Marxism: The Making of the Black Radical Tradition* (Carolina: University of North Carolina Press, 2000).

37   Ruth Wilson Gilmore, *Golden Gulag: Prisons, Surplus, Crisis, and Opposition in Globalizing California* (California: University of California Press, 2007), 247.

38   For instance, see Niamh Eastwood, Mike Shiner and Daniel Bear, *The Numbers in Black and White: Ethnic Disparities in the Policing and Prosecution of Drug Offences in England and Wales* (London: Release & LSE Consulting, 2013); Harmit Athwal and Jon Burnett, 'Investigated or ignored? An analysis of race-related deaths since the Macpherson Report', *Race & Class*, 56:1 (2014), 22–42; Patrick Williams and Becky Clarke, *Dangerous Associations: Joint Enterprise, Gangs and Racism* (London: Centre for Crime and Justice Studies, 2016); Inquest, 'BAME Deaths in Custody' (2019) www.inquest.org.uk/statistics/bame-deaths-in-police-custody (accessed 12 September 2020).

39   Monish Bhatia, Scott Poynting and Waqas Tufail (eds), *Media, Crime and Racism* (London: Palgrave, 2018).

40   David Theo Goldberg, *The Threat of Race: Reflections on Racial Neoliberalism* (Malden: Blackwell, 2009); Eduardo Bonilla-Silva, *Racism without Racists: Color-Blind Racism and the Persistence of Racial Inequality in the United States* (New York: Rowman & Littlefield, 2010); Ian Haney López, *Dog Whistle Politics: How Coded Racial Appeals Reinvented Racism and Wrecked the Middle Class* (Oxford: Oxford University Press, 2014).

41   Karim Murji, *Racism, Policy and Politics* (London: Policy Press, 2017).

42   Hannah Jones, Yasmin Gunaratnam, Gargi Bhattacharyya, William Davies, Sukhwant Dhaliwal, Emma Jackson and Roiyah Saltus, *Go Home? The Politics of Immigration Controversies* (Manchester: Manchester University Press, 2017).

43   Noel Cazenave, *Conceptualizing Racism: Breaking the Chains of Racially Accommodative Language* (Maryland: Rowman & Littlefield, 2015).

44   Shirley Anne Tate and Damien Page, 'Whiteliness and institutional racism: hiding behind (un)conscious bias', *Ethics and Education*, 13:1 (2018), 141–155.

45   Jon Burnett, 'Britain: racial violence and the politics of hate', *Race & Class*, 54:4 (2013), 5–21.

46   Frantz Fanon, *The Wretched of the Earth* (London: Penguin Books, 1967).

47   For a brilliant critique of this kind of narrow nationalist politics, see Annie Olaloku-Teriba, 'Afro-pessimism and the (un)logic of anti-blackness: historical materialism', *Historical Materialism* (2018), www.historicalmaterialism.org/articles/afro-pessimism-and-unlogic-anti-blackness (accessed 1 October 2020).

Notes

Chapter 1 – 'We did not come alive in Britain': histories of Black resistance to British policing

1 John La Rose, 'We did not come alive in Britain', in Paul Field, Robin Bunce, Leila Hassan and Margaret Peacock (eds), *Here to Stay, Here to Fight: A* Race Today *Anthology* (London: Pluto Press, 2019).

2 Satnam Virdee, *Racism, Class and the Racialized Outsider* (London: Palgrave 2014).

3 Arthur Lewis, *Labour in the West Indies: The Birth of a Workers' Movement* (London: New Beacon Books, 1977).

4 Steve Garner, *Whiteness: An Introduction* (London: Routledge, 2007).

5 David Featherstone, 'Politicizing in/security, transnational resistance, and the 1919 riots in Cardiff and Liverpool', *Small Axe*, 22:3 (2018), 56–67.

6 David Featherstone, 'Anti-colonialism, subaltern anti-fascism and the contested spaces of maritime organising', in Kasper Braskén, Nigel Copsey and David Featherstone (eds), *Anti-Fascism in a Global Perspective: Transnational Networks, Exile Communities, and Radical Internationalism* (London: Routledge, 2020).

7 Rhoda Reddock, *Elma Francois: The NWCSA (Negro Welfare Cultural and Social Association) and the Workers' Struggle for Change in the Caribbean in the 1930s* (London: New Beacon Books, 1988), 3.

8 Richard Jacobs, 'The politics of protest in Trinidad: the strikes and disturbances of 1937', *Caribbean Studies*, 17: 1/2 (1977), 5–54.

9 Reddock, *Elma Francois*, 35–6.

10 *Ibid.*

11 George Padmore, 'Fascism in the colonies', *Controversy*, 2:17 (February 1938).

12 Lewis, *Labour in the West Indies*.

13 Kate Quinn, *Black Power in the Caribbean* (Florida: University Press of Florida, 2015).

14 Virdee, *Racism, Class and the Racialised Outsider*.

15 Michael Banton, *The Coloured Quarter: Coloured Immigrants in an English City* (London: Cape, 1955).

16 Roy May and Robin Cohen, 'The interaction between race and colonialism: a case study of the Liverpool race riots of 1919', *Race & Class*, 16:2 (1974), 111–126.

17 Kennetta Hammond Perry, *London is the Place for Me: Black Britons, Citizenship and the Politics of Race* (Oxford: Oxford University Press, 2015).

18 Ed Pilkington, *Beyond the Mother Country: West Indians and the Notting Hill White Riots* (London: I. B. Tauris, 1988).

19 Marika Sherwood, 'Lynching in Britain', *History Today*, 49:3 (1999), 21–23.

20 Hammond Perry, *London is the Place for Me*, 130.

21 Keisha N. Blain, *Set the World on Fire: Black Nationalist Women and the Global Struggle for Freedom* (Pennsylvania: University of Pennsylvania Press, 2018).

22 Hakim Adi, *Pan-Africanism and Communism: The Communist International, Africa and the Diaspora, 1919–1939* (London: African World Press, 2013).

23 Carole Boyce Davies, *Left of Karl Marx: The Life of Black Communist Claudia Jones* (North Carolina: Duke University Press, 2008).

24 Colin A. Palme, *Eric Williams and the Making of the Modern Caribbean* (Carolina: University of North Carolina Press, 2006).

25 Waters, *Thinking Black*.

26 Walter Rodney, *The Groundings with my Brothers* (London: Verso 2019).

27 Steve Biko, *I Write What I Like* (Chicago: University of Chicago Press, 2002).

28 *Battle Front*: Paper of the Black Parents Movement, February 1989.

29 Bryan, Dadzie and Scafe, *The Heart of the Race*.

30 John Solomos, *Race and Racism in Britain*, 3rd edition (Basingstoke: Macmillan, 2003).

31 Stuart Hall, Chas Critcher, Tony Jefferson, John Clarke and Brian Roberts, *Policing the Crisis: Mugging, the State, and Law and Order* (London: Palgrave Macmillan, 1976), 150.

32 *Ibid.* p. 45.

33 Simon Peplow, *Race and Riots in Thatcher's Britain* (Manchester: Manchester University Press, 2019).

34 Martha Otito Osamor, Black Cultural Archives, ref. BWM15.

35 Beverley Bryan and Stella Dadzie, together with Suzanne Scafe, in 1985 co-authored *Heart of the Race: Black Women's Lives in Britain* (London: Virago).

36 Gee Bernard remained prominent in local politics in Croydon, south London, until her death in 2016.

37 Many thanks to Dean Sealey, former organiser with Scrap Sus, for his insights.

38 IRR, 'Fighting Sus! Then and now', *Institute of Race Relations* (2019), www.irr.org.uk/news/fighting-sus-then-and-now (accessed 12 October 2020).

39 Robin Bunce and Paul Field, *Darcus Howe: A Political Biography* (London: Bloomsbury Publishing, 2014).

40 Jude McCulloch and Vicki Sentas, 'The killing of Jean Charles de Menezes: hyper-militarism in the neoliberal economic free-fire zone', *Social Justice*, 33:4 (2006), 92–106.

41 Peplow, *Race and Riots in Thatcher's Britain*.

42 Gerry Northam, *Shooting in the Dark* (London: Faber & Faber, 1988).

43 Peplow, *Race and Riots in Thatcher's Britain*.

44 *Race Today*, February/March 1982, p. 52.

45 Peplow, *Race and Riots in Thatcher's Britain*.

46 Maev Kennedy, 'Tottenham: echoes of a history not forgotten as rioting returns', *Guardian*, 7 August 2011.

47 'Toxteth riots 30 years on: David Sullivan a senior manager with North West Regional Ambulance Service was on duty during the riot', *Liverpool Echo* (2011), www.liverpoolecho.co.uk/news/liverpool-news/toxteth-riots -30-years-on-3369403 (accessed 12 July 2020).

48 Peplow, *Race and Riots in Thatcher's Britain*.

49 Neil Wain and Peter Joyce, 'Disaffected communities, riots and policing: Manchester 1981 and 2011', *Safer Communities*, 11:3 (2012), 125–134.

50 Peplow, *Race and Riots in Thatcher's Britain*.

51 Gus John, *Moss Side 1981 – More Than Just A Riot* (London: New Beacon Books, 2011).

52 *Race Today*, February/March 1982, p. 52.

53 Peplow, *Race and Riots in Thatcher's Britain*.

54 Erik Linstrum, 'Domesticating chemical weapons: tear gas and the militarization of policing in the British imperial world, 1919–1981', *Journal of Modern History*, 91:3 (2019), 557–585.

55 Georgina Sinclair, '"Get into a crack force and earn £20 a month and all found …": The influence of the Palestine police upon colonial policing 1922–1948', *European Review of History: Revue européenne d'histoire*, 13:1 (2006), 49–65.

56 Keith Jeffery, 'Security policy in Northern Ireland: some reflections on the management of violent conflict', *Terrorism and Political Violence*, 2:1 (1990), 21–34.

57 Groce, Brixton Field Notes, 3 October 2015.

58 Northam, *Shooting in the Dark*.

59 Stafford Scott, Brixton Field Notes, 3 October 2015.

60 Jonathan Rosenhead, 'Plastic bullets – a reasonable force?', *New Scientist* (1985), https://apps.dtic.mil/sti/pdfs/ADA385684.pdf (accessed 12 October 2020).

61 Northam, *Shooting in the Dark*.

62 Lee Bridges, 'UK commentary: beyond accountability: Labour and policing after the 1985 rebellions', *Race & Class*, 27:78 (1986), 77–85.

63 *Race Today*, January 1986, p. 13.

64 *Ibid.*

65 David Rose, *Climate of Fear: The Murder of PC Blakelock and the Case of the Tottenham Three* (London: Bloomsbury, 1992).

66 Jed Fazakarley, 'Racisms "old" and "new" at Handsworth, 1985', *University of Sussex Journal of Contemporary History* (2009), 13.

67 *Ibid.* p. 2.

68 Hall *et al.*, *Policing the Crisis*, 394.

69 *Asian Youth News*, Special Edition, September 1985, Police Hypocrisy and Media Conspiracy, npn.

70 *Ibid.*

71 *Ibid.*

72 Fanon, *The Wretched of the Earth*, 118–120.

73 Regional Policy, 'Inner cities policy and problems: regeneration of Liverpool and London; Docklands Urban Development Corporation; Docklands Light Railway and Canary Wharf; South Cardiff urban renewal: Part 8', 4 Feb–29 Nov 1986, p. 179 (accessed The National Archives, Kew, 5 January 2016).

74 *Ibid.* p. 166.

75 *Ibid.*

76 Wendy Larner, 'Theorising neoliberalism: policy, ideology, governmentality', *Studies in Political Economy*, 6:3 (2000), 5–26.

77 Alan Travis, 'Oliver Letwin blocked help for Black youth after 1985 riots', *Guardian* (2015), www.theguardian.com/politics/2015/dec/30/oliver-letwin-blocked-help-for-black-youth-after-1985–riots (accessed 10 January 2016).

78 Jon Burnett, 'Britain's "civilising project": community cohesion and core values', *Policy & Politics*, 35:2 (2007), 353–357.

Chapter 2 – Into the twenty-first century: resistance, respectability and Black deaths in police custody

1 Sir William Macpherson, 'The Stephen Lawrence Inquiry: Report of an Inquiry by Sir William Macpherson', Command Paper 4262 (2000), www.archive.official-documents.co.uk/document/cm42/4262/4262.htm (accessed 15 February 2015).

2 Virdee, *Racism, Class and the Racialized Outsider*, 80.

3 Robert Miles, 'The riots of 1958: notes on the ideological construction of "race relations" as a political issue in Britain', *Immigrants & Minorities*, 3:3 (1984), 252–275.

4 Doreen Lawrence, quoted in Macpherson Report, 1999.

5 Macpherson, 'Stephen Lawrence Inquiry', 91.

6 Doreen Lawrence, 'UK Lawrence Mother Calls Police "Racist"', quoted in BBC News (1998), http://news.bbc.co.uk/1/hi/uk/110842.stm (accessed 22 December 2017).

7 Les Back, 'Whiteness in the dramaturgy of racism', in Patricia Hill Collins and John Solomos, *The SAGE Handbook of Race and Ethnic Studies* (Los Angeles: SAGE, 2010).

Notes

8 Nicola Rollock, 'The Stephen Lawrence Inquiry 10 Years On: An Analysis of the Literature', *Runnymede Trust* (2009), www.runnymedetrust. org/uploads/publications/pdfs/StephenLawrenceInquiryReport-2009. pdf (accessed 3 January 2015).

9 Hazel Carby, 'White women, listen! Black feminism and the boundaries of sisterhood', in Centre for Contemporary Cultural Studies (eds), *The Empire Strikes Back*.

10 Hortense Spillers, 'Mama's baby, papa's maybe: an American grammar book', *Culture and Countermemory: The 'American' Connection*, 17:2 (1987), 69.

11 Rahul Rao, 'Queer Questions', *International Feminist Journal of Politics*, 16:2 (2014), 199–217.

12 Alison Blunt and Gillian Rose (eds), *Writing Women and Space: Colonial and Postcolonial Geographies* (New York: Guilford Press, 1994); Catherine Hall, *Civilising Subjects: Metropole and Colony in the English Imagination, 1830–1867* (Cambridge: Polity 2002); Beverley Skeggs, 'Refusing to be civilised: "race", sexuality, and power', in Haleh Afshar and Mary Maynard (eds), *The Dynamics of Race and Gender: Some Feminist Interventions* (Basingstoke: Taylor and Francis, 1994).

13 Edward Long, 'Candid Reflections Upon The Judgement Lately Awarded By The Court Of King's Bench', in *On What Is Commonly Called The Negroe Cause, By A Planter* (1772), 49.

14 Moss, *Nationalism and Sexuality*.

15 Jasbir Puar, *Terrorist Assemblages: Homonationalism in Queer Times* (London: Duke University Press, 2017).

16 Marshall, 'From sexual denigration to self-respect'.

17 Philip Curtin, *The Image of Africa: British Ideas and Action 1780–1850* (London: Macmillan & Co., 1965), 252.

18 Hilary Beckles, *Centering Woman: Gender Discourses in Caribbean Slave Society* (Kingston: Ian Randle, 1999); Marietta Morrissey, *Slave Women in the New World: Gender Stratification in the Caribbean* (Lawrence: University Press of Kansas, 1989); Jennifer L. Morgan, *Laboring Women: Reproduction and Gender in New World Slavery* (Philadelphia: University of Pennsylvania Press, 2004).

19 It is worth noting that some accounts of Black women in the Caribbean presented them as loyal housewives who engaged in loving, sexual relationships with their masters. This was an attempt by pro-slavery advocates to legitimise these coercive sexual relations by presenting them as comparable to respectable relations associated with middle-class England. Henrice Altink, 'Deviant and dangerous: pro-slavery representations of Jamaican slave women's sexuality, c. 1780–1834', *Slavery and Abolition*, 26:2 (2005), 271–288.

20   Charles Leslie, *A new and exact account of Jamaica, wherein the antient and present state of that colony, its importance to Great Britain, laws, trade, manners and religion; together with the most remarkable and curious animals, plants and trees* (Edinburgh, MDCCXL/1740), 364.

21   Altink, 'Deviant and dangerous'.

22   Edward Long (4 vols, 1735), 'The History of Jamaica', *Gentleman's Magazine* (London, 1774), 271.

23   Kathleen Wilson, 'Empire, gender and modernity in the eighteenth century', in Philippa Levine (ed.), *Gender and Empire* (Oxford: Oxford University Press, 2004).

24   Leslie, *A new and exact account of Jamaica*, 92.

25   Morrissey, *Slave Women in the New World*.

26   Nivi Manchanda, *Imagining Afghanistan: The History and Politics of Imperial Knowledge* (Cambridge: Cambridge University Press, 2020).

27   In Fanon's analysis, the colonisers project the negative characteristics of their own society onto the colonised, including sexual deviancy and violence. See Frantz Fanon, *Black Skins, White Masks* (London: Pluto Press, 1986).

28   Rhoda E. Reddock, 'Women and slavery in the Caribbean: a feminist perspective', *Latin American Perspectives*, 12:1 (1985), 63–80.

29   Barbara Bush, *Slave Women in Caribbean Society 1650–1838* (Bloomington: Indiana University Press, 1990); Jessica Marie Johnson, *Wicked Flesh: Black Women, Intimacy and Freedom in the Atlantic World* (Philadelphia: University of Pennsylvania Press, 2020).

30   David Dickson, 'No Scythians here: women and marriage in seventeenth-century Ireland', in Margaret MacCurtain and Mary O'Dowd (eds), *Women in Early Modern Ireland* (Dublin: Wolfhound Press, 1992), 224.

31   Barbara Harlow and Mia Carter (eds), *Archives of Empire: Volume I, From the East India Company to the Suez Canal* (London: Duke University Press, 2003), 377–379.

32   Gayatri Chakravorty Spivak, 'Can the subaltern speak?', in Patrick Williams and Laura Chrisman, *Colonial Discourse and Postcolonial Theory: A Reader* (Hertfordshire: Harvester Wheatsheaf, 1994).

33   Angela Woollacott, *Gender and Empire* (London: Palgrave Macmillan, 2006).

34   Stephanie Jones-Rogers, *They Were Her Property: White Women as Slave Owners in the American South* (New Haven: Yale University Press, 2019).

35   This was in contrast to Millicent Fawcett's more radical anti-war contemporaries such as Emily Hobhouse. See Vron Ware, 'All the rage: decolonizing the history of the British women's suffrage movement', *Cultural Studies* 34:4 (2020), 521–545. For a more detailed account of the complicated relationship between feminism, whiteness and slavery, and

colonialism and racism, see Vron Ware, *Beyond the Pale: White Women, Racism and History* (London: Verso 2015).

36 Susan Kent, *Gender and Power in Britain, 1640–1990* (London: Routledge, 1999).

37 Carby, 'White women, listen!'.

38 Chamion Caballero and Peter J. Aspinall, *Mixed Race Britain* (London: Palgrave, 2018), 349.

39 *Race Today*, 'Black women and nursing: a job like any other', in Field *et al.* (eds), *Here to Stay, Here to Fight: A* Race Today *Anthology*.

40 Amrit Wilson, *Dreams, Questions, Struggles: South Asian Women in Britain* (London: Pluto Press, 2006).

41 Nicole M. Jackson, A Black woman's choice: depo-provera and reproductive rights, *Journal of Research on Women and Gender* 2:2 (2011), https://journals.tdl.org/jrwg/index.php/jrwg/article/view/52 (accessed 10 December 2020).

42 Margaret Thatcher, *The Downing Street Years*, 2nd edition (London: Harper Press, 1993), 626.

43 Wendy Brown, *In the Ruins of Neoliberalism: The Rise of Antidemocratic Politics in the West* (New York: Columbia University Press, 2019).

44 Paul Gilroy, *There Ain't No Black in the Union Jack: The Cultural Politics of Race and Nation* (London: Routledge, 1987); John Solomos, *Black Youth, Racism and the State: The Politics of Ideology and Policy* (Cambridge: Cambridge University Press, 1988).

45 Tara Young, Wendy Fitzgibbon and Daniel Silverstone, 'A question of family? Youth and gangs', *Youth Justice*, 14:2 (2014), 171–185.

46 Alana Lentin, *Why Race Still Matters* (Cambridge: Polity, 2020).

47 Ed West, 'Black pupils and bad behaviour – only a Black academic can state the obvious', *Daily Telegraph* (2010), http://blogs.telegraph.co.uk/news/edwest/100055001/black-pupils-and-bad-behaviour-only-a-black-academic-can-statethe-obvious (accessed 5 February 2014).

48 Tony Sewell, 'Black boys are too feminised', *Guardian* (2010), www.theguardian.com/commentisfree/2010/mar/15/black-boys-too-feminised-fathers (accessed 25 November 2020).

49 The Moynihan Report, published in the US in 1965, focused on the disorder of the Black family as the source of racial inequalities. Moynihan reported high levels of Black male unemployment and relatively high Black female employment, which he claimed exacerbated Black familial disorder.

50 Spillers, 'Mama's baby, papa's maybe'.

51 *Ibid.*

52 Shaun Bailey, *No Man's Land: How Britain's Inner City Young are Being Failed* (London: Centre for Young Policy Studies, 2005), 21.

53 *Ibid.* p. 22.

54 Kathy Gyngell and Ray Lewis, *From Latchkey to Leadership: A Practical Blueprint for Channelling the Talents of Inner City Youth* (London: Centre for Young Policy Studies, 2006), 10.

55 Greater London Authority, 'Mayor's Mentoring Programme' (2010), www.london.gov.uk/get-involved/public/types-of-volunteering/mentoring (accessed 10 February 2013).

56 Marcia Rigg, interview, 8 July 2018.

57 *Ibid.*

58 *Ibid.*

59 LCAPSV, interview, 30 March 2014.

60 *Ibid.*

61 Trayvon Martin solidarity, interview, 17 May 2016.

62 Black Activists Rising Against Cuts, interview, 7 October 2013.

63 iNAPP, interview, 26 November 2014.

64 Carby, 'White women, listen!'.

65 *Ibid.*

66 TDC, interview, 14 November 2014.

67 Phoenix, 'Theories of gender and Black families'; Reynolds, '(Mis)representing the Black (super)woman'.

68 One Voice, interview, 5 March 2014.

69 Marcia Rigg, interview, 9 July 2018.

70 Claire Alexander, 'Rethinking Gangs', *Runnymede Trust* (2008), www.runnymedetrust.org/uploads/publications/pdfs/RethinkingGangs-2008.pdf (accessed 30 June 2020); Paul Gilroy, 'Police and thieves', in Centre for Contemporary Cultural Studies (eds), *The Empire Strikes Back*; bell hooks, *We Real Cool*; Rashad Shabazz, *Spatializing Blackness: Architectures of Confinement and Black Masculinity in Chicago* (Illinois: University of Illinois Press, 2015).

71 Dot Wordsworth, 'Where did "No justice, no peace" come from?', *The Spectator* (2014), www.spectator.co.uk/article/where-did-no-justice-no-peace-come-from- (accessed 10 October 2020).

72 Marcia Rigg, interview, 9 July 2018.

73 BBC News, 'Mark Duggan "Among Europe's Most Violent Criminals", Inquest Told', *BBC News London* (2013), www.bbc.co.uk/news/uk-england-london-24210480 (accessed 4 April 2014).

74 Richard Littlejohn, 'Duggan was a gangster, not Nelson Mandela', *Daily Mail* (2014), www.dailymail.co.uk/debate/article-2536869/RICHARD-LITTLEJOHN-Duggan-gangster-not-Nelson-Mandela.html (accessed 4 April 2014); Arthur Martin, 'Duggan "was one of Britain's most violent gangsters": inquest hears he was linked to ten shootings and two murders', *Daily Mail* (2013), www.dailymail.co.uk/news/article-2430081/Mark-Duggan-Britains-violent-gangsters-Inquest-hears-linked-shootings.html (accessed 7 July 2020).

75   Adam Elliott-Cooper, 'Riots, raids and building resistance', *Ceasefire Magazine* (2013), http://ceasefiremagazine.co.uk/anti-imperialist-13 (accessed 3 February 2013).

76   Williams and Clarke, *Dangerous Associations*.

77   Littlejohn, 'Duggan was a gangster, not Nelson Mandela'.

78   Joan Anim-Addo, 'Activist-mothers maybe, sisters surely? Black British feminism, absence, and transformation', *Feminist Review* 108 (2014), 44–60.

79   Michelle Wallace, *The Black Macho and the Myth of the Superwoman* (New York: Verso, 1979); Reynolds, '(Mis)representing the Black (super) woman'; Yasmin Gunaratnam and Gail Lewis, 'Racialising emotional labour and emotionalising racialised labour: anger, fear, and shame in social welfare', *Journal of Social Work Practice*, 15:2 (2001), 125–142; Megan Comfort, 'In the tube at San Quentin: the "secondary prisonization" of women visiting inmates', *Journal of Contemporary Ethnography*, 32:1 (2003), 77–107; Rachel Condry, 'Stigmatised women: relatives of serious offenders and the broader impact of crime', in Frances Heidensohn (ed.), *Gender and Justice: New Concepts and Approaches* (London: Willan, 2006).

80   Carby, 'White women, listen!'

81   Reynolds, '(Mis)representing the Black (super)woman'.

82   Mama, 'Black women and the police'.

83   Spillers, 'Mama's baby, papa's maybe'.

84   *Ibid.*

85   Luke De Noronha, *Deporting Black Britons: Portraits of Deportation to Jamaica* (Manchester: Manchester University Press, 2020).

86   Many thanks to Aviah Day and Shanice McBean for their insights on this question.

Chapter 3 – Black masculinity and criminalisation: the 2011 'riots' in context

1   Runnymede Trust, 'Section 60 Stop and Search Powers' (2013), www.runnymedetrust.org/section-60-stop-and-search-powers.html (accessed 13 October 2020).

2   Eugene K, 'Section 60 – A Brief History of Mission Creep', Stop Watch (2017), www.stop-watch.org/news-comment/story/section-60-a-brief-history-of-mission-creep (accessed 13 October 2020).

3   Equality and Human Rights Commission, 'Stop and Think: A Critical Review of the Use of Stop and Search Powers in England and Wales' (2010), www.equalityhumanrights.com/sites/default/files/documents/raceinbritain/ehrc_stop_and_search_report.pdf (accessed 3 June 2014).

Notes

4   MayorWatch, Metropolitan Police, 'Blunt 2 Has Reduced Knife Crime' (2009), www.mayorwatch.co.uk/met-police-%E2%80%98blunt-2-has-reduced-knife-crime%E2%80%99 (accessed 22 October 2016).

5   Rhydian McCandless, Andy Feist, James Allan and Nick Morgan, 'Do Initiatives Involving Substantial Increases in Stop and Search Reduce Crime? Assessing the Impact of Operation BLUNT 2, Home Office' (2016) https://assets.publishing.service.gov.uk/government/uploads/sy stem/uploads/attachment_data/file/508661/stop-search-operation-blu nt-2.pdf (accessed 10 October 2020).

6   Vikram Dodd, 'Police in talks to scrap "reasonable grounds" condition for stop and search', *Guardian* (2018), www.theguardian.com/law/2018/nov/11/uk-police-chiefs-hold-talks-to-expand-stop-and-search (accessed 13 March 2019).

7   Hall *et al.*, *Policing the Crisis*.

8   Phil Scraton, 'Scientific knowledge or masculine discourse? Challenging patriarchy in criminology', in Loraine Gelsthorpe and Allison Morris (eds), *Feminist Perspectives in Criminology* (Milton Keynes: Open University, 1990).

9   Hazel Waters, *Racism on the Victorian Stage: Representation of Slavery and the Black Character* (Cambridge: Cambridge University Press, 2007).

10   Robert Norris, *Memoirs of the Reign of Bossa Ahadee, King of Dahomy, an Inland Country of Guiney; To Which Are Added, the Author's Journey to Abomey, the Capital; And a Short Account of the African Slave Trade* (London: printed for W. Lowndes, 1789), 173.

11   Bryan Edwards Esq., FRS, SA, *The history, civil and commercial, of the British colonies in the West Indies, in three volumes*, 1801.

12   John Stewart, *A view of the past and present state of the island of Jamaica: With remarks on the moral and physical condition of the slaves, and on the abolition of slavery*, 1823.

13   Biko Agozino, 'Imperialism, crime and criminology: towards the decolonisation of criminology', *Crime, Law & Social Change* 41 (2004), 343–358.

14   Lisa Lowe, *Intimacies of Four Continents* (Duke University Press: North Carolina, 2015).

15   William Wilberforce, *A Letter on the Abolition of the Slave Trade, Addressed to the Freeholders and other Inhabitants of Yorkshire* (London, 1807), 73–74, cited in Philip Curtin, *The Image of Africa: British Ideas and Action 1780–1850* (London: Macmillan & Co., 1965), 252.

16   John Stuart Mill, *On Liberty* (1859), ch. 1, npn, www.gutenberg.org/files/34901/34901-h/34901-h.htm (accessed 30 November 2020).

17   Thomas Carlyle, 'Occasional Discourse on the Nigger Question' [1853], in Barbara Harlow and Mia Carter (eds), *Archives of Empire: Volume II, The Scramble for Africa* (London: Duke University Press 2003), 123. Original

version (published anonymously): 'Occasional Discourse on the Negro Question', *Fraser's Magazine*, 1849.

18 David Theo Goldberg, 'Liberalism's limits: Carlyle and Mill on "the negro question"', *Nineteenth-Century Contexts: An Interdisciplinary Journal*, 22:2 (2000), 203–216.

19 Jonathan R. Dalby, '"Such a mass of disgusting and revolting cases": moral panic and the "discovery" of sexual deviance in post-emancipation Jamaica (1835–1855)', *Slavery & Abolition*, 36:1 (2015), 136–159.

20 It is worth noting that this pattern of sexualised governance is likely to have influenced modern laws and forms of violence against LGBTQI people and communities in the British Caribbean. Many thanks to Dr Nathaniel Coleman in helping me to think through this issue.

21 Dalby, '"Such a mass of disgusting and revolting cases"'.

22 Dickens also draws parallels with the Irish, claiming that 'several of these scenes of savage life bear a strong generic resemblance to an Irish election, and I think would be extremely well received and understood at Cork'.

23 Alan Lester and Fae Dussart, 'Masculinity, "race" and family in the colonies: protecting Aborigines in the early nineteenth century', *Gender, Place & Culture*, 16:1 (2009), 63–75.

24 William Cobbett, quoted in Robbie Shilliam, *'Race' and the Undeserving Poor: From Abolition to Brexit* (London: Agenda Publishing, 2017), 17.

25 Bradley Deane, *Masculinity and the New Imperialism: Rewriting Manhood in British Popular Literature, 1870–1914* (Cambridge: Cambridge University Press, 2014).

26 Pamela Lothspeich, 'Unspeakable outrages and unbearable defilements: rape narratives in the literature of colonial India', *Postcolonial Text*, 3:1 (2007), 1–19.

27 Edward Spiers, *The Victorian Soldier in Africa* (Manchester: Manchester University Press, 2004).

28 Bhabha, *The Location of Culture*.

29 Catherine Hall, 'Of gender and Empire: reflections on the nineteenth century', in Philippa Levine (ed.), *Gender and Empire* (Oxford: Oxford University Press, 2004).

30 Robinson, *Forgeries of Memory and Meaning*, 4.

31 Jock Mcculloch, 'Empire and violence, 1900–1939', in Levine (ed.), *Gender and Empire*.

32 Elkins, *Britain's Gulag*.

33 John Moore, 'Is the empire coming home? Liberalism, exclusion and the punitiveness of the British State', *Papers from the British Criminology Conference*, 14:1 (2014), 31–48; Jasbinder Nijjar, 'Echoes of empire: excavating the colonial roots of Britain's "war on gangs"', *Social Justice* 45, 2/3 (2018), 147–161.

34 Raewyn Connell, 'Hegemonic masculinity: rethinking the concept', *Gender & Society*, 19:6 (2005), 829–859.

35 David Featherstone, 'Politicizing in/security, transnational resistance, and the 1919 riots in Cardiff and Liverpool', *Small Axe*, 22:3 (2018), 56–67.

36 Robert Miles, 'The riots of 1958: notes on the ideological construction of "race relations" as a political issue in Britain', *Immigrants & Minorities: Historical Studies in Ethnicity, Migration and Diaspora*, 3:3 (1984), 252–275.

37 Caballero and Aspinall, *Mixed Race Britain*, 348.

38 Carby, *Imperial intimacies*.

39 Shirin Hirsch, *In the Shadow of Enoch Powell: Race, Locality and Resistance* (Manchester: Manchester University Press, 2018).

40 Shaun Bailey, *No Man's Land: How Britain's Inner City Young are Being Failed* (London: Centre for Young Policy Studies, 2005), 3.

41 This is also reflected in liberal and state-sanctioned LGBTQI+ campaigns in Europe and North America, which support imperial interventions in parts of the Global South, particularly Muslim-majority countries, on the basis that Western dominance will solve homophobia in these regions. See Puar, *Terrorist Assemblage*.

42 Raewyn Connell and James Messerschmidt, 'Hegemonic masculinity: rethinking the concept', *Gender & Society*, 19:6 (2005), 832.

43 This reflects similar tropes, including the 'good Muslim, bad Muslim'. See Mahmood Mamdani, *Good Muslim, Bad Muslim: Islam, the USA, and the Global War Against Terror* (Delhi: Permanent Black, 2005). Also, Jasbir Puar, 'Good queer, bad queer', in Puar, *Terrorist Assemblages*.

44 Bailey, *No Man's Land*, 3.

45 Burnett, 'Britain's "civilising project"'.

46 bell hooks, *We Real Cool*.

47 Beth Richie, *Arrested Justice: Black Women, Violence, and America's Prison Nation* (New York: New York University Press, 2012).

48 Interview with member of iNAPP, 26 November 2014.

49 Mama 'Black women and the police'.

50 JJ Bola, *Mask Off: Masculinity Redefined* (London: Pluto Press, 2019).

51 *Guardian* and London School of Economics, 'Reading the Riots' (2012), http://eprints.lse.ac.uk/46297/1/Reading%20the%20riots(published).pdf (accessed 15 June 2015).

Chapter 4 – 2011: revolt and community defence

1 Mark Sebba and Shirley Tate, '"Global" and "local" identities in the discourses of British-born Caribbeans', *International Journal of Bilingualism*, 6:1 (2002), 75–89.

2 Matt Lloyd, 'Kingsley Burrell death in custody was neglect, rules inquest', *Birmingham Mail* (2015), www.birminghammail.co.uk/news/midlands-news/kingsley-burrell-birmingham-inquest-neglect-9263823 (accessed 15 January 2015).

3 Paul Gilroy, '1981 and 2011: from social democratic to neoliberal rioting', *South Atlantic Quarterly*, 112:3 (2013), 550–558.

4 Lee Bridges, 'Four days in August: the UK riots', *Race & Class*, 54:1 (2012), 1–12.

5 Joanne McCabe, 'Nottingham riots: arrests to hit 100 after police station is firebombed', *The Metro* (2011), http://metro.co.uk/2011/08/10/nottingham-riots-canning-circuspolice-station-firebombed-84-arrested-109735/#ixzz3viYVyCyw (accessed 28 December 2015).

6 Joseph Kay, 'Intakes: Communities, Commodities and Class in the August 2011 riots' (2011), http://libcom.org/library/intakes-communities-commodities-class-august-2011-riots-aufheben (accessed 16 November 2012).

7 John Solomos, 'Race, rumours and riots: past, present and future', *Sociological Research Online*, 16:4 (2011), 210–215.

8 A version of the analysis of Mauro's case appears in Adam Elliott-Cooper, Estelle du Boulay and Eleanor Kilroy, 'Moral panic(s) in the 21st century', *City*, 18:2 (2014), 160–166. Many thanks to Newham Monitoring Project for the work they did on this case.

9 Jordan Camp, *Incarcerating the Crisis: Freedom Struggles and the Rise of the Neoliberal State* (London: Verso, 2016).

10 David Cameron, 'David Cameron Riot Statement in Full' (2011), www.politics.co.uk/comment-analysis/2011/08/11/david-cameron-riot-statement-in-full (accessed 18 November 2012).

11 *Guardian* and London School of Economics, 'Reading the Riots'.

12 Williams and Clarke, *Dangerous Associations*.

13 Home Affairs, 'Gangs and Youth Crime Report' (2015), UK Parliament, https://publications.parliament.uk/pa/cm201415/cmselect/cmhaff/199/19905.htm (accessed 1 October 2020).

14 'Frontline London, day 1: the gangs of London', *Evening Standard* (2013), www.standard.co.uk/news/london/frontline-london-day-1-the-gangs-of-london-8838696.html (accessed 12 June 2016).

15 Press Association, 'Stop and search ruling due', *Guardian* (2014), www.theguardian.com/law/2014/feb/04/stop-and-search-ruling-due (accessed 15 July 2016).

16 The full quote from the Metropolitan Police website reads: 'To further demonstrate our commitment to fairness, the Met continues to record stop and account, unlike the majority of other forces. In 2016, just under 90,000 people were stopped and asked to account for themselves. 64% were white, 20% Black and 12% Asian.

There is disparity in the use of stop and search in relation to gender, age and race. The reasons for disparity are complex and include the use of the power to tackle gangs and specific crimes.' Metropolitan Police, 'Stop and Search' (undated, *c*. 2017), www.met.police.uk/police-forces/metropolitan-police/areas/about-us/about-the-met/stop-and-search (accessed 13 October 2020).

17 'Frontline London: these young gangsters have lost so many friends, they've stopped going to their funerals', *Evening Standard* (2013), www.stand ard.co.uk/news/london/frontline-london-these-young-gangsters-have -lost-so-many-friends-theyve-stopped-going-to-their-funerals-8838684.html (accessed 1 November 2013).

18 Karim Murji, 'Rioting and the politics of crisis', *Ethnic and Racial Studies*, 41:10 (2018), 1820–1836; Sivamohan Valluvan, Nisha Kapoor and Virinder Kalra, 'Critical consumers run riot in Manchester', *Journal for Cultural Research*, 17:2 (2013), 164–182.

19 David Harvey, 'Capitalism Hits the Streets' (2011), http://davidharvey. org/2011/08/feral-capitalism-hits-the-streets (accessed 29 December 2015).

20 Ambalavaner Sivanandan, 'This is not the end of rebellion – it is the beginning', *Socialist Worker* (2011), www.socialistworker.co.uk/art.php?id=25716 (accessed 12 November 2014).

21 Owen Bowcott and Stephen Bates, 'Riots: magistrates advised to "disregard normal sentencing"', *Guardian* (2011), www.guardian.co.uk/uk/2011/aug/15/riots-magistrates-sentencing?CMP=twt_fd (accessed 17 November 2012).

22 Haringey Council, 'Summary of Tottenham Profiles' (May 2012), www.har ingey.gov.uk/summary_of_tottenham_profiles.pdf (accessed 12 November 2014).

23 Michael Keith, *Race, Riots and Policing: Lore and Disorder in a Multi-Racist Society* (London: University College London Press, 1993).

24 Stafford Scott, 7 February 2015, author's field notes in Tottenham.

25 'Frontline London', *Evening Standard*.

26 Hall *et al.*, *Policing the Crisis*.

27 Peter Walker, 'PC Alex MacFarlane cleared of racist abuse after second trial without verdict', *Guardian* (2012), www.theguardian.com/uk/2012/oct/25/pc-alex-macfarlane-jury-discharged (accessed 1 November 2013).

28 The Monitoring Group (2013), 'The enduring effects of slavery and institutional racism' (2013), www.tmg-uk.org/the-enduring-effects-of-slavery-and-institutional-racism (accessed 15 March 2015).

29 Metropolitan Police Volunteer Welcome Pack (2011), www.metpolice careers.co.uk/corporate_induction/pdf/volunteer-welcome-pack.pdf (accessed 10 October 2020).

30 Bridges, 'Four days in August'.

31 Martin, 'Duggan "was one of Britain's most violent gangsters"'.

32 H. M. Coroner, 'Transcript of the Hearing 11 December 2013', *Inquest into the Death of Mark Duggan*, http://dugganinquest.independent.gov.uk/transcripts/1711.htm (accessed 22 September 2014).

33 Inquest, 'BAME Deaths in Custody'.

34 His Honour Judge Cutler, quoted in H M Coroner, 'Transcript of the Hearing 11 December 2013', *Inquest into the Death of Mark Duggan*.

35 Arthur Martin, 'Mark Duggan, the man who lived by the gun: arms draped around two violent gangsters, the thug whose death sparked riots – but who his family insist was a peacemaker', *Daily Mail* (2014), www.dailymail.co.uk/news/article-2536197/Mark-Duggan-Arms-draped-two-violent-gangsters-thug-death-sparked-riots.html (accessed 14 March 2018).

36 David Williams, 'Shooting inquiry: answers to the key questions behind the man who was gunned down by police triggering the riots', *Daily Mail* (2011), www.dailymail.co.uk/news/article-2023951/Mark-Duggan-shooting-inquiry-Answers-key-questions-triggered-Tottenham-riots.html (accessed 10 October 2020); Diane Taylor, 'Mark Duggan's mother says she is still waiting for answers about shooting', *Guardian* (2012), www.theguardian.com/uk/2012/aug/03/mark-duggan-mother-waiting-answers (accessed 10 June 2017); James Rush, 'Officer in charge of firearms operation which led to shooting of Mark Duggan "was told he came towards officers firing a gun"', *Daily Mail* (2013), www.dailymail.co.uk/news/article-2431912/Mark-Duggan-Officer-firearms-operation-led-shooting-told-came-officers-firing-gun.html#ixzz3PweyDBEl (accessed 10 October 2020).

37 Martin, 'Duggan "was one of Britain's most violent gangsters"'.

38 BBC News, 'Met Launches "Total War on Crime"' (2012), www.bbc.co.uk/news/uk-england-london-16954257 (accessed 13 October 2018).

39 Alan Travis, 'What policies lie behind Cameron's "all-out war on gangs"?', *Guardian* (2011), www.theguardian.com/politics/2011/aug/15/policies-cameron-all-out-war-gangs (accessed 21 April 2012).

40 Essi Viding and Eamon McCrory, 'Special Investigation: The Gangs of London', University College London (2013), www.ucl.ac.uk/news/headlines/2013/sep/special-investigation-gangs-london (accessed 11 December 2014).

41 David Cohen, 'The ex-cons who'll take away your stuff … but only if you pay them!', *Evening Standard* (2013), www.standard.co.uk/news/london/the-excons-wholl-take-away-your-stuff-but-only-if-you-hire-them-8863625.html (accessed 25 January 2013).

42 David Cohen, 'Party Leaders David Cameron, Ed Miliband and Nick Clegg hail our gang campaign', *Evening Standard* (2013), www.standard.

co.uk/news/london/party-leaders-david-cameron-ed-miliband-and-nick-clegg-hail-our-gangs-campaign-8866448.html (accessed 1 November 2013).

43 Inquest, 'BAME Deaths in Custody'.

Chapter 5 – All-out war: surveillance, collective punishment and the cutting edge of police power

1 Williams and Clarke, *Dangerous Associations*.

2 City Hall, 'Mayor Hosts International Summit as London Turns a Corner on Gang Crime', Greater London Authority (2014), www.london.gov.uk/press-releases-6168 (accessed 12 August 2016).

3 De Noronha, *Deporting Black Britons*.

4 Jon Robins, 'Caught in the joint enterprise dragnet', *The Justice Gap* (2015), www.thejusticegap.com/caught-in-the-joint-enterprise-dragnet (accessed 12 May 2019).

5 JENGbA, 'Tireless campaigners', *Inside Times* (2020), https://insidetime.org/tireless-campaigners (accessed 12 May 2019).

6 Mr T. Smith, quoted in Gloria Morrison, 'How many angels can dance on the head of a pin?', *The Justice Gap* (2019), www.thejusticegap.com/how-many-angels-can-dance-on-the-head-of-a-pin (accessed 12 May 2019).

7 Spillers, 'Mama's baby, papa's maybe', 69.

8 David French, 'Nasty not nice: British counter-insurgency doctrine and practice, 1945–1967', *Small Wars & Insurgencies*, 23:4–5 (2012), 744–761.

9 Frank Kitson, *Low Intensity Operations: Subversion, Insurgency and Peacekeeping* (London: Faber & Faber, 1971).

10 John Newsinger, *British Counterinsurgency* (London: Palgrave, 2nd edition, 2015).

11 *Ibid.*

12 Robert Thompson, *Defeating Communist Insurgency: Lessons from Malaya and Vietnam* (London: F. A. Praeger, 1960), 20.

13 Karl Hack, 'Malaya – between two terrors: "people's history" and the Malayan Emergency', in Hannah Gurman (ed.), *Hearts and Minds: A People's History of Counterinsurgency* (New York: The New Press, 2013), 20.

14 Bernice Chauly, 'Truth still denied: the Batang Kali massacre', *The Griffith Review* (2018), www.griffithreview.com/articles/truth-still-denied-batang-kali-massacre (accessed 2 April 2020).

15 Paul Dixon (ed.), *The British Approach to Counterinsurgency: From Malaya and Northern Ireland to Iraq and Afghanistan* (London: Palgrave, 2012).

16 Hack, 'Malaya – between two terrors', 23.

17 *Ibid.*

Notes

18 Maureen Sioh, 'An ecology of postcoloniality: disciplining nature and society in Malaya, 1948–1957', *Journal of Historical Geography*, 30:4 (2004), 729–746.

19 Thompson, *Defeating Communist Insurgency*, 16.

20 John Cloake, *Templer, Tiger of Malaya: The Life of Field Marshal Sir Gerald Templer* (London: Harrap, 1985), 212.

21 Kitson, *Low Intensity Operations*.

22 Levi Izuakor, 'Kenya: demographic constraints on the growth of European settlement, 1900–1956', *Africa: Rivista Trimestrale di Studi e Documentazione dell'Istituto Italiano per L'Africa e L'Oriente*, 42:3 (1987), 400–416.

23 David Anderson, *The Histories of the Hanged* (London: Weidenfeld & Nicolson, 2005), 77–80.

24 Frank Kitson, *Gangs and Counter Gangs* (London: Barrie & Rockliff, 1960).

25 *Ibid.* p. 15.

26 Dane Kennedy, 'Constructing the colonial myth of Mau Mau', *The International Journal of African Historical Studies*, 2:2 (1992), 245.

27 Kitson, *Gangs and Counter Gangs*, 63.

28 Elkins, *Britain's Gulag*, 121.

29 *Ibid.* p. 143.

30 Anderson, *The Histories of the Hanged*, 293–295.

31 Kitson, *Gangs and Counter Gangs*, 45.

32 Kennedy, 'Constructing the colonial myth of Mau Mau', 254.

33 *Ibid.* p. 253.

34 Agozino, 'Imperialism, crime and criminology'.

35 Thompson, *Defeating Communist Insurgency*, 54.

36 Pat Conway, 'Critical reflections: a response to paramilitary policing in Northern Ireland', *Critical Criminology*, 8:1 (1997), 109–121. Conway, at the start of the article, informs the reader: 'This essay arises from the experiences of a practitioner who has, until recently, managed a project offering services to those under threat from paramilitary organisations'.

37 Northam, *Shooting in the Dark*.

38 McCulloch and Sentas, 'The killing of Jean Charles de Menezes'.

39 Ian Loader, 'Fall of the "platonic guardians": liberalism, criminology and political responses to crime in England and Wales', *British Journal of Criminology*, 46:4 (2006), 561–586.

40 Hall *et al.*, *Policing the Crisis*.

41 Gilroy, *There Ain't No Black in the Union Jack*.

42 Robert Reiner, 'Success or statistics? New Labour and crime control', *Criminal Justice Matters*, 67:1 (2007), 4–37.

43 Arun Kundnani, *The End of Tolerance: Racism in 21st Century Britain* (London: Pluto Press, 2007).

44 Michael Shiner, 'Drug policy reform and the reclassification of cannabis

in England and Wales: a cautionary tale', *International Journal of Drug Policy*, 26:7 (2015), 696–704.

45 Will McMahon and Rebecca Roberts, 'Ethnicity, Harm and Crime: A Discussion Paper', Centre for Crime and Justice Studies, Kings College London (2008), www.crimeandjustice.org.uk/sites/crimeandjustice.org. uk/files/ETHNICITY%20HARM%20AND%20CRIME%20A%20DIS CUSSION%20PAPER.pdf (accessed 13 October 2020).

46 Sweet & Maxwell, *Blair: 54% More New Laws Every Year Than Thatcher* (London: Sweet & Maxwell's Westlaw UK and Lawtel, 2007), www. sweetandmaxwell.co.uk/about-us/press-releases/260607.pdf (accessed 1 October 2020).

47 Prison Reform Trust, 'Prison: the facts', *Bromley Briefings*, Summer 2019.

48 Ines Hasselberg, 'Coerced to leave: punishment and the surveillance of foreign-national offenders in the UK', *Surveillance & Society*, 12:4 (2001), 471–484.

49 Monish Bhatia, 'Crimmigration, imprisonment and racist violence: narratives of people seeking asylum in Great Britain', Special Issue – Asylum Seekers in the Global Context of Xenophobia, *Journal of Sociology* (2019), 1–17.

50 Liz Fekete and Frances Webber, 'Foreign nationals, enemy penology and the criminal justice system', *Race & Class*, 51:4 (2010), 1–25.

51 De Noronha, *Deporting Black Britons*.

52 Gary Younge, 'Beyond the blade: the truth about knife crime in Britain', *Guardian* (2017), www.theguardian.com/uk-news/2017/mar/28/beyond-the-blade-the-truth-about-knife-in-britain (accessed 22 March 2019).

53 David K. Humphreys, Michelle Degli Esposti, Frances Gardner and Jonathan Shepherd, 'Violence in England and Wales: does media reporting match the data?', *British Medical Journal*, 367 (2019), https://doi. org/10.1136/bmj.l6040 (accessed 2 December 2020).

54 Roger Grimshaw and Matt Ford, 'Young people, violence and knives – revisiting the evidence and policy discussions. UK Justice Policy Review', *Centre for Crime and Justice Studies*, 3 (2018), www.crimeandjustice.org.uk/ publications/young-people-violence-and-knives-revisiting-evidence-and-policy-discussions (accessed 2 December 2020).

55 Luke de Noronha, Gargi Bhattacharyya, Nadine El-Enany, Dalia Gebrial, Adam Elliott-Cooper, Kojo Koram, Sita Balani and Kerem Nisancioglu, *Empire's Endgame: Race and Racism in Britain* (London: Pluto, 2021).

56 Liberty, 'Knife Crime Prevention Orders Would Only Harm The Fight Against Violent Crime' (2019), www.libertyhumanrights.org.uk/news/ blog/knife-crime-prevention-orders-would-only-harm-fight-against-vio lent-crime (accessed 22 September 2020).

57 Amnesty International, 'Trapped in the Matrix'.

58 Gary Younge and Caelainn Barr, 'How Scotland reduced knife deaths among young people', *Guardian* (2017), www.theguardian.com/member ship/2017/dec/03/how-scotland-reduced-knife-deaths-among-young-people (accessed 2 October 2020).

59 Joseph-Salisbury, 'Race and Racism in English Secondary Schools'.

60 Northern Police Monitoring Project, 'No Police in Schools' (2019), http://npolicemonitor.co.uk/no-police-in-schools (accessed 13 October 2020).

61 Bradley, 'A Prevent-style plan for knife crime is not just misguided, it's dangerous'.

62 Shaun Bailey, in Freddie Jordan, 'London bloodbath: Shaun Bailey offers solution to knife crime epidemic under Sadiq Khan', *The Express* (2019), www.express.co.uk/news/uk/1137928/Sadiq-Khan-london-knife-crime-stabbings-shaun-bailey-2020-election-shaun-bailey (accessed 13 October 2020).

63 Dan Hancox, 'The war against rap: censoring drill may seem radical but it's not new', *Guardian* (2018), www.theguardian.com/music/2018/jun/22/the-war-against-rap-censoring-drill-may-seem-radical-but-its-not-new (accessed 12 July 2019).

64 Ellen Peirson-Hagger, 'Why banning rappers from using certain words won't work', *New Statesman* (2019), www.newstatesman.com/culture/music-theatre/2019/10/why-banning-rappers-using-certain-words-wont-work (accessed 10 October 2020).

65 'Police use "rap translator" to convict gang leader who threatened to shoot rivals in drill song', *Telegraph* (2019), www.telegraph.co.uk/news/2019/10/04/police-use-rap-translator-convict-gang-leader-threatened-shoot (accessed 10 September 2020).

66 *Ibid.*

67 Lambros Fatsis, 'Policing the beats: the criminalisation of UK drill and grime music by the London Metropolitan Police', *The Sociological Review* 67:6 (2019), 1300–1316.

68 'Rappers Skengdo and AM Breached Injunction by Performing Drill Music', *BBC Newsbeat*, 2019, www.bbc.co.uk/news/newsbeat-46932655 (accessed 29 July 2020).

69 Simon Hallsworth and Tara Young, 'Gang talk and gang talkers: a critique', *Crime Media Culture*, 4 (2008), 175–195.

70 Amnesty International, 'Trapped in the Matrix'.

71 Patrick Williams and Eric Kind, *Data-Driven Policing: The Hardwiring of Discriminatory Policing Practices across Europe – Project Report* (European Network Against Racism, 2019).

72 *Ibid.*

73 Amnesty International, 'Trapped in the Matrix'.

74 Metropolitan Police & National Physical Laboratory, *Metropolitan Police Service Live Facial Recognition Trials* (2020), 17, www.met.police. uk/SysSiteAssets/media/downloads/central/advice/met/facial-recogni tion/met-evaluation-report.pdf (accessed 13 October 2020).

75 Williams and Kind, *Data-Driven Policing*.

76 Virinder Kalra and Tariq Mehmood, 'Resisting technologies of surveillance and suspicion', in Nisha Kapoor, Virinder Kalra and James Rhodes, *The State of Race* (London: Palgrave, 2013).

77 Moore, 'Is the empire coming home?' Nisha Kapoor, 'Blind justice and blinding crime', in *Deport, Deprive, Extradite: 21st Century State Extremism* (London: Verso, 2018); Nijjar, 'Echoes of empire'.

78 Rod Ardehali, 'Police watchdog urges the government to crack down on county lines drug gangs using anonymous pay-as-you-go "burner phones"', *Daily Mail* (2020), www.dailymail.co.uk/news/article-7872187/ Police-watchdog-urges-government-crack-county-lines-drug-gangs.html (accessed 1 October 2020).

79 M Huncho, 'M Huncho "Bando Ballads", Official Lyrics & Meaning', *Genius* (2020). www.youtube.com/watch?time_continue=327&v=3b4Zyz srrCM&feature=emb_title (accessed 12 June 2020).

80 James Keith, 'Last Night, Krept & Konan Spoke in the House of Commons in Defence of Drill', *Complex* (2019), www.complex.com/ music/2019/06/krept-and-konan-diane-abbott-ban-drill (accessed 10 June 2020).

Chapter 6 – Futures of Black resistance: disruption, rebellion, abolition

1 For more on the violence of Britain's border system, and some of the ways it is being resisted, see El-Enany, *Bordering Britain*.

2 Channel 4 News, '"We Can't Breathe": 76 Arrested at London Eric Garner Demo' (2014), www.channel4.com/news/eric-garner-protests-london-westfield-die-in (accessed 12 April 2015).

3 BBC News, 'Black Lives Matter Protests Stop Cars and Trams Across England' (2016), www.bbc.co.uk/news/uk-england-nottinghamshire-36983852 (accessed 20 May 2019).

4 Don Mitchell, *The Right to the City* (New York: Guilford Press, 2003); Margaret Kohn, *Brave New Neighbourhoods: The Privatization of Public Space* (London and New York: Routledge, 2004).

5 Peter Jackson and Dan Holbrook, 'Multiple meanings: shopping and the cultural politics of identity', *Environment and Planning A: Economy and Space*,

27:12 (1995), 1913–1930; John Flint, 'Surveillance and exclusion practices in the governance of access to shopping centres on periphery estates in the UK', *Surveillance and Society*, 4:1 (2002), 52–68.

6 Kai Koddenbrock, 'What money does: an inquiry into the backbone of capitalist political economy', *MPIfG, Discussion Paper from Max Planck Institute for the Study of Societies*, 17:9 (2017); Peter Dauvergne, *Will Big Business Destroy Our Planet?* (Boston: Polity, 2018).

7 Ann Phizacklea and Robert Miles, 'The strike at Grunwick', *Journal of Ethnic and Migration Studies*, 6:3 (1978), 268–278.

8 John La Rose, in 'Alliance of Black Parents Movement, Black Youth Movement and Race Today Collective', in *The New Cross Massacre Story: Interviews with John La Rose* (London: New Beacon Press, 2011).

9 John Kelly, *Working for the Union: British Trade Union Officers* (Cambridge: Cambridge University Press, 1994); Seumas Milne, *The Enemy Within: The Secret War Against the Miners* (London: Verso, 2014).

10 Jamie Woodcock, *Working the Phones: Control and Resistance in Call Centres* (London: Pluto Press, 2016).

11 David Harvey, *Rebel Cities: From the Right to the City to the Urban Revolution* (London: Verso Books, 2012).

12 Adam Elliott-Cooper, 'Britain is not innocent', *Network for Police Monitoring* (2020).

13 Mike Noon, 'Pointless diversity training: unconscious bias, new racism and agency', *Work, Employment and Society*, 32:1 (2017), 198–209.

14 Linda Moore and Phil Scraton, *The Incarceration of Women: Punishing Bodies, Breaking Spirits* (London: Routledge, 2014).

15 Angela Davis, 'Masked racism: reflections on the prison industrial complex', *ColorLines* (1998).

16 Ruth Wilson Gilmore, *Golden Gulag: Prisons, Surplus, Crisis, and Opposition in Globalizing California* (California: University of California Press, 2007).

17 Robert R. Ross, Elizabeth A. Fabiano and Crystal D. Ewles, 'Reasoning and rehabilitation', *International Journal of Offender Therapy and Comparative Criminology*, 32:1 (1988), 29–35, cited in Alan Clarke, Rosemary Simmonds and Sarah Wydall, 'Delivering Cognitive Skills Programmes in Prison: A Qualitative Study', The Home Office (2002), https://delta.bipsolutions. com/docstore/pdf/7384.pdf (accessed 13 October 2020).

18 Jack Cattell, Alan Mackie, Yvette Prestage and Martin Wood, 'Results from the Offender Management Community Cohort Study (OMCCS): assessment and sentence planning', *Ministry of Justice Analytical Series* (2013), 24.

19 Mark Neocleous, *War Power, Police Power* (Edinburgh: Edinburgh University Press, 2014).

20 McCulloch and Sentas, 'The killing of Jean Charles de Menezes'.

Notes

21 Kojo Koram, *The War on Drugs and the Global Colour Line* (London: Pluto Press, 2019).

22 Derecka Purnell, 'How I became a police abolitionist', *The Atlantic* (2020).

23 Erica Meiners and Judith Levine, *The Feminist and the Sex Offender* (London: Verso, 2020).

24 David Scott, 'What is to be done? Thinking about abolitionist alternatives', *Prison Service Journal*, 231 (May 2017), 36–42.

25 Sophie Evans, 'Young dad who died after police struggle "boasted of drug dealing on Facebook and dubbed himself 'hard to kill'"', *The Mirror* (2017), www.mirror.co.uk/news/uk-news/rashan-charles-hackney-dead-police-10908953 (accessed 13 October 2020).

26 Ruth Wilson Gilmore, 'Abolition geography and the problem of innocence', in Gaye Theresa Johnson and Alex Lubin (eds), *Futures of Black Radicalism* (London: Verso, 2017).

27 Jon Sharman, 'Met police officer must "justify use of force" after video shows constables attacked in Hackney McDonald's during arrest', *The Independent* (2018), www.independent.co.uk/news/uk/crime/met-police-hackney-mcdonalds-video-arrest-taser-punch-kick-assault-footage-a8511481.html (accessed 13 October 2020); Jon Sharman, 'Hackney McDonald's fight: Police Federation chief claims "breakdown in society" after fracas involving officers', *The Independent* (2018), www.independent.co.uk/news/uk/crime/hackney-mcdonalds-police-fight-video-met-police-federation-officers-a8512191.html (accessed 13 October 2020).

Conclusion

1 Derek Peterson, 'The intellectual lives of Mau Mau detainees', *Journal of African History*, 49:1 (2008), 73–91.

2 David Lowe, 'The envy of the world', *The Sun* (2011), www.thesun.co.uk/archives/news/654714/the-envy-of-the-world (accessed 13 October 2020).

3 Dan Bulley, Jenny Edkins and Nadine El-Enany, *After Grenfell: Violence, Resistance and Response* (London: Pluto, 2019).

4 John Solomos and Les Back, *Racism and Society* (London: Palgrave Macmillan, 1996).

Index

(Note: 'n.' after a page reference indicates the number of a note on that page; likewise '*fig.*' refers to figure.)

Index

Index

Index

Index

Macpherson, Sir William
  Report (Stephen Lawrence
    Inquiry, 1999) 55, 128,
    195n.38, 199n.1, 200n.8
Malaya (now Malaysia) 139–144,
    211n.12, 211n.13, 211n.15,
    212n.18, 212n.20
  Batang Kali 141, 211n.14
  Emergency 141–143
  Malayan National Liberation
    Army (MNLA) 141–143
Manchester 4, 32–33, 38, 42,
    79, 115, 154, 168, 198n.49,
    209n.18
  Moss Side 38, 42, 198n.51
  Moss Side Defence Committee 42
March Against Deaths in Custody
    77–78
Marx, Karl 197n.23
  Marxism 16, 51, 195n.36
  Marxists 33
masculinity 61, 69–72, 99–108
  see also hegemonic masculinity;
    hegemony
Mau Mau see Kenya
McCarran Act 32
McKenley, Jan 39
mental health 10, 15, 107, 111–112,
    119, 153, 174, 178, 193n.17
mentoring 71–72, 203n.55
M Huncho 161, 215n.79
migration 8, 22, 30, 52, 67, 138
Mill, John Stuart 92–93, 205n.16,
    206n.18
missionaries 65, 83, 101, 146
mobile phones 130, 159, 161, 180
  data collection 156, 159
Monitoring Group, The 126,
    209n.28
Moss Side see Manchester
Moynihan Report (US, 1965)
    202n.49
mugging 38, 151, 197n.31
  muggers 8, 38, 187
Mujinga, Belly 4
multiculturalism 51, 90
Muslims 188, 207n.41

anti-Muslim racism 160, 162,
    194n.30, 207n.43
  Muslim women 61

National Front 39
National Unemployed Movement
    (Trinidad) 25
Negro Welfare Association (UK) 25
Negro Welfare, Cultural and
    Social Association (NWCSA,
    Trinidad) 25, 27–28, 197n.7
Newcastle-upon-Tyne 99
New Cross (south-east London)
  New Cross Fire (1981) 39, 170,
    216n.8
  see also Lewisham
New Labour 86, 149, 212n.42
Newham (London Borough of) 122,
    127
  Newham Monitoring Project
    (NMP) 17, 122, 124, 208n.8
Newman, Sir Kenneth 43, 45
NHS 3
Nigeria 25, 189
Nkrumah, Kwame 32
Norris, Robert 91, 205n.10
Northern Ireland 40–43, 138–139,
    147, 198n.56, 211n.15,
    212n.36
  Royal Ulster Constabulary
    (RUC) 43
  Troubles 40, 147
  see also Ireland, Irish
Northern Police Monitoring Project
    (NPMP) 154, 214n.60
Nottingham (West Midlands) 1, 30,
    41, 54, 66, 113, 168, 208n.5,
    215n.3
Notting Hill (west London) 30, 54,
    99, 122, 196n.18
  Notting Hill Carnival 30, 32,
    159

Occupy 172
Offensive Weapons Act (2019) 152
Operation Blunt 2 (2008–11) 86–87,
    110, 205n.4, 205n.5